D0141774

HARD TIMES

HARD TIMES

IMPOVERISHMENT AND PROTEST IN THE PERESTROIKA YEARS

The Soviet Union 1985-1991

William Moskoff

M. E. Sharpe

ARMONK, NEW YORK
LONDON, ENGLAND

Library of Congress Cataloging-in-Publication Data

Moskoff, William
Hard times—impoverishment and protest in the Perestroika years :
the Soviet Union 1985–1991 / William Moskoff.
p.   cm.
Includes bibliographical references and index
ISBN 1-56324-213-3 (cloth)
ISBN 1-56324-214-1 (pbk)
1. Soviet Union—Economic conditions—1985–1991.
2. Cost and standard of living—Soviet Union.
3. Perestroika—Social Aspects.
4. Protest movements—Soviet Union.
I. Title.
HC336.26.M69   1993
330.947'0854—dc20
93-20098
CIP

Printed in the United States of America

The paper used in this publication meets the minimum requirements of
American National Standard for Information Sciences—
Permanence of Paper for Printed Library Materials,
ANSI Z 39.48-1984.

⊗∞

BM (c) 10   9   8   7   6   5   4   3   2   1
BM (p) 10   9   8   7   6   5   4   3   2   1

For Eugene Hotchkiss

Contents

List of Tables

Acknowledgments

This book owes a great deal to a number of people and institutions. First I would like to thank The National Council for Soviet and East European Research for a grant which allowed me the time to complete the research and write this book. The James S. Kemper Foundation also provided research support.

I would also like to thank Dean David Spadafora of Lake Forest College for his constant encouragement during the entire process. My colleague Jeffrey Sundberg read the entire manuscript in detail and provided many valuable suggestions, most of which I was wise enough to take. At an early stage in my thinking I benefited from conversations with Anthony Jones. My student assistant, Mark Peysakhovich, was also very helpful. Most especially, I want to thank my wife and colleague, Carol Gayle, whose careful readings always make my work better.

These contributions notwithstanding, I alone bear responsibility for the contents and findings of the book.

Introduction

The nearly seven years that Mikhail Gorbachev held office in the Soviet Union were remarkable. They were the years when the Communist party surrendered its monopoly over political life in the Soviet Union and the spirit of intellectual and political discourse arose as never before. During this period the great divide between the west and the east disappeared when the iron curtain melted away in 1989. The long suppressed nationalities militantly began to assert their belief that they had a fundamental right to self-determination.

But these were also the years when the pretense that central planning was the most efficient way to organize the Soviet economy was essentially relinquished. Gorbachev and others frankly declared to the whole world that the economy was really in desperate condition, that it was hopelessly inefficient, and that in its existing state it was incapable of achieving the lofty goals promised for so long by the communist regime. Change, Gorbachev said, had to come soon or the Soviet Union would fall forever behind the advanced nations. People were more shocked by the messenger's public admission than they were by the message, because they had been living with a stagnant economy for at least a decade.

The recognition that the Soviet economy was in trouble meant that alternative ways had to be found to run it. But it was not a simple matter suddenly to put on the brakes and change course; because more than fifty years of central planning had wrought many changes in Soviet society, most of them quite enduring and powerful. Institutions established by the regime had socialized two complete generations of Soviet citizens. These included the Soviet strategy of economic development that had rapidly industrialized and urbanized a formerly agrarian society and created a new nation; and the communist idea, including the promise to provide material goods in great abundance, had created expectations of a future beyond the wildest imaginings of any previous society. These high expectations were reinforced by an extraordinary increase in the level of education, and supported by a set of entitlements—such as a free education, guaranteed employment, inexpensive housing, and free medical care—which made such dreams seem plausible. The elevated goals, however, were tempered by the experience of hardship, and the persistence of scarcity, and by the time Gorbachev came to power, few still had illusions that prosperity was just around the corner. Yet Gorbachev's sober words neither lowered expectations nor diminished the population's sense of entitlement. They wanted the goods and services that they had long been promised, but they also wanted to retain their entitlements. They expected more, but they did not want to pay for it.

There were two broad sets of illusions that people had about the country. The first, those that had to do with the building of a communist society and with justice and abundance for all, was already dying a natural death by the time Gorbachev took office. In retrospect, it is clear that these illusions were held together by thin threads. By 1985, only the staunchest and most loyal ideologues still believed there was sanctity and truth in the writings of their patriarchs, Marx and Lenin. The second set of illusions had been created around Gorbachev's promises that he could rescue this sinking but still noble ship from stormy waters and bring it safely home to port. Almost immediately after taking office, Gorbachev had assured the Soviet population that many more goods and services would be available if only people would work harder.[1] This was the first promise of restructuring, or *pere-stroika*. It was associated with the promises of glasnost and democratization—that people would no longer have to speak in whispers or write in secret and that they would have a greater voice in choosing their leaders. All of these promises created great expectations. Some of them were fulfilled; most were not. Certainly the hope that perestroika could rescue the economy had died before December 1991, when Gorbachev resigned and the Union of Soviet Socialist Republics was dissolved; it had died even before August 1991, when some of Gorbachev's most trusted aides had tried to remove him from office.

Opinion polls help us to chart the slide of people's faith in and optimism about perestroika. In 1989 Soviet sociologist Tatiana Zaslavskaia said that perestroika had had the support of about 35 percent of the population from 1985 to 1986, a figure that climbed to 43 percent in 1987 and then fell to 41 percent in 1988.[2] Much higher levels of support were reported in a telephone poll of 939 Muscovites in May 1988 which was done for *The New York Times* and CBS News. It showed that 73 percent of those interviewed strongly supported perestroika and only 23 percent had reservations about it—this despite the fact that, when people were asked how the material well-being of their families had fared over the previous three years, only 33 percent said it had improved, 53 percent said it had not changed, and 12 percent said it had worsened. Moreover, less than half of those polled, some 40 percent, believed that perestroika would improve the standard of living.[3] By early 1989, public confidence in perestroika had slipped badly: very few people (13 percent) reported that they were better off under perestroika, while more than 29 percent said that their standard of living had declined.[4] At the end of that year, the government published the results of a public opinion poll it had commissioned which showed that 56 percent of those surveyed considered the situation "critical" and 38 percent considered it "bad." Only 18 percent said they had "confidence in tomorrow," and fully 25 percent of them thought that perestroika would never succeed.[5]

The deterioration of the material conditions of their lives had made a cynical people even more cynical, a pessimistic people even more pessimistic. But it also had made them angry. And unlike the past, when anger was an emotion best contained, or drowned in a bottle of vodka, now the people became openly angry. They expressed their anger in public opinion polls, in the destruction of property, in strikes, and in political revolt against the presumptions of an unwanted master.

It is a fundamental argument of this book that perestroika was a disastrous failure. Instead of the economy's recovery, it contributed to its steady disintegration after mid-1988 and, by the end of 1991, its complete collapse. Although at first the promise that material life would be better under perestroika engendered some hope, it in fact not only failed to improve economic conditions but also came to be viewed by the population as the chief contributor to their wretched existence. Material life before perestroika had not been good, but it was sufficiently stable and predictable that the population had been willing to tolerate its deficiencies. The instability created by perestroika and its failure to make life better were, if not the root causes of the collapse of the Soviet Union, without question among the chief sources of the demise of Gorbachev and the Soviet system. In this sense, the attempted coup of August 1991 did not end the Gorbachev era; it verified that Gorbachev and his perestroika were already obsolete.

The casualties of this failed effort at reforming the Soviet system were the people of the Soviet Union, and it is the people of the Soviet Union who stand at the center of this book. The book is about how perestroika affected the day-to-day material conditions of life for ordinary Soviet citizens. It is divided into three major parts. The first part deals with the Soviet people as consumers and how their experience of mounting and persistent shortages of everyday goods created disillusionment and anger. The second part deals with the population as producers and how perestroika and Gorbachev's policies led to the emergence of unemployment—or the fear of it—as new burdens in the lives of the Soviet people. The final part of the book shows how strikes came to represent the primary weapon of protest against the failed policies of perestroika; the strike became a basic way in which people could peacefully display their anger and disenchantment.

This book is ultimately about ordinary people and the way their ordinary concerns about everyday life grew to become extraordinary apprehensions. It is not about great men or grand schemes, but about the collapse of economic life in the Soviet Union and the death of people's hope for their country's future.

Notes

1. Elizabeth Teague, "Gorbachev's First Four Years," *Report on the USSR* (March 3, 1989), 2.

2. *The New York Times* (November 5, 1989), A13.

3. *The New York Times* (May 27, 1988), A1, A10. All polls have their limitations. In this one, the pollsters said that many seemed "guarded" in their responses and others seemed to provide the "politically correct" answer. But the general direction of support seems indisputable.

4. *Pravda* (September 17, 1989), 2.

5. *The New York Times* (November 5, 1989), A13.

1

The Soviet Economy
Under Gorbachev

The deeply troubled economy that Gorbachev inherited was obviously not of his own making. When he was chosen head of the Communist Party of the Soviet Union in March 1985, Gorbachev's legacy had been shaped by the so-called era of stagnation, the name given to the years from 1964 to 1982 when, under Leonid Brezhnev's stewardship, the USSR saw a serious slowing of the economy. Growth rates had been falling for a long time, factor productivity was extremely low, and goods were in short supply.

The stagnation of the economy could be seen in the significant decline in rates of economic growth in the quarter century preceding Gorbachev's ascent to power. Economic growth, which during the decade 1961–70 averaged 4.8 percent annually, fell by fully half, to 2.4 percent a year, from 1971 to 1980, and to a mere 1.7 percent a year from 1981 to 1985.[1]

Moreover, there was a widening gap between the Soviet Union and its traditional adversaries—the United States, Western Europe, and Japan. An economist from the Soviet Academy of Sciences said that Soviet gross national product was no more than 28 percent of the U.S. level, a remarkable revelation considering the general view in the United States that Soviet aggregate output was about half the American level.[2] Soviet industrial equipment was also extremely outmoded. In contrast to the average life span of ten to twelve years in the industrialized west, equipment in the Soviet Union was used on average for twenty years.[3] Even more discouraging for the USSR was the fact that the gap was narrowing between it and a number of the newly industrialized nations such as South Korea and Singapore. The world was passing the Soviet Union by. By 1985, it seemed clear that Soviet economic institutions were not only irrelevant, they were dead. So, too, was the quality of economic life.

A nation that was a military superpower and could mount a major space program could not provide adequate housing for its people; nor could it feed them properly. The transportation system in many parts of the country remained in a primitive state, pollution was rampant in the air, on the land, and in the water, and resources were being depleted at frightening rates. The health of the people was literally deteriorating; and quality medical care was rare. The Soviet people had endured a great deal of suffering for a very long time and they had done it with a patience borne of a well-tempered resignation to deprivation, and because terror had ruled so much of their lives. But terror had been largely eliminated as a central feature of Soviet economic life after Stalin's death in 1953. In addition to the serious slowing of its economy during the "era of stagnation," the nation had begun to eat away at its remaining moral fabric; corruption became routine, and the so-called second economy became the supplier of last resort. The fight for scarce goods and resources made most everyone a player in the underground economy. By 1985, the most prominent items produced by the economy were inefficiency and corruption. It was Gorbachev's task to pull the nation out of the quicksand. He dubbed the effort *perestroika*, or restructuring.

The era of perestroika can be divided into two roughly equal periods. The first period lasted from 1985 to late 1988. If not a honeymoon, these three and a half years were ones during which the population accepted, at times even enthusiastically, the changes Gorbachev was trying to bring about. The second period began toward the end of 1988, when it became apparent that the economy was floundering badly. From that point until the Soviet Union dissolved at the end of 1991, the economy slid downhill at an accelerating rate. It was a bumpy ride to the bottom from the feeling of high hope that people had had in 1985 to the crisis that developed and reached a head at the time of the August 1991 coup attempt and the subsequent unraveling of the USSR.

In fact, from 1985 to 1991, the story of perestroika was one of economic destabilization and crisis. There is simply no other way to describe the state of the Soviet economy at the end of the Gorbachev era. Perhaps the saddest part of all is that for all the sacrifice and hardship experienced during these years, there was nothing to show for it: not the building of a new nation, not a victory over a treacherous enemy, and certainly not the establishment of a new economic system. In a material sense, the people had virtually nothing to show for all their suffering.

The First Phase of Perestroika

In a real sense, in the first phase of perestroika, Gorbachev's efforts to deal with the economy reflected no strategy at all. Indeed, we can say that his initial actions reflected his party roots. This meant that his first efforts were to enhance the party's role in dealing with the economy, to correct the undisciplined behavior of workers, and to eliminate ineptitude. In other words, Gorbachev wanted to wager on the so-called human factor. He mounted an antialcohol campaign two months after he came to office and made efforts to get workers off shopping queues and back to their jobs. But there was no systematic effort at structural change in the economy. A second aspect of the early Gorbachev program was his effort to modernize the country's stock of plant and equipment. By improving the technological base in the economy, Gorbachev hoped for a spurt of growth that would have a self-perpetuating character. At the same time, he called for improved quality, an aspect of production that previously had been secondary to high growth rates in the Soviet system. But

Gorbachev sought these goals without changing the incentive system which had always encouraged the economy to attempt to maximize aggregate output and was therefore antithetical to the goals he was enunciating with so much energy. In fact, there was early resistance to Gorbachev's agenda, from both the economic bureaucracy and enterprise managers. For them, quality and quantity were incompatible goals; they were not used to operating in a world of ambiguity.

During the first full year when Gorbachev was in office, economic growth was a quite respectable 4.1 percent, the best overall performance in years. However, much of that growth was attributable to the good weather which had resulted in excellent agricultural production and to a honeymoon period in industry where the impact of Gorbachev's campaign of strict discipline had a positive effect on productivity. The results were much worse in 1987 and 1988, when neither of these factors was present and the growth rate again fell to a low level. Economic growth, according to western estimates, was only 1.3 percent in 1987 and 2.1 percent in 1988.[4] By the All-Union Party Conference in June 1988, Gorbachev recognized that things were going badly. He described the "new economic mechanism" as "spin[ning] its wheels."[5]

Economic Reform

It is certainly not as if there were no efforts to change the system. There were several years of effort, although they were mostly half-hearted attempts to institute change. There were a number of important reforms introduced in 1988, the key ones being the Law on the State Enterprise and the Law on Cooperatives.

The Law on the State Enterprise went into effect on January 1, 1988.[6] Its main objective was to have enterprises shoulder complete responsibility for the economic outcomes of their activities. Investment would no longer be financed by the state, but would come from the enterprise's own resources. Enterprises were also to have much greater freedom in determining what they would produce, and state orders for goods were to comprise a much reduced proportion of total enterprise output. Enterprise inputs were to be distributed through a new wholesale network and only scarce producer goods would be rationed by the old state system. The entire pay structure of the country was to be redone, and, most important, any wage increases were to be determined by an enterprise's capacity to pay and were supposed to be linked to productivity.

In fact, the actual results fell short of the goals. By the end of 1988, about 60 percent of total output was being produced in enterprises that were functioning under self-financing, state orders constituted 86 percent of industrial output, a mere 4 percent of industrial production went through the promised wholesale trade network, and wages well exceeded productivity.[7] There were three dysfunctional responses to the law: the state severely diminished enterprise authority; enterprises misused the authority they were given; and the law was incompletely implemented.

The second major piece of legislation was the Law on Cooperatives, passed in May 1988. It was the culmination of a process to create a legal private sector that had begun some eighteen months earlier. The 1986 Law on Individual Labor Activity had been a timid effort to provide the private sector with a framework of support, but was almost hopelessly compromised by official and unofficial interference. The May 1988 law removed a number of barriers and effectively removed the semantic distinction between a capitalist private enterprise and a socialist cooperative or personal business. Capitalism was given a legal status it had not enjoyed since the New Economic Policy of the 1920s. Nonetheless, the economic and political bureaucracies would continue to raise barriers against the new cooperatives' activities.[8] In many ways, the substantial roadblocks erected in 1989 by conservatives in the country and the considerable popular hostility that arose as a direct result of the high prices charged by the cooperatives were a useful measure of the standing of private economic activity in the country. There was a definite contradiction between the rhetoric of radical economic reform espoused by the country's leaders and the retrograde legislation and day-to-day intrusions on the activities of the cooperatives. These attitudes were reflected in what happened, or rather did not happen, in 1989, 1990, and 1991.

Economic growth slowed during 1987 and 1988 for several reasons. There was an inability to commission about one-third of the priority investment projects. The new reforms created disorder for managers; the Law on the State Enterprise especially differed from the old way of the state providing all investment funds, to which managers were accustomed. Moreover, inflationary pressure began to build as budget revenues declined and expenditures rose. The population also began to voice complaints about the rising shortages.[9]

In view of the problems that emerged with special force toward the end of 1988, Gorbachev shifted direction in 1989, making a clear effort to please the Soviet people by diverting resources to consumer goods.[10] He proposed several schemes to increase the output of consumer goods, lower the budget deficit, and defer any reforms which might impose an undue burden on the population. Thus, consumption was given a higher priority in the 1989 plan, at the expense of investment which declined in absolute terms for the first time since the end of World War II. At the same time, Gorbachev proposed to cut defense spending by more than 14 percent over a two-year period. The increasing popular outrage over rising prices of consumer goods also led Gorbachev to pledge that price reform would be deferred indefinitely.

The search for a reform program lost its momentum in 1989, in part because the government appeared to give more attention to stabilizing consumer goods markets and in part because it was rethinking its next moves. By the end of the year, the only important piece of legislation to emerge from the Supreme Soviet was the Law on Leasing, the government's effort to bolster the economy's dismal performance in agriculture and to supply the population with food.[11]

But matters only worsened in 1989. Economic growth fell to only 1.5 percent and, while agricultural output rose briskly, industrial output actually fell.[12] For the population, it was the first of three consecutive years of severe, crisis-level shortages. At the end of 1989, of 1,200 kinds of goods, the government identified shortages in 1,150 of them.[13] Irresponsible increases in wages and the money supply fueled these shortages. These same problems worsened in 1990. In that year, the government said that at existing prices there was a shortage of 250 billion rubles in goods.[14] The budget deficit and inflationary pressures escalated, and the recklessness of Soviet policy caused a monetary and fiscal crisis of a proportion that had not existed since the 1920s. Things were falling apart simultaneously in the economic, social, and political realms, so that at times it was difficult to separate one from the other.

The economic disintegration occurred because central planning broke down and was not replaced by any other way of organizing the economy. Without exception, the republics declared their sovereignty in 1990. The logical consequence was a battle between the center and the republics for control over economic resources. Rights to raw materials, budget receipts, control over banks, and control over hard currency earnings were all contested. In a goods-poor environment, the republics jealously and vigorously protected their own people by withholding deliveries to the center or to any others outside their own boundaries.

The total collapse of the economy came in 1991. Aggregate output had dropped by 17 percent, a magnitude of decline not seen since the devastating Nazi invasion.[15] The process that had begun in 1988 and picked up momentum in 1989 had snowballed into a giant, unstoppable boulder rolling through the economy. The statistics for the monetary and fiscal sectors were shocking. Prices and deficits rose to unprecedented levels, and fear spread through the nation about prices exploding out of sight. Unemployment began to increase, and fears of high unemployment were always in the back of people's minds. Twenty-six percent of the people interviewed in a Moscow survey said they believed they would lose their jobs if a market economy was introduced.[16] As the standard of living fell and many more people became impoverished, the idea that the Soviet Union was susceptible to collapse began to seem more likely; the social fabric had become extremely fragile. Perestroika had turned out to be a process of economic destabilization.

The Dimensions of Economic
Destabilization under Perestroika

First among the many dimensions to economic destabilization was the crisis created by a soaring budget deficit. The deficit, which was hidden from the public until October 1988, amounted to an estimated 131 billion rubles for the years 1985–88. Gorbachev attributed the deficit to the war in Afghanistan, the Chernobyl catastrophe, the earthquake in Armenia, the decline in world oil prices, and the drop in state revenues because of the decline in sales of alcohol beverages as a result of the antialcohol campaign.[17] Although these were not trivial factors in the budget deficit issue, there were other, more serious, structural problems that gave rise to the problem.

The budget was used to bail out unprofitable enterprises. Because the financial performance of an enterprise did not matter, the difference between an enterprise's revenues and its costs was covered by an allocation from the central budget. Second, the government provided huge subsidies to Soviet consumers so that food prices could be kept low. Subsidies for consumer goods equaled 110 billion rubles in 1989.[18]

The budget deficit continued to mount even after the war was over and alcohol revenues were once again flowing. In 1989, it was 120 billion rubles,[19] and in 1991, a deficit planned to be 26.7 billion rubles for the entire year had already reached 84.4 billion rubles by the end of September.[20] More important, as a percentage of gross domestic product (GDP) the deficit kept rising, from 2.4 percent in 1985 to 6.2 percent in 1986 to 9.2 percent in 1988 to 17 percent in 1991.[21] This created enormous inflationary pressure within the economy. As is discussed in detail in chapter 3, a substantial part of the deficit was caused by workers' wages, which rose at startling rates, much faster than productivity, and were funded by the central bank's unchecked use of the printing press. Moreover, the breakdown in relations between the center and the republics led republics to withhold revenues for their own purposes.[22] Finally, in an effort to appease the population, several social programs to which the government committed enormous sums were introduced or expanded in 1990, such as a new pensions law and the return of about one billion rubles to rural families to reimburse them for their electricity bills.[23]

A second source of instability was the decline of the Soviet Union's foreign trade position. In 1989, for the first time in many years, Soviet imports exceeded exports. That year, the trade deficit was $5.4 billion. In 1990, it nearly tripled, to about $15 billion. The primary cause was the loss of export earnings, itself a product of falling raw material prices, especially oil. The goods whose export prices fell accounted for about 40 percent of total exports. But there were also internal problems which contributed to the trade deficit. Oil production fell from 640 million tons in 1988 to 570 million tons in 1990.[24] The low point came in 1991, when total trade fell by 38 percent for the year.[25] The Soviet Union was also vulnerable in foreign trade because it depended on imports of consumer goods to satisfy the basic demands of its people, especially for food and for about 40 percent of its inputs for light industry.

The fall in export earnings forced the Soviet Union into western capital markets to borrow money not only to purchase imports but also to service its foreign debt. While estimates of the extent of Soviet foreign debt vary, everyone agrees that it was climbing. External debt, which had been no more than about $16 billion in 1985, rose to $42.3 billion in 1988, and by the end of 1991 it was estimated at between $64 and $90 billion.[26] The mounting debt meant that more and more export earnings went to service it, that is, to pay the interest on the debt. Whereas 22 percent of export earnings went to pay the interest on the debt in 1988—a figure considered reasonable by international authorities—by the end of 1991, the debt service ratio had more than doubled, to 50 percent.[27] Thus half of all export earnings, which were already shrinking, went to pay interest on the debt. The problem took on even more dangerous dimensions for the nation because at least three-fourths of its 1990 hard currency borrowings were used to service the debt.[28] As a consequence, relatively little was available for direct investment in the economy. In a relatively few years, the status of the Soviet Union shifted from that of a creditworthy nation to an international financial pariah.

A third source of instability was the increase in the amount of rubles in the hands of the population that could not be spent. In 1988, enterprises were given more freedom to determine wages, and the money incomes of Soviet households grew rapidly. Wages went up by 3.4 percent in 1987, by 8.5 percent in 1988, and by 14.4 percent in 1990. By early 1991, excess demand was estimated at 250 billion rubles.[29] The inflationary pressure embedded in high wage increases was reinforced by enterprises that also used their new economic freedom to produce a more expensive assortment of goods.

This leads us to the fourth element in the destabilization of the economy, the explosion in the price level that brought the economy to the brink of hyperinflation by the time the perestroika era ended. It is sufficient here to state the problem in general terms. In a period of only six years, inflation rose from essentially zero to double digits in 1989 and to triple digits by the end of 1991. The excessive wages were only one element in the equation. The money supply also grew rapidly, in support of the rising wages. When the government increased prices in April 1991, 70 percent of the increase was offset by subsidies, in effect indexing prices upward.[30] The rise in prices was also stimulated by the new freedom for private entrepreneurs, who took full advantage of the deep shortages in food and consumer goods markets to charge prices that the market would bear. The private sector did what the government did not have the courage to do: it allowed markets to find their equilibrium level. Instead of allowing that process to run its course, however, a generous government kept pumping rubles into the economy at alarming rates, which translated into rapidly rising prices.

As the economy deteriorated, all the reformers, including Gorbachev, recognized that it was necessary to go beyond the desultory modifications of perestroika and move to some kind of market system. A number of comprehensive programs were produced, but as we will see, none of them were put into operation. They were the pipe dreams of pretenders.

The Grand Plans for a Market Economy

The key year for comprehensive economic reform was 1990, when three major reform plans were offered for consideration. The first was that of Nikolai Ryzhkov, then the prime minister. Ryzhkov's plan was followed in August by the so-called 500-Day Plan, a program issued by a commission that had been appointed jointly by Gorbachev and Boris Yeltsin and headed by Stanislav Shatalin. This plan attracted the most attention domestically and worldwide. The final plan was Gorbachev's own proposal, which he made public in October.

Ryzhkov's plan called for a five-year transition to a "regulated market economy."[31] Although the program advocated the development of market institutions, it limited their development in several ways, most notably by not allowing the market to set prices. Rather, there would be three categories of prices: fixed prices determined solely by the state; regulated prices to be determined from lists produced by state organizations; and free prices which would cover only 10 to 15 percent of all retail goods. In the interest of protecting the population from the arbitrariness of the market, the prices on all basic consumer goods would be either fixed or regulated. Without allowing prices to reflect relative scarcity, the plan meant that ruble convertibility was out of the question. In addition to his defense of the old pricing mechanism, Ryzhkov took the position that everyone was entitled to a job and that full employment was the state's responsibility.

The highly conservative Ryzhkov plan received little support from any group, and the reformers continued to demand change. In an effort to secure a more acceptable program, the commission appointed by Gorbachev and Yeltsin was given the responsibility of coming up with a plan for a transition to a market economy. The commission produced the most radical plan to date and, although it was rejected by Gorbachev, in many ways it set the tone for Yeltsin's later approach to Russian reform.

The idea of a 500-day transition to the market was never meant by its authors to be taken literally; in fact, it was meant only to signal a sense of urgency for reforming the economy.[32] At the heart of the program were the rapid decontrol of prices, the privatization of state-owned industry, and large budget cuts, especially slashes in defense spending and foreign aid. The 500-Day Plan envisioned a four-stage transition to the market economy. During the first 100 days, emergency measures would be taken to denationalize the economy and institute the legalization of all entrepreneurial activity. Some fifty to sixty enterprises would be privatized; private land ownership would be initiated; the budget deficit would be cut significantly (by means that included the elimination of all subsidies); a central bank not unlike the U.S. Federal Reserve Bank would be established; and price decontrol would be introduced for all goods with the exception of necessities. During the second stage, coinciding with the next 150 days, privatization and price liberalization would continue and privatization of housing would begin. During the third stage, 30 to 40 percent of state industry, half of the transportation stock, and 60 percent of commercial business would be sold to the public, and the ruble would be made convertible. In the last 100 days, almost three-fourths of state enterprises would be denationalized, and an even higher percentage of transportation, construction, and trade would be in private hands.

Gorbachev found the Shatalin plan much too radical for his tastes and asked Abel Aganbegian, a long-time economic adviser, to develop a compromise which would blend the government's plan, the Shatalin plan, and the views of various interest groups who had made their own suggestions.[33] As it turned out, Aganbegian's version of a reform plan hewed very closely to the Shatalin 500-day, four-stage model.

Since this last compromise program did little to satisfy Gorbachev, he offered his own program in October 1990.[34] Like the Shatalin plan, Gorbachev's program called for four stages, but whereas the Shatalin program was specific on timing, Gorbachev's was vague. The first stage was devoted to stabilization, particularly to dealing with the high rates of inflation which had afflicted the nation. During the second stage, price decontrols would begin and privatization, begun in stage one, would continue. The social safety net, with a set of programs designed to protect the population, would be introduced. The market would begin to play a major role in consumer and capital goods during stage three, and during the fourth stage the marketization begun earlier would be solidified. The ruble would also become convertible. Gorbachev's proposal was ambiguous, cautious, and only partially committed to the market. For example, on the matter of letting the market determine prices, Gorbachev's plan allowed republics and local organs the right to determine the maximum level of freed prices.

When all was said and done, there were many words spoken on behalf of the market, but little accomplished. There were three reasons for the failure to make serious headway toward a radical restructuring of Soviet economic institutions. First, Gorbachev vacillated. The leadership he had shown in international affairs was never in evidence at home, as he delicately tried to balance the competing demands on shrinking economic resources. Gorbachev was never fully comfortable with the institutions that constituted a market economy. As late as November 1990, for example, he stated his firm opposition to the buying and selling of land.[35]

Second, popular support for a market economy was weak and ambivalent. The people did not have a consistent or resolute commitment to a market economy. What the population wanted was an outpouring of goods with low and stable prices. If that was what constituted a market economy, then they were for it.

Understandably, the people wanted the transition to be pain-less. In the best of all worlds, there would be no unemployment while inefficient enterprises cleaned house to become more cost-conscious and no rising prices while markets adjusted. Many people were naïve about a market economy, but others under-stood that unemployment and (more) inflation were likely by-products of the shift.

The weak popular support for a market economy can be seen in the results of a poll taken at the time. At the end of 1989, a Moscow survey found 34 percent of its respondents had a posi-tive reaction to the word "capitalism."[36] In May and June of 1990, the All-Union Center for the Study of Public Opinion asked people what they thought about the market economy. In May, 56 percent said they favored the market economy, and in June, that number jumped to 66 percent.[37] But at virtually the same time, in June, a poll of 30,000 people by *Goskomstat*, the State Committee on Statistics, reflected dramatically different attitudes toward the market. The *Goskomstat* poll was quite spe-cific in probing popular attitudes about price changes under the specific conditions of a transition to a market economy. Asked about in this way, the people gave the idea of a market economy quite unfavorable reviews: Only 9.9 percent had a "favorable" opinion of a regulated market economy, while 78 percent thought that prices would rise rapidly once the transition toward the mar-ket took place.[38] In yet a third poll, taken early in 1990, 87 percent of those interviewed said they favored socialism.[39]

Finally, Gorbachev and his supporters faced some formidable, well-established foes at every mention of reform. The first group of opponents to a market economy was the economic bureau-cracy. Central planning had invented this group, which was com-prised of millions of people who worked in the ministries in Moscow and in every provincial branch of the state bank. They and their families were absolutely dependent on the preservation of the status quo. The second group who opposed reform was the working class. If Gorbachev could deliver on his promises of more goods, they stood to gain a great deal in the long run after the economy became more efficient. But workers lived in the short run, and for them market reform meant that their jobs were no longer secure. For the working class, a job was an entitlement, not an aspiration. They had been told for decades that the greatest evil of capitalism was unemployment—and they believed this. In the late 1980s and early 1990s they could not support what they and their parents and their grandparents had been told for more than half a century was evil. A third group that was opposed to economic reform was the Soviet version of the military-industrial complex. The first threat to this group came in Gorbachev's speech in December 1988 at the United Nations in which he announced a unilateral reduction of 500,000 troops in Eastern Europe and an equally impressive decrease in the number of offensive weapons that were located in the region. The subsequent cuts in the military budget and the idea that the military's privileged budgetary status was reduced were hard pills to swallow. The notion that resources would be redirected to build a new technological base in the civilian sector made the military-industrial complex an opponent of reform. The conservative opposition showed its true colors on August 19, 1991, when key government, party, military, and KGB leaders led an unsuccessful attempt to overthrow Gorbachev.

But it was only a matter of months before the Gorbachev era would end. For all the problems the Soviet economy had, and for all of Gorbachev's awareness that fundamental change was necessary, by the time he left office in December 1991, there had been in fact no radical changes in the economic organization of the Soviet Union. What was left behind were several proposals to introduce change, some more radical than others, but none with a broad-based mandate.

The ensuing chapters attempt to explain how the material conditions of life under perestroika deteriorated for the Soviet population to the point where people lost all faith in the possibility of perestroika resurrecting their lives. The final years under Gorbachev constituted a great crisis in the lives of working people. Rising unemployment, rampant inflation, severe difficulties in finding food, and the absence of many basic consumer goods were only some of the more important causes for the anger that surfaced with such great force. For the working men and women of the Soviet Union, there was not a trace of justice left.

Notes

1. Central Intelligence Agency, *Handbook of Economic Statistics* (1991), 62.
2. *The New York Times* (April 24, 1990), A6.
3. Defense Intelligence Agency, "Gorbachev's Modernization Program: A Status Report," mimeo (March 19, 1987), 3.
4. CIA, *Handbook of Economic Statistics*, 62.
5. *Current Digest of the Soviet Press* 40, no. 26: 8.
6. Ibid., nos. 30 and 31 (1987).
7. Central Intelligence Agency and Defense Intelligence Agency, "The Soviet Economy in 1988: Gorbachev Changes Course," (April 14, 1989), 8.
8. See Anthony Jones and William Moskoff, *Ko-ops: The Rebirth of Entrepreneurship in the Soviet Union*. Bloomington, IN: Indiana University Press, 1991.
9. *Pravda* (September 14, 1988), 1–2.
10. A detailed accoun of Soviet economic activity in 1988 and the plans for 1989 can be found in "The Soviet Economy in 1988: Gorbachev Changes Course."
11. A good overview of the leasing issue can be found in Karen Brooks, "Lease Contracting in Soviet Agriculture in 1989," in *Perestroika in the Countryside*, ed. William Moskoff, 63–80. Armonk, NY: M.E. Sharpe, 1990.
12. CIA, *Handbook of Economic Statistics*, 62.
13. *Planovoe khoziaistvo*, no. 6 (June 1990), 61–71.
14. *Pravitel'stvennyi vestnik*, no. 51 (1990), 1.
15. Keith Bush, "The Disastrous Last Year of the USSR," *RFE/RL Research Report* (March 20, 1992), 39.
16. *Moskovskie novosti* (May 13, 1990), 10.
17. *Report on the USSR* (January 20, 1989), 27.
18. Central Intelligence Agency and Defense Intelligence Agency, "The Soviet Economy Stumbles Badly in 1989," mimeo (April 20, 1990), 18.
19. Moscow Interfax (October 18, 1991). From Foreign Broadcast Information Service–Soviet Union (FBIS-SOV)-91-204 (October 22, 1991), 37.
20. *Izvestiia* (October 19, 1991), 2.
21. International Monetary Fund et al., *The Economy of the USSR: Summary and Recommendations* (1991), 10; *RFE/RL Research Report* (February 7, 1992), 44.
22. *Pravda* (October 18, 1991), 1.
23. John Tedstrom, "The Soviet Economy: Planning for the 1990s," *Report on the USSR* (December 22, 1989), 2.

24. *Izvestiia* (July 29, 1990), 7.

25. Moscow Postfaktum (February 21, 1992). From FBIS-SOV-92-036, (February 24, 1992), 22.

26. John Tedstrom, "Soviet Foreign Trade in 1990," *Report on the USSR* (April 12, 1991), 10; Keith Bush, "Commonwealth of Independent States: Foreign Indebtedness," *RFE/RL Research Report* (January 10, 1992), 21; *RFE/RL Research Report* (March 6, 1992), 45.

27. Bush, 21.

28. *Izvestiia* (July 29, 1991), 7.

29. Anders Aslund, Lecture at the Kennan Institute for Advanced Russian Studies, April 22, 1991, *Meeting Report* 8, no. 15.

30. Aslund, Lecture.

31. Translated in FBIS-SOV-90-102, (May 25, 1990).

32. For an English translation of the Five-Hundred-Day Plan, see "Transition to a Market Economy," Foreign Broadcast Information Service, JPRS-UEA-90-034 (September 28, 1990).

33. A synopsis of the Aganbegian compromise plan was published in *Rabochaia tribuna* (September 21, 1990), 1–2; (September 22, 1990), 1–2; (September 25, 1990), 1–2; and (September 26, 1990), 1–2.

34. The full text of Gorbachev's plan can be found in *Izvestiia*, (October 27, 1990). An abbreviated version was translated in FBIS-SOV-90-202 (October 18, 1990).

35. *Pravda* (December 1, 1990), 4. Gorbachev said: ". . . while I am for a market, I cannot, for example, accept the private ownership of land, no matter what you do to me."

36. *Moscow News*, no. 2 (1990), 9.

37. *Rabochaia tribuna* (July 29, 1990), 1.

38. *Rabochaia tribuna* (December 8, 1990), 3.

39. Moscow World Service in English (April 24, 1990). From FBIS-SOV-90-180 (April 25, 1990), 68.

2

The Shortage Economy

Neither Mikhail Gorbachev nor perestroika created shortages; central planning did. But the consequence of perestroika was to exacerbate the shortages that already existed in many important areas, such as food supply, beyond limits that were tolerable to the population. The shortage economy that grew under Gorbachev from 1985 through 1991 significantly reduced the Soviet Union's standard of living and contributed mightily to the anger, despair, and cynicism that came to abide daily in the land.[1]

One result of shortages, especially during the Brezhnev years, had been a burgeoning second economy; that is, free-market economic activity that took place outside the dominant and legal state economy. This included everything from stealing state property and selling or using it to the sale of food in legal collective farm markets, to illegally buying positions of power in the party. During the perestroika era, the shortage economy that dominated the economic scene predictably grew to a new level of importance. In the view of the population, its growing presence confirmed suspicions that they were victims and not beneficiaries of Gorbachev's policies.

But the second economy was only one of three responses to the growing shortages under perestroika. The other two involved hoarding. Private hoarding was the response of a panicked population to real and imagined shortages; it developed in unsystematic and unpredictable ways and either aggravated the existing difficulties or created new ones. Public hoarding was the response of city, regional, and republic governments to protect their local populations from "outsiders" who took goods out of their city or region or republic. Beginning in 1989, policies to restrict the movement of goods spread like wildfire through the USSR. Although they were nominally described as rationing techniques to protect the local populations, in essence they were a form of local protectionism, and they significantly contributed to the demise of the Soviet Union as a unified political and economic entity.

Food Shortages: Real or Imagined?

No issue was more visible during the era of perestroika than the insufficient supply of food. As it had in earlier eras—the 1917 Revolution, the Civil War, collectivization and its aftermath, and World War II—like the proverbial bad penny, the food question arose once again in Soviet history. This time, the failure of the regime to ensure an adequate and stable food supply evoked visible anger among the population.

During the Gorbachev years, food became scarce suddenly and in many places. It should be said, however, that the country was never placed on the brink of starvation, and in fact there is scant evidence that any people starved. Instead, there was genuine anxiety and even greater anger that life had become a little more miserable and a lot more expensive because of the food shortages.[2]

At the heart of all the food problems was the failure of producers to deliver according to stipulated targets. Beginning in 1988, this became the dominant factor in the food shortages of 1990 and 1991. Local authorities reneged on their contractual obligations for three reasons. First, they wanted to keep more food for their own populations because total food supplies were diminishing. The idea of officials retaining food for their local populations was something quite new. For years, the old administrative-command system had stripped local authorities of the right to decide where food would go; local producers had been required to meet delivery obligations to the central government no matter what the consequences for the local population. As the primacy of central economic authority diminished, the well-defined boundaries of authority broke down. This emboldened local producers and many local political leaders, who no longer felt required to give the center a large piece of the pie when that meant giving themselves an even smaller piece. Second, in the climate of food shortages, producers of agricultural products, negotiating privately, could sell their output at higher prices than the state would pay. Third, local authorities quickly recognized that they could use food to barter for goods they could not get through normal channels, that is, through the state.

The failures to provide stable food supplies can be contrasted to the lofty aspirations that had been expressed in Brezhnev's Food Program, which had been approved in 1982 and slated to end in 1990, the end of the twelfth Five-Year Plan. At that time, according to the program, Soviet citizens were supposed to be consuming 70 kilograms of meat, 260 eggs, 110 kilograms of potatoes, 19 kilograms of fish, 46 kilograms of sugar, 13 kilograms of vegetable oil, 135 kilograms of bread, and 340 kilograms of milk on an annual per capita basis.[3] Even before the end of the Food Program, it was obvious that the 1982 goals were only a distant dream. In spite of this, as late as October 1988, the government harbored illusions that the population could be well-fed. In discussing the subject of food in the republic for the years 1988–1990, the RSFSR Council of Ministers said, "[T]here is a real possibility . . . to fully meet the population's requirements in terms of rational food norms for dairy products, poultry, vegetables, fish products, groats, margarine, eggs, tea, confectionery goods, and of course, bread and macaroni."[4]

Keeping the goals of the Food Program in mind, one can get a sense of the shortfalls by examining the data on food production. Crop production declined in both 1987 and 1988.[5] Gross agricultural output in 1989 was only about two percent higher than the 1986–1988 average, when food production was virtually unchanged. At the end of 1989, consumption of meat was at best 40 kilograms per capita. Prime Minister Ryzhkov summarized the quantitative shortfall of food when he told the Agro-Industrial Workers Congress that the level of unsatisfied demand for food products was 50 billion rubles for 1990.[6] And in late 1991, while the country was said to have "adequate supplies of potatoes, butter and vegetables," there was a shortage of 1.5 million tons of meat, 5.7 million tons of milk, and 3.6 billion eggs.[7]

As 1990 ended, Soviet citizens were far from satisfied with the food situation. A poll published in the magazine *Ogonek* in early 1990 showed enormous dissatisfaction with both the quantity and quality of food. Some 73 percent of those polled experienced shortages either quite often or constantly; more than 75 percent could not get enough meat, fish, and poultry; and almost two-thirds could not get enough vegetables, fruit, and berries. Only bread, macaroni, and groats were in plentiful supply (83 percent), as were vegetable oil, butter, and lard (67 percent). Twenty-five percent found Soviet food monotonous and more than 40 percent thought it was of low quality. Perhaps the most significant finding was that only 18.1 percent of the people interviewed thought their diet was "sufficient in amount and good quality." For the rest, food was deficient in some way.[8] This coincides with the findings of polls taken in Ukraine and Russia. In Ukraine, of 528 people polled, 33.5 percent were dissatisfied with their diet and of the 1,606 Russians surveyed, only 7 percent were completely satisfied with their diets, while 65 percent were dissatisfied.[9] A poll published in late 1990 showed that only 34.7 percent drank milk every day or almost every day, and 47 percent never used fresh frozen products.[10]

The seriousness and the unevenness of the food supply situation can better be seen by looking at some different places in the country. Although it may seem obvious, it is worth pointing out that when the system of central planning broke down for food deliveries, the major cities in the country were far worse off than the smaller provincial cities or rural towns because the larger cities were dependent on other cities for their food. The commanding presence that the major industrial and political centers had held in the pre-Gorbachev days dissipated as rigid centralism diminished. This generalization is confirmed by the data collected from some 6,000 interviews of Soviet emigres from 1985 to 1990 which were carried out by the Radio Free Europe/Radio Liberty (RFE/RL) Soviet Area Audience and Opinion Research (SAAOR). The surveys found that, until 1988, the larger cities in the country had a better food supply than the smaller cities. After 1988, while dairy products and staples were more available in the largest cities, and meat supplies were everywhere about the same, the smaller cities had a better supply of vegetables.[11]

The Food Supply in Moscow and Leningrad

The destruction of the once clearly delineated obligations of the old system reduced the two leading cities of the Soviet Union to the status of mere mortals. Moscow's position as the political center of the USSR had always made it a privileged city. Those who wielded power not only made sure that they themselves were well taken care of, they also made sure that the city was well fed. Witness Boris Yeltsin's successful effort in 1986, when he was head of the Moscow party organization, to get an additional thousand tons of various food products allocated to Moscow.[12] But as the discipline of central planning broke down, and the center began to lose its political hold over the rest of the country, the food supply in Moscow declined. Relative to that of the rest of the country, Moscow's ability to supply its citizens with all major foods deteriorated. In the fall of 1989, the city reported shortages of virtually all foods, particularly meat. On October 14, for example, 88 Moscow stores had no meat at all, 221 were without beef, and 323 without pork. Much the same was true for macaroni products and flour. On October 14 and 15, 154 Moscow stores had no pancake flour. A trade union newspaper summarized the situation in the fall of 1990: "There is a crisis situation with food goods. One must stand in line for many hours to buy meat, eggs, or sausage. There are only a few vegetables

Table 2.1

Per Capita Consumption of Food, in Kilograms: Moscow

	1980	1985	1986	1987	1988	1989
Potatoes	94	84	84	84	84	81
Vegetables and melons	135	131	133	134	135	127
Fruit	61	58	60	57	57	56

Source: Rabochaia tribuna (November 30, 1990), 1–2.

and fruits in the city; one can only purchase onions, carrots, and potatoes."[13] More systematic evidence of the worsening of the food situation can be seen in Table 2.1, which details the decline in the consumption of several staples.

Even bread supplies were down, leading one statistician in 1989 to observe that if the current shortfall in the delivery of bread products to Moscow was the same as the city being without any bread for one day, then by 1990, shortfalls would be equal to three days without any bread.[14]

The most important item in the Soviet diet has always been the daily bread. Indeed, the government had always given a high priority to a plentiful supply of good, cheap bread by providing a large subsidy to producers. As long as there was certainty that bread was available, even when all else was in short supply, other hardships were endured, if not with enthusiasm at least with tolerance. But in the fall of 1990, even the supply of bread became problematical. People often wandered from store to store looking in vain for bread.[15] Indeed, one commentator said that Russia was experiencing its worst bread shortage since the early sixties.[16] The primary reason was that Soviet farmers were withholding grain deliveries from the state. In part, this represented opportunistic hoarding in the grain-producing areas.[17] Gorbachev understood this, and on September 4 he sent telegrams to regional party heads in the relevant areas telling them to ensure that grain was sent to the state.[18] His efforts did not succeed.

There were other reasons for the bread shortage. People were trying to substitute bread for other food products that were also in short supply, such as meat, pasta, and herring.[19] In some areas, such as the central *oblasts* (regions) of Russia, farmers were feeding cheap, subsidized bread to their livestock because they were not receiving the fodder that was supposed to have been delivered under state orders.[20] Further, as some argued, the bread industry's plant and equipment in Moscow were at the same levels as they had been in the 1950s when there were only half as many people living in the city as there were in 1990. Moreover, wages in the industry were so low that people did not want to work as bakers.[21] About 1,500 workers left the industry early in 1990 and, consequently, there was a shortage of skilled bakery workers. The decline in the number of the industry's workers forced a dozen production lines to go out of operation and another seven bakeries to operate at only about fifty percent of capacity.[22]

Moscow's supplies of milk and other dairy products also suffered during the Gorbachev era. As in the case of bread shortages, the main reason was that the deliveries of dairy products fell short of the state's stipulated targets. In 1990, a number of milk-producing regions refused to ship milk to Moscow.[23] Moscow should have been receiving 2,300 tons of raw milk a day for processing, but actual supplies were 1,000 tons less, a decline of about 40 percent.[24] Three reasons were given for reduced deliveries: milk producers were keeping the milk to satisfy the needs of the local population, they were suffering from a shortage of processing capacity, and the transportation distances were great.[25] But much of this was untrue. There is convincing evidence that local political authorities in some dairy-producing regions were ordering cutbacks in deliveries to the cities. On September 19, for example, the Penza Oblast Soviet Executive Committee stated that no cottage cheese or sour cream was to be delivered to Moscow in the fourth quarter of 1990. And in November 1990, the director of the Kaluga Dairy Agro-Industrial Association wrote that a decision of the Kaluga Oblast Soviet Executive Committee obliged him to stop shipping whole milk to Moscow.[26] The failure to meet delivery targets also resulted in meat shortages in Moscow. In the eight-month period of January to August 1990, Moscow did not receive its scheduled 71,000 tons of meat.[27]

Whenever shortages occurred, people not only looked for sensible explanations, they also looked for scapegoats. As things got worse, paranoia rose along with frustration. In Moscow, the "mafia" became the focus of blame for the meat shortage, a theory ultimately rejected by the Moscow militia, although not until after serious investigation. The mafia conspiracy story went as follows: Local residents said that the mafia was prohibiting meat from getting into Moscow by stopping trucks on the roads that led into the city and forcing them at gunpoint to turn around. To check out these rumors, the Moscow Administration for Struggle Against Embezzlement of Socialist Property (UBKhSS) said it sent a thousand people to investigate meat combines and meat procurement stations; and Moscow police even escorted meat trucks twenty-four hours a day, right up to the food stores where they were supposed to deliver meat. UBKhSS personnel questioned more than three hundred drivers and could not substantiate the theft of meat. The upshot of the investigation was that there was no proof of mafia involvement in the meat shortage.[28] The explanation provided by Moscow Deputy Mayor Sergei Stankevich, that 15 to 20 percent of the food that was supposed to go to Moscow's stores was actually sold through other channels, seems much more plausible.[29]

Food shortages in Leningrad is an emotional issue, one informed by the horrible experiences of World War II when perhaps a million people died of starvation. The new shortages under Gorbachev were extremely troubling for the city's population. By the end of August 1990, there was a daily shortage of 300 to 400 tons of vegetables.[30] A month later, at the end of September, the vegetable storage facilities in the city had taken in only one-third the amount of potatoes they were supposed to have received. Cities like Brest, Vilnius, Vitebsk, and Grodno had failed to deliver potatoes as scheduled.[31] Although the shortfall in deliveries was due in part to excessive rains that flooded fields and in part to the unwillingness of urbanites to work in the harvest, much of it had to do with suppliers breaking their contracts. As a result, in October, the heads of the various departments in Leningrad were traveling great distances to find vegetables, because their usual supplies were nowhere close to meeting their needs.[32]

A *Pravda* reporter traveling about the city in November vividly described the shortage of food and the high prices it engendered: "Some stores were completely empty, while in others there was a fierce crush of people after a piece of pork gristle described as meat or a soggy cooked sausage. Groats and sunflower oil have disappeared and salt and matches are not to be had. . . ."[33] Leningrad Mayor Anatolii Sobchak blamed the food shortages on "separatist tendencies" and "economic war" in the country.[34] In spelling out his views on December 11, Sobchak used apocalyptic terms: "This is a disaster. Famine will start if our emergency steps fail these few days or, at most, a fortnight. Moscow and Leningrad have always been supplied out of [central supplies]. Now that republics and regions no longer supply these [goods], the center can't guarantee us a gram of food. So we have to rely on ourselves or demand emergency steps from the central authorities."[35]

Food Problems in the Provinces

If life was difficult in Moscow and Leningrad, what it was like in the provinces could be seen in Sverdlovsk, a major industrial city on the eastern edge of the Ural Mountains. At the very end of 1989 and throughout 1990, the city experienced what its leaders described as a crisis. At the end of December 1989, just before the holidays, both food and vodka had disappeared from the stores. There were spontaneous demonstrations on December 29 when people had been issued ration coupons for vodka that did not exist on the shelves. But the absence of vodka was only the precipitating cause. The root of the people's anger was the perpetual absence of both food and other consumer goods in their city. But despite the demonstrations, the shortages grew worse.

By the fall of 1990, stores were described as empty, and it was said that for six months local residents were not able to exchange their ration coupons for sausage and sugar. There was no poultry, no canned fish, no flour, no fat. Moreover, the agricultural situation in regions near the city was in a deplorable state. The worst conditions existed in the potato harvest. It was estimated that the oblast's population needed 97,000 tons of potatoes to make it through a normal winter, but as of early September less than one-tenth of this amount had been transported and an even smaller amount stored.[36]

The Sverdlovsk deputies issued an ultimatum to Gorbachev, the central government, and the RSFSR Supreme Soviet, saying that if their food supply was not guaranteed, they would stop delivering industrial and defense goods.[37] The specifics of the Sverdlovsk charges were that other areas had failed to send thousands of tons of meat and that the city had not received its quota of sugar and imported tobacco products. The city of Sverdlovsk demanded that they be allowed to keep up to 20 percent of the food they were supposed to deliver under state orders and that they be given control over the foreign currency they earned.[38] In early October, the deputies in the Sverdlovsk Oblast council sent another telegram indicating that if the food situation did not improve within a week, they would consider taking "extreme measures to protect the interest of the population, including halting materials produced in the Sverdlovsk Oblast."[39]

There were similar problems in the Kemerovo Oblast during September 1990; thousands of tons of meat had not been shipped from Voronezh, Penza, and the Altai *Krai* (territory).[40] The Komi Autonomous Republic, in the northern part of Russia, also experienced severe food shortages in 1990 because other parts of the country failed to meet their delivery obligations. As Sverdlovsk officials did, the Komi leadership sent telegrams insisting that steps be taken to ensure they were supplied with food. Although they did not issue any ultimatums, the telegrams said that they would "switch to exchanges in kind" if deliveries were not honored.[41] The following April, the first party secretary in Komi directed all enterprises in the republic to deliver 15 percent of their output to the government so that it could be used to barter for food. At the same time, rationing was also introduced. Residents of the city of Syktyvkar were allowed one chicken and one pound of sausage every three months.[42]

As these examples illustrate, breaching contracts became a regular practice throughout the country in 1990. Only 73 percent of the 1990 plan for interrepublic deliveries of grain, flour, and cereals was fulfilled by the RSFSR; for Ukraine, this figure was 74 percent, and for Kazakhstan, 57 percent. All told, the shipments of grain products between republics and oblasts was 5.4 million tons shy of the plan.[43] The Krasnodar district of the Russian republic was a prime violator of state obligations. Its collective and state farms sold 31,000 tons of meat on the side and kept 16,500 tons more than they did in 1989 in order to meet local needs. Critics claimed that as a consequence, Murmansk did not receive even half the meat they were supposed to from Krasnodar farmers, Karelia got less than a third, and the Komi Autonomous Republic received only slightly more than half of its allocation.[44] In Tadzhikistan, rather than meeting their state orders for fruits and vegetables, farmers negotiated to sell their produce to the highest bidder. As a result of this and of farmers breaking their contracts, the state's canneries saw a shortfall of 6,000 tons of vegetables from Tadzhikistan. Tadzhik farmers also bartered fruits and vegetables in Siberia and in the Ural cities in exchange for needed lumber, cement, slate, metal, gasoline, and industrial equipment.[45] And Ukrainian farmers withheld four million tons of grain to barter for slate, timber, cement, and farm equipment.[46]

The following tale illustrates how the shortage of meat turned local authorities into criminals: A New Zealand cargo plane carrying $900,000 worth of New Zealand meat for sale in Europe ran out of fuel evading Stinger missiles on the Afghan-Soviet border and was forced to land in Tashkent. The local airport authorities refused to accept American dollars for fuel and instead briefly hijacked the plane and its precious cargo, demanding five tons of meat (valued at $37,200) in exchange for the fuel. Finally, the New Zealanders negotiated their way out of the situation by exchanging an unspecified amount of meat for fuel.[47]

The food shortfalls were not caused simply by the producers' unwillingness to meet their contractual obligations. The greater freedom of perestroika caused the breakdown of the patchwork system that had previously operated during the harvest seasons; perestroika also highlighted the country's dependence on administrative measures rather than economic incentives to move food successfully from field to table. For many years, one of the critical factors in the successful harvesting of field crops was the system whereby urban workers were bussed to collective and state farms to pick crops or to work at vegetable distribution centers. Industrial enterprises were required to release a certain number of their workers for several weeks to allow them to help in the harvest, and these workers were often joined by professionals such as engineers and doctors.

Quite independent of the economic and social costs of such a system, including the slowdowns in production and services, it was uniformly resented by both workers and enterprise directors. In a public opinion poll of 1,100 urbanites from ten large- and eleven medium-sized cities in several republics, the people's hostility toward work in vegetable storage facilities was obvious. Twenty-five percent said that neither he nor any member of his family would go to work at a vegetable storage facility. And even though 25 percent said that in principle people should help with the harvest, only 16 percent said that people should in principle help with the storage of vegetables. The negative attitude toward this kind of work prevailed in spite of the fact that only 6 percent of those interviewed believed that their city had a better supply of fruits and vegetables in 1990 than they did in 1989 and more than 50 percent felt that the opposite was true.[48]

When the most pernicious elements of the command system began to fall away, industrial enterprises and other types of organizations rebelled and refused to send workers for the harvest. The number of workers absent from their regular jobs during the harvest season of 1987 averaged 700,000 a day, but only 150,000 at the beginning of August 1990, suggesting how successful the boycott of the harvest became.[49] But there were also some costs. In 1989, in the city of Tomsk, the population refused to help with the harvest, with the result that a large part of the potato crop was lost. Tomsk was then left without a substantial part of its main food source, and potato prices rose as a result.[50] In August 1990, it was reported that in Minsk eighty of the city's enterprises and organizations were refusing to help with the harvest. Consequently, about 440 hectares became overrun with weeds for lack of workers. In retaliation, the agro-industrial authorities decided not to send vegetables to dozens of Minsk's cafeterias.[51] In essence, the industrial and agro-industrial bureaucracies went to war with each other. Many farms in the Saratov Oblast said that due to the absence of workers, they might have to plow under as much as 30 percent of their fields.[52] In the fall, one Moscow *raion* (district) sent a mere fourteen workers to help with the harvest even though their contract called for 1,420 people.[53]

The decline in the number of agricultural workers created by the urban boycott created an emergency to which the government responded with a multifold strategy. One part of the response focused on the workers themselves. In the Krasnodar Krai, local authorities threatened workers with the loss of their jobs if they did not help with the harvest. They also appealed to worker self-interest by announcing on television that urbanites could keep half the potatoes they harvested, an offer which substantially increased the number of volunteers.[54] A second tactic was to enlist the services of the military. The USSR Ministry of Defense sent 94 motor transport battalions, or about 45,000 vehicles to assist with the 1990 harvest.[55] In the republics of Russia and Kazakhstan, military drivers carried 30 million tons of agricultural produce, including 16.8 million tons of grain.[56] Still, the military equipment was seriously underutilized in 1990 because of what the Soviet Army general in charge described as serious inefficiencies in the organization of the harvest as well as the shortage of gasoline and oil. Consequently, on average, military trucks carried about 30 to 40 percent less of the harvest in 1990 than they had in 1989.[57]

Other critical factors disrupting the food supply in the provinces were the shortages of fuel and spare parts, the serious morale problem in the countryside because of the shortage of cigarettes (only 39 of the Soviet Union's 50 tobacco factories were operating), and the availability of only about one-third of the crates and jars that were needed for canning and shipping.[58] Krasnodar, for instance, needed 48,000 metric tons of fuel in order to harvest its hay and wheat, but had only 21,000. This meant that only one-third of their combines could be used in the harvest.[59] The Zaporozhe Oblast in Ukraine had no reserves of gasoline by June 1990 because the fuel depots in the Russian republic were not sending any under the instructions of its State Committee for Petroleum Products. Predictably, the oblast reacted by announcing that it would stop delivering meat until it received gasoline.[60] The links in the food production system had broken apart, with disastrous effects.

These problems were magnified by the disruptions in the storage, transportation, and distribution of food. Most of these problems had existed well before Gorbachev came to office. For a long time, one of the great failings of Soviet agriculture was the high percentage of food lost because it rotted in fields, or was not properly stored, or was shipped via inadequately refrigerated transportation and was not unloaded in a timely fashion. Perhaps as much as 30–40 percent of Soviet food never made it to the homes of the citizenry. In 1990, the amount of substandard and rotten food as a proportion of all the food delivered to state retail stores accounted for 11 percent of potatoes, 20 percent of cabbages, 14 percent of onions, and 30 to 40 percent of tomatoes.[61] This does not include the crops that rotted in the fields or barns or at points along the way to its destinations. In August of that year, there were reports that at least a million tons of grain was spoiling every day because of deficiencies in storage and transportation.[62] Refrigeration storage facilities were so inadequate that more than 40 percent of refrigeration equipment was regarded as past its usable life.[63]

Table 2.2

**Food Prices in Urban Markets (264 Cities) May 1990,
in Percent of May 1989 Food Prices**

Potatoes	89
Fresh cabbage	116
Onions	148
Green onions	134
Beets	129
Carrots	123
Fresh cucumbers	122
Fresh tomatoes	127
Garlic	92
Dill	119
Parsley	131
Apples	124
Beef	128
Lamb	114
Pork	129
Lard	104
Butter	108

Source: Merkurii, no. 5 (July 12, 1990), 3.

Rail cars loaded with food sat in railroad stations when there was little to buy in the stores. In mid-September 1990, not long before Leningrad instituted rationing, 174 rail cars carrying meat were standing unloaded in the city.[64] And on November 21, 1990, rail cars carrying meat were delivered to a meat-processing plant in Moscow where they sat still unloaded more than two weeks later on December 6.[65] This was at a time when Moscow stores were empty because of local fears of a winter famine.

All the previous problems of agriculture combined with the failings of perestroika to produce the first sustained food crisis since World War II.

Increasing Food Prices

As food supplies diminished, prices rose everywhere. Predictably, they were highest in the areas with the most substantial food deficits, namely the largest cities, particularly Moscow and Leningrad. Table 2.2 shows the increase in food prices in Soviet

Table 2.3

Food Prices in Collective Farm Markets, in Rubles per Kilogram, 1990

	Beef	Pork	Cucumbers	Apples	Onions
Moscow	18–20	18–30	6–10	3–5	2–3
Leningrad	20–30	15–20	6–10	5–7	1.5–2
Minsk	9	9	5	1–3	1.7
Tashkent	8	4	1.5	1.5	0.6
Alma-Ata	6	5	1.2	0.8	0.6
Frunze	7	5	1.0	0.7–1.0	0.6
Ashkhabad	8	6	4.0	2	0.7

Source: Izvestiia (November 1, 1990), 2.

urban markets from 1989 to 1990. For all but a few items, the increases were substantial, ranging from 16 to 48 percent.

The sometimes dramatic differences in prices between cities can be seen in Table 2.3. The prices in the collective farm markets of Moscow and Leningrad were substantially higher than those of other cities.

Rising food prices created anger. As early as mid-1989, for example, many Leningraders boycotted the collective farm markets one weekend, following the call of people's deputy Aleksei Levashev to protest the high and rising prices farmers were charging. The city supported the boycott by setting up stalls outside the collective farm market and selling fruits and vegetables at much reduced prices, although this was a symbolic gesture at best.[66] In the long run, the boycott had no effect on market prices because the absence of food in state stores did not leave Leningraders many options; they had to buy many foods in the free market or go without. There was also outrage in January 1991 after the Altai Krai government increased the price of meat and some dairy products. At angry rallies over the course of several days, people called for the resignation of the local leadership and the recall of all their deputies.[67]

Constant increases in food prices meant that Soviet households were forced to spend an ever increasing share of their income on food. Of those interviewed for a 1989 survey, 22.1 percent said they spent almost all their income on food, 38.2 percent said they spent more than half, and 24.6 percent said they spent approximately half their income on food.[68] By the end of the Gorbachev era, the situation seems to have worsened. An August 1991 poll of 3,000 people found that one-fourth of the population spent almost all their income on food, and more than one-third spent more than half their income this way.[69]

Private Hoarding

The hoarding of goods is a rational response by a citizenry that has lost faith in the capacity of its leaders to guarantee the supply of essential commodities and that has expectations of future inflation. Although the old Soviet system of centralized supply had many well-known failings, the population was sufficiently secure with it not to feel the need to resort to hoarding on a large-scale basis. There had always been shortages, but people had felt that a minimum supply would be available; there had been few fears that the system would not consistently provide at least the minimum. But during perestroika, people lost faith in the system's ability to guarantee the supply of even minimum amounts of food and other consumer goods, and private hoarding began. It accelerated when food prices rose rapidly in 1990 and 1991. The fear that prices would rise even higher led people to buy food at existing prices rather than risk waiting until the next day or the next week. As panic spread throughout the nation, hoarding became routine. Expectations of shortages were realized as people grabbed what they could when they could. The prophesy of rising shortages was fulfilled.

Hoarding began as early as 1987 when, according to one estimate, as much as a quarter of the population, fueled by rumors, was already stockpiling goods, especially food.[70] Panic buying of food never stopped after that. In the fall of 1989, rumors spread in Moscow that stores were running out of food and that it would be worse during the winter; housewives began to stockpile such staples as rice, pasta, and flour. People did not accept assurances from central authorities. The head of *Glavprodtorg* (the main administration of food trade) said, "We have sufficient amounts of . . . 'cereal-flour' type groceries not only in Moscow, but in the country as a whole," but panicked Muscovites were buying 140 tons of rice every day, compared to the usual daily sales of 95 to 96 tons.[71] In May 1990, panic buying of food in Leningrad led the local authorities to impose a system requiring a passport as proof of people's city residence before they could shop there. Flour sales in Leningrad were three times the normal level, groats were selling at four times the usual rate, and twice as much butter as normal was sold. For reasons that no one seemed able to explain, there was a run on salt and matches as well.[72]

A year later, in 1991, it seemed as though the entire population was trying to buy as much as possible; their wallets were full of rubles, but their cupboards were bare. Everything seemed fair game in what appeared to be a feeding frenzy brought on by fears that nothing would be available the next day and that the bottom might fall out at any moment. Reports suggested that the population was buying 50 percent more meat, twice the amount of tea and canned food normally purchased, "150 percent more sugar, . . . 50 percent more refrigerators, electric irons and television sets and 70 percent more footwear than they actually need."[73] A survey of 49,000 urban Soviet households confirmed the widespread hoarding. As of January 1, 1991, the stocks of individual food items held by families was considerably higher than it had been in 1990. The average urban family (blue-collar and white-collar families) held 9 percent more meat and meat products, 17 percent more milk and dairy products, 65 percent more eggs, 68 percent more fish and fish products, 12 percent more sugar, twice as much sugar, 11 percent more potatoes, 54 percent more flour, 83 percent more flour, 70 percent more cereals, and more than twice as much macaroni products as they had in 1990.[74]

As the price increases scheduled for April 1 approached, Soviet households went about buying goods even more furiously. The amounts of certain food products held by the average household as of the first of April were staggering: 3.5 months' supply of flour and cereals, 58 days' worth of sugar, 45 days' store of rice, 37 days' worth of macaroni, 15 days' supply of meat products, and 4 to 8 days' store of dairy products, fish products, and eggs.[75] The massive hoarding represented a rush to accumulate food both as nonmonetary assets as a hedge against inflation, and as security against fears of hunger.

Other factors, such as the tense nationality politics of the perestroika era, also contributed to private hoarding. On June 1, 1990, the Latvian republican government introduced rationing for food products, including flour, cereal, and pasta, that had recently been in significantly greater demand. The reason for this so-called pasta panic was that immediately after Latvia declared its independence, the republic's citizens went on a shopping spree, buying everything in sight, including some foods no one would touch before, like canned fish. People were fearful that the central government would punish their maverick politics by slowing down the flow of food to Latvia. They remembered the central government embargo imposed on Lithuania when it had declared its independence, and they believed that they too could become victims of a similar policy.[76] Fears about the consequences of the transition to a market economy also sparked private hoarding in a number of places. In Kaluga, for instance, people panicked over the announcement on May 25, 1990, that the central government was going to move to economic reform.[77]

By the time the Gorbachev era came to an end, most households were hoarding goods. A survey of some 3,000 people carried out by the All-Union Center for the Study of Public Opinion found that 57 percent of the people were "stocking up on products for future use," while only 37 percent said they were not. Of those who were not hoarding goods, just under half—47 percent—said it was because there was nothing to buy anyway, 29 percent said they did not have the financial capacity to stockpile goods, 15 percent said they had nowhere to store extra goods, and only 19 percent were not stocking up because they did not believe there would be a justification for doing so.[78] In other words, about 80 percent of the population either was hoarding or wanted to but could not because of their circumstance.

Public Hoarding

The hoarding by individuals paled in comparison to the massive scale of public hoarding, which became a dominant policy of the republics. It was called rationing, and nominally that is what it was. Scarce goods, food and nonfood alike, were allocated among the citizenry in city after city and republic after republic. But it was not done in the interests of an equitable sharing of the shrinking pie; it was done to protect the local population and to provide the local rationing authority with control over certain goods they could use as barter for goods they did not have. Past nationwide rationing policies, such as those that had been in effect during World War II, had been intended to create a national sense of equity; but during the perestroika years, there was never any sense of national unity behind local rationing policies. In simple truth, protection barriers were erected internally; the cities and republics of the USSR declared economic war against each other. In retrospect, it is arguable that the Soviet Union ceased to exist as an entity once localism had begun to rule the land.

The Moscow passport system reflected all the harmful consequences of protectionism that developed during the Gorbachev era. The decision to ration goods in Moscow evolved over a period of several months. In August 1989, the Moscow City Trade Administration worked on a set of procedures for selling goods that were scarce in the city, basing their ideas on the assumption that 40 percent of all food and other goods sold in Moscow, and as much as half of certain of these, actually left the city. At first, the only major step taken was to concentrate scarce food products in special "orders" stores or in "orders" departments of large grocery stores in the areas of the city with the highest population concentrations. It was also decided to sell consumer goods that were in high demand at work places, through an arrangement called "on-site sale."[79]

The following May, however, the Moscow City Council introduced a rationing system. It acted in the wake of a frenzy of food buying when many Moscow stores were said to have sold their monthly allotment of tea, sugar, cereals, flour, eggs, vegetable oil, and pasta in two days. Under the new system, food could be purchased only by residents of Moscow or the Moscow Oblast who presented an internal passport.

Initially, the passport identification system was to be in force for two weeks only.[80] But once the two-week period ended, the Moscow City Council decided to extend the rationing system indefinitely and issued each resident a special shopping identification "visiting" card (*torgovaia vizitnaia kartochka*), which entitled them to shop in the city's stores.[81] In order to ensure that restricted goods did not leave the city, the police and representatives of the Department for Combating the Embezzlement of Socialist Property and Speculation patrolled the railroad stations and inspected departing trains. The executive committee of the Moscow City Council also empowered law enforcement agencies to inspect baggage that they thought looked suspicious, without any special authority from the city prosecutor's office.[82] By taking such measures, the radical democrats of the Moscow City Council were retreating to the heavy-handed methods of their predecessors in an effort to protect the economic well-being of their constituents.

The passport system drew an angry response from those who lived outside Moscow but shopped in the city. On May 29, 1990, for example, the city of Kalinin asked Moscow to rescind the decision and sent telegrams to the councils of ministers for USSR and the RSFSR to gather support for its cause. Kalinin also wielded its own club: it threatened temporarily to stop sending livestock products to Moscow as of June 1 and to introduce their own passport system if Moscow persisted in selling goods only to Muscovites.[83] A number of cities surrounding Moscow also introduced their own rationing systems. Kaluga instituted the rationing of flour, cereals, vegetable oil, and butter and a passport system for the purchase of all other foods on June first and decreased its deliveries of meat and milk to Moscow. Yaroslavl, Tula, and Riazan also either broached the subject of a rationing system or actually put some form of one into effect.[84]

In an effort to deal with the situation, virtually all these cities simultaneously held discussions with the Moscow administration to persuade it to back off from its rigid policy.[85] Faced with retaliation, Moscow agreed to a compromise that would allow 1,500 stores to open on Sundays to serve nonresidents of Moscow, who were then able to buy the same amount as city residents.[86]

The Moscow city council also tried to mollify the strong sense of their own citizens' aggrievance. Muscovites produced some 6 percent of the country's manufactured consumer goods, but could buy only a small percentage of what they produced because the rest was shipped outside the city. In mid-1990 the city asked the governments of both the USSR and the RSFSR to allow Moscow to keep an additional 12.5 percent of their output in 1990.[87]

The goods shortages continued throughout 1990, and, as the situation worsened, the city administration sought other answers. In July, at the city's request, the All-Union Center for the Study of Public Opinion conducted a poll of almost 2,900 Muscovites to solicit their views on how to distribute food and other consumer goods in the near future. Fifty-four percent favored a continuation of the special visiting card, 17 percent wanted a return to the passport system, and 24 percent wanted a return to the old unrestricted system. Forty-five percent wanted a rationing system, and 27 percent wanted a market with freely determined prices.[88] The people who wanted rationing got what they asked for, although not for nearly a year. On October 22, the Moscow City Council's presidium announced plans to use ration coupons for basic foods to protect the population during the transition to the market economy. At the same time, the city said that Moscow food would be for Moscow citizens alone.[89] However, it was not until January 1991 that the government announced actual plans for rationing, to go into operation on March 1 for meat, lard, sausage, grains, vodka, and wine.[90]

Ukraine developed similar policies to protect its own population. The republic faced a highly inflationary situation, claiming that three billion rubles was chasing one billion rubles worth of goods on the market.[91] Its rationing program began with a ban on the export of grain and sunflower seeds early in September 1990, because there was a shortage of grain to produce the bread and pasta demanded by Ukrainians.[92] Later that month, the presidium of the Ukrainian Supreme Soviet banned the export of all agricultural products above the levels already designated for export, because the Russian republic had raised its purchase prices for meat and other key agricultural products, providing neighboring southern Ukrainian farmers with an incentive to sell these products to Russia.[93]

The centerpiece of Ukraine's effort to deal with the empty shelves in its stores was the introduction of a policy on November 1, 1990, to protect the republic's consumers. The essence of this policy was the issuance of consumer coupons; 70 percent of a Ukrainian worker's after-tax monthly salary was paid in coupons.[94] The remaining 30 percent was paid in cash, which was used to buy goods in the collective farm markets, in commercial stores, and in restaurants. Most food and consumer goods were sold for coupons. The main exceptions were expensive consumer durables costing more than 1,500 rubles, but even in these cases, cash was not the medium of exchange; people had to use checks from the state savings bank, and these checks could be used only by those who lived in the republic.

In the early days of the Ukrainian policy, there was a great deal of uncertainty about how it would work. Many wanted the measure postponed because they feared that the second economy would benefit. The Odessa Oblast Trade Union Council, for example, opposed the measures on several grounds: workers could not get food for their families without a coupon, the coupons did not guarantee that goods would be in supply, and there was a belief that prices would rise and that the second economy would grow.[95] The popular view was perhaps captured best by a letter from a Ukrainian that was cited in *Pravda*. The writer said cynically, "If there are goods in the stores, I will accept and be in favor of ration cards. If not, I don't need any innovations."[96]

By the end of 1990, the Ukrainian leadership optimistically claimed that it had ended panic buying in the republic. As evidence, it pointed to the fact that gross sales receipts for November were 500 billion rubles less than the government target and 1.8 billion rubles less than receipts for October, when the buying fever was at its height. Simultaneously, such foods as cereals, eggs, and a variety of canned and smoked goods that had disappeared during the panic buying reappeared.[97] The government was so confident that sufficient stability had been achieved on the local consumer goods market that it abolished the special coupons on July 1, 1991; perhaps ironically, in Odessa, where there had originally been vocal opposition to the plan, it was decided to keep the program in place until September 1 to prevent nonresidents from buying up goods in the city's stores.[98]

But Ukraine's problems were not solved; they were just dealt with in a more politically palatable way. The optimism of December 1990 disappeared in the heat of the summer. On August 10, slightly more than a month after the special-coupon program was lifted, Prime Minister Fokin announced that the republic was temporarily banning the export of sixty consumer items, including foods. Once again, Ukrainian farmers began sending goods to areas where the purchase prices were higher. Like Moscow, Ukraine felt it necessary to administer the new policy by using police authority. They created 95 new border posts and 152 mobile border units. At the same time, the republic resurrected ration coupons.[99]

The beggar-thy-neighbor policy that was pursued with such energy in Moscow and Ukraine also dominated the Leningrad response to the shortages. The Leningrad city government's first response to the goods shortages came on January 10, 1990, with new residents-only consumer regulations, under which the sale of cigarettes, furniture, meat, lemons, butter, cooking oil, and luxury items was restricted to those who held documented proof of residency (initially of an internal passport and later an identification card).[100] The action resulted in the predictable responses from such neighboring areas as Novgorod and Pskov, whose own citizens' welfare was dependent on their ability to buy goods in Leningrad. The local governments of the surrounding areas threatened everything, from cutting the deliveries of meat and dairy products to Leningrad, to cutting the city off completely.

The variations in reactive economic policies among the different republics and cities, combined with newly open borders, created an incentive for goods to move out of places with fixed prices and toward places with more freely determined prices in the goods market. Leningrad faced a serious dilemma so long as it maintained subsidized prices. Either it had essentially to seal its borders or risk the continued outflow of scarce goods to outsiders; Estonians, for instance, came to Leningrad to buy goods at fixed state prices, then resold them at prices which were rising rapidly within Estonia.[101]

This discrepancy between a market in Estonia and the command system still operating in Leningrad prompted the latter to enact further restrictive food-distribution policies. When Estonia decided to raise certain food prices in the fall of 1990, city authorities assumed that Estonians would once again pour into Leningrad to buy food at lower prices. In order to prevent this, the city decided to expand its proof-of-residence regulations to cover the sale and purchase of all foods.[102] This was not a real solution to Leningrad's continuing food shortages, and in mid-November the city council voted to introduce food rationing on December 1, 1990. Meat, vegetables, oil and animal fats, eggs, cereals, and certain other foods were to be rationed. It was a policy which suited many Leningraders, especially elderly citizens who felt that rationing would create stability in the food supply.[103] But the monthly ration allowances were slender: 1.5 kilograms of meat, 1 kilogram of sausage, 0.5 kilogram of butter, 0.25 kilogram of vegetable oil, 10 eggs, 0.5 kilogram of flour, and 1 kilogram of cereals or macaroni.[104] These rations were not very different from the ration allowances for some groups during the first part of World War II.[105]

Regional protectionism spread through the country like a virus, and it was a disease for which there was no cure in the short term. The republic of Kirgizia, whose vegetable production was important to cities in Siberia, the Urals, and the far north, banned the export of vegetables to any part of the country in October 1989. The Kirgiz government justified the policy with the rather dubious argument that it would diminish the "speculative activity of trading and production cooperatives and the primary necessity of fulfilling economic tasks with regard to state deliveries," even though the export ban extended to surplus vegetable production.[106] The republic of Georgia also introduced an emergency measure to deal with food shortages whereby all goods in state stores could only be sold upon presentation of an identity card. In this case, one of the primary goals was to prevent the export of Georgia's citrus fruits.[107]

Beginning in April 1990, the Russian city of Kostroma issued to its citizens resident-consumer identification booklets for the purchase of certain goods. There were two types of booklets: family booklets, for the purchase of large, expensive items such as furniture and major appliances; and individual booklets, for the purchase of such personal items as shoes.[108] On October 1, 1990, in the wake of critical food shortages, the city of Saratov instituted a policy whereby local stores could sell certain basic food products and tobacco only to those with proof-of-residence identification.[109] Rationing of food to local citizens only was introduced in the city of Cheliabinsk on November 1, 1990, and then was expanded to the entire oblast on December 5, 1990. The monthly entitlement was only half a kilogram each of pasta and margarine, ten eggs, and three bottles of alcohol, and citizens had to show their identity cards three times within the same store— once to register in the store's card index, once to get a receipt printed out, and a third time to receive their goods.[110]

Lithuania responded to the problem of goods shortages in stages as part of its struggle toward autonomy. Limitations were imposed in the wake of Gorbachev's efforts to bring to heel a rebellious republic which had declared independence and was now being punished for its single-minded efforts to achieve sovereignty.[111] It had foolishly supposed it could cut Moscow and

Leningrad off from food, but it did not have the resources to accomplish this and instead became a victim of rather severe food shortages.[112] Meat, for example, became extremely scarce in the capital of Vilnius. Food rationing in Lithuania began in May 1990, when monthly personal allowances were set as two kilograms each of flour, cereals, oil and butter, and sugar.[113] The second stage of Lithuania's effort to cope with the shortages came on January 1, 1991, when it adopted a coupon system for allocating basic foods and some industrial consumer goods.[114] All dairy products except butter and milk were excluded from the original list of rationed products. People were able to buy 400 grams of butter a month per "sugar" coupon and ten eggs per "groats" coupon. Consumer goods were rationed to one pair of socks or stockings a month for "sock" coupons, one item for the "knitted underwear" coupon, and one item every six months for the "table linen" and "towel" coupons. In July 1991, Lithuania adopted a coupon program similar to Ukraine's. One-fifth of an individual's wages was paid out in so-called general checks and four-fifths were paid in rubles. The coupons were not only for purchasing food, but were also to be used for purchasing such consumer goods as electrical and household appliances, furniture, high-fashion clothing, shoes, and fabrics.[115]

A great deal of conflict among cities, between cities and republics, and between republics and the central government was caused by the parochialism of local interests. The Soviet republics' retaliatory responses to each other's protective economic measures were textbook examples of the sorts of reprisals against tariffs and quotas that take place in international trade. Krasnodar's conflict with the RSFSR government is a case in point. At the beginning of February 1991, the Krasnodar region of the RSFSR introduced food rationing. Coincidentally, at the end of January there had been an emergency meeting of the Extraordinary Commission of the Congress of RSFSR People's Deputies to discuss the 1990 shortfalls in the Krasnodar Krai's agreed-upon meat deliveries to the Russian government. The commission instructed the RSFSR procurator's office to file charges against N. Kondratenko, the chairman of the Krasnodar Krai's council, under a relatively new law that defined mutual obligations during the period of economic reform and allowed the court to impose fines of up to 10,000 rubles against Krasnodar for failing to meet those obligations. There was anger in Krasnodar at the decision because there was a great shortage of meat in the Kuban region, and the meat that was being demanded by the RSFSR authorities did not exist, which was why rationing had been introduced.[116] Much the same thing happened the following January when the Irkutsk Oblast Party Committee was reprimanded by the Russian government for not delivering all the timber required under state orders. The oblast committee responded that, until it received guarantees of food deliveries, it would continue its policy of establishing direct trading ties with other areas in order to ensure the needs of its own people.[117]

Another almost textbook case involved the area around Vologda, in northern Russia. The city of Vologda instituted a rationing system in January 1990, whereby goods were sold "by invitation": Residents of the city received a chit on their birthday entitling them to buy a scarce consumer good in one of thirty-two stores in the city. But the 62,000 people who lived in the rural areas around the city and did their shopping for furniture and high-fashion shoes and clothing in the city proper were ineligible for this program and were understandably angry. Rumors abounded that certain state farms in the area were going to retaliate against the city by not shipping it food.[118]

Gorbachev finally responded to the problem of public hoarding, but his response had almost no effect on the national preoccupation with elevating local interests above all other considerations. In April 1991, no more than four months before his opponents attempted to remove him from office, he issued a decree entreating enterprises to honor all their contracts and economic ties for 1991. To deal with the pernicious economic divisions, he gave the local and republican governments one week to rescind all decrees that obstructed exports.[119] The unpleasant fact is that Gorbachev's effort was too little, too late. Too substantial a part of the economic system that had existed before perestroika had been significantly altered, and the country was out of control.

The Shortage of Consumer Goods

Along with the food shortages, the lack of consumer goods was a visible failure of the Gorbachev era. It was especially noticeable because a great deal had been promised. On April 18, 1985, a month after Gorbachev became head of the Communist Party of the Soviet Union, the CPSU Central Committee adopted a resolution entitled "On Measures for the Further Development of Local Industry in 1986–1990 and in the Period up to the Year 2000." The resolution called for an increase in consumer goods production over the 1985 level of at least 33 percent by 1990 and 80 percent by the year 2000.[120] These goals were then translated into the Comprehensive Program for the Development of Consumer Goods Production and the Service Sphere from 1986 to 2000, which set out more detailed quantitative goals, such as increasing housing and municipal services, long a sore point with the population.[121]

But much less was delivered than was promised, and the shortages multiplied. It was not only a matter of too much money chasing too few goods. In 1989 there was an *absolute* decline in the production of certain goods. The number of television sets produced that year fell short of the state plan by 420,000, radios by 740,000, and washing machines by 353,000; and the shortfall in furniture production was valued at 294 million rubles. Targets for refrigerators, sewing machines, and electric vacuum cleaners were also not met.[122] The result was that, in 1991, of 1,100 types of consumer goods, only twenty were routinely available in the country's stores and only ten percent of all types of goods were not in some way rationed.[123]

These shortfalls were exacerbated by two circumstances. Most important was the increase in incomes during the Gorbachev years, which far outstripped the increase in consumer goods; excess demand was a constant problem during perestroika. In 1988, money income increased by 9 percent, well above the 3 to 5 percent increases of the previous decade. In 1989 and the first half of 1990, the amount of consumer goods going into the state retail network rose by 9 percent, but money incomes went up by 12.9 percent.[124] The gap between supply and demand kept growing. In 1987, the gap between the supply of goods and the population's money incomes was 9.5 billion rubles; in 1988 it was 20.7 billion rubles; in 1989, 22.5 billion rubles; and for the first half of 1990, it was already 21.4 billion rubles (for a projected annual level of 42.8 billion rubles).[125] Second, during the three-year period from 1986 through 1988, the reduction in the imports of consumer goods was valued at almost 9 billion rubles.[126] Even the combination of domestic production and imports met only 40 to 70 percent of the population's demands for many types of goods.[127]

Early in 1989, the weekly *Nedelia* asked its readership to send in answers to a questionnaire on their experiences with "new" shortages: What specific goods, which they had had no problems buying before, did they now find in short supply? From 5,008 responses, *Nedelia* drew up a long list. Although the list contained items that had previously been in short supply and therefore somewhat limited the accuracy of the findings, the exercise suggested that people were prepared to use any means they could find to express publicly their frustrations over the shortages.

In certain ways, the consumer goods shortages stemmed from the same circumstances that caused the food shortages, but there were also some different problems.

Hoarding Consumer Goods

As in the food economy, there was hoarding of consumer goods. In this instance, however, in addition to private hoarding by citizens and public hoarding by republics and cities, there was also hoarding by the central government, which sought to restrict the export of consumer goods. Hoarding by a republic was an attempt to ensure that its goods did not benefit some other

Table 2.4

"New Shortages" of Nonfood Consumer Goods

Item	Number of Times Mentioned per 1,000 Questionnaires
Soap	433
Laundry powder	405
Cosmetics, perfumery	353
Toothpaste	203
Shampoo	65
Hair spray	12
Razor blades	36
Compact cassettes	84
Footwear	53
Hosiery items	46
Outer clothing	42
Underwear	16
Sporting goods	15
Fabrics and wool	13
Photographic supplies	11
Zippers	10
Television sets, refrigerators, washing machines	90
Furniture	30
Automobiles	10
Medicine	15
Contraceptives	15

Source: Nedelia no. 20 (May1989), 6.

republic's citizens at the expense of its own people, a policy which ran absolutely counter to the central government's wishes. But the fortress mentality of the regions was reinforced by the national policy of export restriction.

Private hoarding emerged as a response to three things: real shortages, groundless fears that particular goods might be in short supply, and official rationing of certain goods which led people to accumulate as much as possible of the rationed products. In the same way they hoarded certain foods, Soviet citizens hoarded excessive amounts of consumer goods. A poll showed that, from 1989 to 1990, 9 to 10 percent of the purchases of men's and women's footwear and 12 percent of the purchases of

children's footwear were for future use and were bought as a
hedge against future shortages.[128] The poll also showed that the
average holding of detergents per household was about 6 kilograms, or more than twice what was considered to be the ordinary needs of a Soviet family.[129] Some families reportedly
accumulated 6 to 8 months' worth of soap and detergents.[130] In
Moscow alone, where normally 80 tons were sold daily, 300 to
600 tons of detergent a day were being sold.[131] The number of
people who hoarded goods rose as items continued to disappear.
While 25 percent of families made purchases in 1987 which they
described as "hoarding," 66 percent did so in 1988, and in 1989,
90 percent were hoarding supplies.[132] By the time of the August
1991 coup, almost everyone feared for a future without goods to
buy and acted in ways that guaranteed that their worst fears
would come true.

There were many examples of republics or localities acting to
protect their own citizens. In Estonia, the city of Tallinn enacted
a law prohibiting the sale of consumer goods to people who did
not live in the city and requiring consumers to present their passports or personal identity cards in the stores. The head of the
Tallinn trade department said that the measure was being taken
because otherwise, in his view, speculators would clean out the
stores and sell the goods in other cities where there were consumer goods shortages.[133] The Kirghiz Council of Ministers pro-
scribed the export of most consumer goods in February 1990 in
order to improve supplies for their own population.[134] The Uzbek
Council of Ministers adopted a resolution permitting the sale of
both food and consumer goods only on presentation of a passport or
some other form of identification, in part as an effort to improve
upon the situation of their citizens and in part as the measure was a
form of protective retaliation against proof-of-residence restrictions
that had been instituted elsewhere.[135]

The central government first imposed a ban on the export of
various foods and consumer goods, televisions, refrigerators and
freezers, washing and sewing machines, children's clothing, and
footwear, some household appliances, some radios and cameras,

and some car parts, on February 1, 1989, to run through the end of 1990. Exports of certain goods out of the Soviet Union were made subject to customs duties that equaled from 20 to 100 percent of retail prices. And the total value of goods that an individual could take out of the country could not exceed 100 rubles.[136] These strict controls resulted from the fact that large numbers of goods had been leaving the Soviet Union: during the first ten months of 1988, about 400,000 televisions, 200,000 refrigerators and freezers, and 50,000 washing machines had been purchased by foreigners, most from Eastern Europe and Mongolia.[137] As the shortages worsened, the list of goods that could not leave the country expanded. In July 1989, the central government added building materials, household linen, and tableware to the catalogue of prohibited goods.[138]

As public anger over the shortages grew, the central government once again intervened. In December 1989, it published new restrictive rules for obtaining licenses to export consumer goods. With the specific goal of increasing supplies of foods and consumer goods, the government also set quotas on the amount of consumer goods that could be exported in 1990.[139] Yet another emergency regulation governing the movement of goods out of the Soviet Union was adopted in March 1990, tightening controls at the border and directing the confiscation of goods from citizens who tried to take even a single item from the lengthened list of banned goods out of the country.[140]

Diminished Output of Consumer Goods

One of the main factors affecting the shortage of consumer goods was the producers' inability to get their allotted supplies of inputs. At the beginning of 1990, the RSFSR's light industry and textile enterprises were guaranteed only 65 percent of the cotton fiber they needed, 86 percent of the raw silk, 86 percent of the dyestuffs, and 75 percent of the plasticized rubber.[141] Much the same held true for other republics. The obvious result was that certain consumer goods could not be produced. For example, in

1988, the Vichuga Clothing Factory in Ivanovo was doing quite well selling popular bleached denim suits. But it had to cut back its production drastically in 1990 when the supply of denim fell from its 1988 level of 120,000 meters to only 20,000.[142]

The main cause of this supply problem was similar to the primary cause of the shortfall in food deliveries: the republics that had previously been relied upon to supply factories in other republics or other cities with production inputs were now protecting themselves. A yarn-producing enterprise in Lithuania, for instance, informed a Georgian knitwear factory that it was saving all its yarn for local factories.[143] This was part of the pattern of retaliation that emerged after republics and cities had imposed either formal ration coupon systems or export barriers.

A second aspect of the supply problem was the result of a shortage of hard currency, which left Soviet factories unable to purchase foreign-produced inputs. As one example, the local knitwear association in Volgograd purchased Italian sewing machines early in 1990 to produce men's socks, an item already in short supply. But the machines were used for only a little more than seven months; the Volgograd factories ran out of needles but could not buy any more because of the foreign exchange crisis.[144]

Clearly, people in the Soviet Union had a sense of being beleaguered. Some tried to fight back. A number of consumer advocate groups were created by ordinary Soviet citizens. A group called the USSR Union of State and Cooperative Information and Reference Services was formed early in 1989. Its goals were not only to develop a nationwide reference and information service about job openings, but also to have a listing of where shoppers could find spare parts, equipment, and other non-perishable consumer goods.[145] But the organization's efforts bore little fruit.

Importing Consumer Goods

The inability of the domestic economy to produce an adequate supply of consumer goods forced the leadership to turn to international markets in an attempt to close the gap between domestic supply and demand and to mollify the increasingly frustrated population. In April 1989, the Ministry of Trade disclosed that it planned to increase imports of consumer goods from the original level of 32 billion rubles to 37 billion rubles, clearly regarding this as an emergency measure.[146] What the regime regarded as the most dire shortages is suggested by examining the shopping list for which these additional 5 billion rubles were used. The plan was to import 15 million pairs of leather shoes, 12 million pairs of women's warm boots, 15 million sewn and knitted items, 300 million razor blades, 150 million dry-cell batteries, 30 million pairs of women's pantyhose, 10 million small cassette players, more than 180,000 tons of soap and detergents, 10,000 tons of toothpaste, as well as quantities of other goods.[147] As if to demonstrate the concern of the Gorbachev leadership, five ministers, including Deputy Prime Minister Aleksandra Biriukova, went to Great Britain in July and spent $165 million for consumer goods, including 50 million pairs of pantyhose and 1.7 million pairs of women's shoes.[148]

But the government's ability to import such goods was severely constrained by the shortage of hard currency which had hit with great force in 1989. The city of Moscow, for example, had 160 million rubles in foreign currency allocated to it in 1988, to buy everything from milk to garbage trucks. By 1990, that amount had dropped to a mere 15 million rubles.[149]

The Cigarette Shortage

A look at the cigarette shortage of 1990 illuminates the picture of consumer goods shortages. Late in the summer of 1990, the country experienced a severe shortage of cigarettes, for a number of reasons. Among these was the antiquated state of the Soviet Union's production equipment, which was in need of constant repair, and the virtual absence of any spare parts during the two previous years.[150] Production materials were also in short supply. Moscow's Yava factory closed down in part because there were no filters for cigarettes, and factories all over the country were

facing the same problem. The only producer of filters for cigarettes since about mid-1989 had been an Armenian plant that was
not operating because it received its fiber from Kirovakan, which
had not produced any since the 1989 earthquake.[151] Several other
problems, such as the shortage of cigarette paper and printer's
ink for cigarette packs, were also connected with the ubiquitous
breakdown in production and supply.[152]

The cigarette shortage led to serious morale problems in the
country. In Tomsk, the 1990 harvest was threatened when some
farm machinery operators said they would not go back to work
until they got their cigarettes. And workers in a number of enterprises broached the subject of a strike over the same issue.[153] A
more explosive response to the sense of deprivation were the
August tobacco riots in Leningrad, which grew to be quite large.
The Leningrad city council responded by imposing fines of
20,000 rubles for those involved and the confiscation and auc-
tioning of cars used in the organization of the riots.[154]

The shortage produced the predictable response in black markets. The price of a pack of cigarettes soared to 10 to 20 times the
regular price.[155] It also produced an example of local protectionism in Moscow, where the city council set a limit on the number
of packs that could be bought at state prices. A person over the
age of sixteen could buy up to five packs a month; after that, they
would have to buy their cigarettes on the black market or go
without.[156] People could buy their September cigarette rations
only with their December 1990 sugar ration coupon. Those who
chose not to use the sugar coupon for cigarettes received 4 kilograms of sugar instead of 2 at the beginning of 1991.[157] With utter
disregard for the rule of the USSR State Committee on Prices,
which prohibited free-market prices, the city council also intention-
ally allowed certain cigarette brands to be sold at market prices.[158]

The Anger of the Population

There was no shortage of popular anger in the country, nor of
efforts to lay blame. Much like the bad old days, it became fash-

ionable to go after the economic and party bureaucracy to find the reasons for deficiencies. At a meeting of the Politburo on September 8, 1989, the issue of the insufficient supply of non-food consumer goods was raised. Describing conditions in the country as "tense," the Politburo decided that "the situation which evolved was the result of mistakes, red tape, and an irresponsible attitude toward this business by the leaders of ministries, departments and enterprises, the permanent organs of the USSR Council of Ministers and the USSR State Planning Committee."[159] At the end of the month, the CPSU Central Committee examined more closely the issue of who within the party was to blame for the shortages of consumer goods. Specific individuals were reprimanded in the press for their failures. These included, among others, the Minister of the Chemical Industry for failing to ensure an adequate supply of synthetic detergents, and the Deputy Chairman of the USSR Council of Ministers Bureau for Social Development for his role in "inadequately monitoring the production and delivery of consumer goods."[160] In the ruling group's analysis, it was not the system that was at fault, but specific individuals who did not do their jobs properly; if only they had, these shortages would not have existed.

For the general population, there were other scapegoats at hand. Foreign workers were seen as victimizers of Russians because they were buying up scarce consumer goods. On several occasions in September 1989, the tension led to fights between Muscovites and some of the 10,000 Vietnamese working in the capital. On September 22, when there was already great tension, a fight erupted after Vietnamese workers apparently bought the entire stock of scarce shampoo at one department store. Two Vietnamese had gotten on line early and were later joined by others. By the time the Russian workers reached the counter, there was no shampoo left, and the fight broke out.[161] If nothing else, the fighting reflected how much tension existed and how easy it was for the citizens to find a way to blame outsiders for their problems.

The frustration of the whole population was turning ugly, and violence was erupting in a number of places. In Vologda, over a four-month period, twenty-nine store workers were reported injured in clashes with consumers. In Irkutsk, angry customers broke store windows, damaged counters, verbally abused and even frisked clerks to look for hidden goods. In Khabarovsk, when a local clothing store sold all its merchandise, the angry customers who had gathered outside broke through barriers and destroyed windows and doors. And in Tula Oblast, a twenty-three-year-old liquor store clerk was killed after he refused to sell vodka after hours.[162] In Chita, in eastern Siberia, there was a liquor riot at the end of 1990 when thousands of people were unable to exchange their ration coupons for liquor. Among other things, the rioters lit bonfires and destroyed lampposts.[163] In Novosibirsk, a person was crushed to death when the queue waiting to buy imported raincoats tried to storm the department store. Riot police were sent to guard the store in the aftermath, but the violence there was not new. The store manager said she occasionally hid in the freight elevator out of fear when the crowds of customers went wild. Once she had had nerve gas sprayed in her face and two of her assistants had been beaten up. In an early 1991 incident, police had to rescue sales clerks trapped at 2 A.M. in the store by customers, and in the rescue process a great deal of damage was done to the store.[164]

The Housing Shortage

It would be hard to find another area in which the Soviets failed so miserably as they did in housing. While the housing shortage was not a new problem, it got worse as perestroika wore on. The predicament was so bad, that in a 1990 nationwide poll of 100 rural and urban areas, housing was rated as the most severe socioeconomic problem in the country.[165] At the end of 1989, some 11 million people were living in dormitories, more than 5 million were living in what the Soviets regarded as dilapidated housing, and 10 percent of all urban families were living in rooms in communal apartments. Almost 50 percent of the population lived in housing with less than 9 square meters per person, an amount considered below sanitary standards. The Twenty-Seventh Party Congress, held in February 1986, announced the Housing–2000 program. Its goal was to provide every Soviet family with an individual apartment or house by the year 2000, an ambition that meant building a minimum of 35 million apartments, the equivalent of about twice the amount of housing space that had been built during the most productive five-year plan. If this announcement raised the hopes of the Soviet people, the pace of investment, which made it possible to build no more than 67 percent of the proposed housing space, quickly dashed them.[166] This was a poorer level than had been achieved before Gorbachev took office. For the years 1981–1984, the plan for opening apartment houses to tenancy was fulfilled by 79 percent; in the first nine months of 1985, that figure was only 73 percent.[167]

The task of building new housing was made more difficult in 1989 and 1990 because the construction industry was faltering so much. In those years, housing starts, both in terms of numbers of residential units and square meters, fell appreciably while the cost of building rose rapidly.[168] Actual construction for the five-year-plan period 1986–1990 proceeded decently for the first three years and then dropped in 1989 and 1990. In 1986, 119.2 million square meters of housing were built; in 1987, 131.4 million; and in 1988, 132.3 million. The decline began in 1989, when only 128.9 million square meters were constructed, and continued through 1990, when new housing space fell to 115 million square meters. In 1990, the housing shortfall amounted to about 600,000 apartments. In early 1991, it was estimated that only 50 percent of the Housing–2000 program would be completed by the target year.[169]

The withdrawal of about 200,000 troops and their families from Eastern Europe only served to exacerbate the housing crisis. The resettlement of these troops meant that even greater pressure was placed on an already inadequate stock that was deteriorating even further due to the construction slowdown in the last years of the Gorbachev era. Under these circumstances, it is not surprising that extreme forms of localism emerged. As early as the spring of 1990, the Moldavian Supreme Soviet revoked certain USSR housing resolutions. Under Soviet law, certain categories of military personnel were entitled to apartments within three months. But Moldavia unilaterally repealed the law and said that only those servicemen who had been drafted from Moldavia itself were entitled to apartments in Moldavia.[170] The issue of the military and housing came to loom large.

The Second Economy

As goods disappeared from normal channels, the size of the second economy and the number of its participants mushroomed. While the inherently illegal nature of the underground economy makes it impossible to measure its size accurately, serious attempts have been made in the Soviet Union to estimate its magnitude. In an article in the respected Soviet journal *Voprosy ekonomiki*, the Soviet economist Tatiana Koriagina said that at the beginning of the 1960s, the second economy was five billion rubles a year, but that at the end of the 1980s, it was equal to 90 billion rubles.[171] Two separate estimates suggested that between 20 and 30 million Soviet citizens were involved in illegal economic activities on the production side.[172] Early in 1991, a Soviet economic paper estimated that in that year the second economy might be as large as 130 billion rubles, with the possibility that it could rise to 200 billion rubles within a few years. That is, illegal business activity could amount to a staggering 30 to 40 percent of gross national product.[173] Such a devastating prediction was doubtlessly based in part on the estimate that in 1990 the size of the black market for nonfood goods had increased 2.8 times over the 1989 level.[174]

A large percentage of the population purchased goods in the black market during the perestroika years to meet their needs. A 1990 survey showed that 30 percent shopped in black markets and that nearly 44 percent planned to use them. There was a direct (although not perfect) correlation between level of income and use of these markets. While 25 percent of those with an income under 100 rubles a month (the lowest income group in the country) shopped in black markets, almost 50 percent of those with monthly incomes over 300 rubles did so.[175] While all income groups were forced to do more of their shopping in the second economy, those with the highest incomes could best afford the high prices that were charged.

Prices in the Second Economy

The rise in the volume of activity in the second economy coincided with a precipitous rise in its prices. The power of those who had access to scarce goods was such that they could charge seemingly limitless prices. This angered the public, who saw the increased prominence of the second economy as the ultimate symbol of the regime's ineptitude. There was a great contradiction at work in the second economy. On the one hand, the population was forced to pay astonishing prices for scarce goods. For those with low salaries or on pensions, the underground economy was like an unrelenting monster; it was the ultimate evidence that they would never live decent and just lives, at least not under perestroika. On the other hand, the continued existence—indeed, the prosperity—of these markets demonstrated that people both needed and used them. Somehow, millions of people found the means to buy black-market goods.

There are a number of studies of black-market prices that provide useful insights into the degree to which shortages existed under perestroika. An RSFSR study toward the end of 1990 looked at 71 republican, district, and provincial centers and found that, on average, black-market prices were 2 to 3 times higher than state retail prices.[176] A detailed study of the December 1990 black market for the entire nation showed that, for a wide variety of food and other consumer goods, black-market prices were roughly 3.3 times state prices (see Table 2.5).

As Table 2.6 shows, there were also striking regional differences in black-market prices, reflecting the differences in the extent of shortages by geographic area.

Table 2.5

**Black-market Prices as a Multiple of
State Retail Prices, USSR, December 1991**

Food Products (per unit of sale)

Meat	4.8
Sausage items	3.2
Tea	3.0
Coffee beans	2.1
Powdered coffee	3.0
Black caviar	3.3
Red caviar	4.0
Delicatessen fish	3.0
Canned fish items	4.4
Candy sold loose	2.4
Packaged candy	4.4
Vodka	2.4
Cognac	2.2
Champagne	3.1
Wine	3.0

Nonfood Items (per unit of sale)

Clothing and Linens

Woman's winter overcoat	2.8
Woman's light overcoat	2.9
Man's winter overcoat	3.6
Man's light overcoat	3.3
Man's suit	2.5
Woman's raincoat	2.9
Man's raincoat	3.0
Jacket	3.2

Leather Footwear

Man's winter overshoes	4.8
Man's low quarters	4.6
Man's summer shoes	4.3
Woman's winter boots	4.5
Woman's spring–fall shoes	3.9
Woman's fashionable shoes	4.4
Woman's summer shoes	3.5
Children's shoes	3.7
Young girl's shoes	3.1
Young boy's shoes	3.6

Table 2.5 *(continued)*

Household Items

Carpets	2.6
Napless woven woollen carpets	2.5
Dinner sets	3.3
Crystal items	3.1
Sewing machines	2.8
Knitting machines	4.0

Electric Items

Refrigerator	2.6
Washing machine	2.6
Vacuum cleaner	2.8
Coffee grinder	3.0
Iron	5.6

Electronic Items

Black and white television	2.6
Color television	2.5
Videotape recorder	2.6

Source: Ekonomika i zhizn', no. 12 (March 1991), 16.

The immensity of the population's frustration over shortages was demonstrated by the remarkable finding that, by late 1990, Soviet citizens were actually willing to pay even more than the going black-market prices in order to obtain the goods they wanted (see Table 2.7).

Fighting the Second Economy

The Gorbachev regime was caught in a vise of growing shortages on the one side, and rising prices in the second economy on the other. Since it really did not have a program for increasing the supply of food and other consumer goods, it went after the second economy. But that effort was quixotic, doomed from the start. The police taking pokes at the second economy could not increase the supply of goods, although their actions may have temporarily deflected popular resentment over shortages and

Table 2.6

Relative Black-market Prices in Different Cities, 1990

	Refrigerators	Color TVs	Vacuum Cleaners	Sewing Machines	Adult Bicycles
Average for all cities	100	100	100	100	100
Moscow	111	88	114	63	81
Leningrad	——	100	——	——	——
Alma-Ata	111	76	114	117	——
Ashkhabad	67	59	91	50	81
Baku	64	65	——	67	——
Vilnius	278	141	189	500	430
Dushanbe	44	59	87	58	91
Yerevan	111	70	——	83	——
Kiev	111	118	152	67	96
Kishinev	111	59	152	208	54
Lvov	67	206	114	83	134
Minsk	128	124	——	——	73
Odessa	50	206	83	67	134
Riga	278	765	227	583	108
Tashkent	69	59	57	35	67
Frunze	100	88	136	116	——
Khabarovsk	89	71	53	83	134
Kharkov	78	88	76	83	75

Source: Ekonomika i zhizn', no. 49 (December 1990), 16.

Table 2.7

Black-market Prices: Actual and Planned Maximums, in Rubles

	Price Prepared to Pay	Actual Price
Fall coat	800	500
Jackets	1,600	600
Raincoats	1,000	500
Boots	700	500
Shoes	200	160
Summer footwear	550	200

Source: Ekonomika i zhizn', no. 47 (November 1990), 8.

high prices. The thrust of police efforts was to re-establish a sense that the state was concerned about justice in the distribution of goods and was fighting the fiercely hated "mafia" and "speculators" who appeared to have so much power. Even the press supported the myth of a conspiracy of profiteers. Indeed, one major newspaper speculated that half of all goods wound up in the hands of profiteers.[177] In fact, not only did the policies and actions against the second economy do little to affect the real condition of people's lives, they occasionally deeply offended the sensibilities of the population, most notably in the case of the 1991 ruble confiscation, with which we deal in detail below.

A first step in the government's crackdown on the black market was the creation in 1989 of a new department in the Soviet Interior Ministry (MVD), called the Department to Fight Organized Crime, necessitated, it was said, because the Soviet mafia was broadening the scope of its operations in the economy.[178] The Leningrad police also organized a special section to combat economic crime, saying they believed that 60 percent of the goods meant for the population were winding up on the black market.[179]

It was not that black-market activities had not existed in the wholesale depots and retail stores before the Gorbachev era; it was that now the illegalities had gotten completely out of hand. The Interior Ministry's special arm for dealing with such matters, the Department for Combating Embezzlement of Socialist Property and Speculation, found that half of the 160,000 trading enterprises they checked in 1990 had committed crimes.[180] A great deal of the problem involved workers in such enterprises withholding food and other consumer goods, either to sell them or to barter them for other goods. Such was the case in the far northwest city of Murmansk, where police found "shelves filled with dozens of imported television sets, video and radio equipment, and thousands of cassettes. . . . Commodities in short supply such as motor vehicle tires, children's sleighs, Japanese fishing tackle, motorcycles, and spare parts were stored at another warehouse."[181] And in a Novgorod department store, 18,000 rubles' worth of goods in high demand were kept from the general public. In a sporting goods store in the same city, another 15,000 rubles' worth were found cached away.[182]

The strongest assault on the second economy began in early December 1990 and signaled a two-month barrage of administrative efforts to deal with its epidemic growth. The first salvos were fired on December 4, when the Soviet parliament granted Gorbachev emergency powers to deal with the problems in the trade network. First, he established a system of workers' control in the trade network: workers would act as the eyes and ears of the state in order to reduce the leakage of goods as they moved from manufacturer to consumer.[183] Second, as this was a time when food aid had begun to move into the Soviet Union and western benefactors were concerned that it might wind up in the wrong hands, the secret police were brought into the picture. To address the concerns of foreign benefactors and also to demonstrate to the population that it could control the situation, the government gave the responsibility for monitoring the arrival of food aid and following its path to the stores to the Sixth Directorate of the KGB.[184]

Third, in January 1991, Gorbachev issued a decree effectively confiscating 50- and 100-ruble notes from the population in an effort to damage the second economy where it would hurt the most. Confiscation of the population's ruble accumulations was not new to the Soviet experience. After World War II, in December 1947, the population was ordered to exchange its holdings of rubles at the rate of ten old rubles for one new ruble, a move that had largely affected the Soviet peasantry who had made a great deal of money selling food to urbanites at highly inflated prices during the war.[185] They had hoarded this money rather than putting it into banks and thereby making the state aware of how much money they had made by taking advantage of wartime shortages. Those who had bank deposits at the time of the 1947 action also had their money revalued, although at a less punitive exchange rate.[186] The Stalin regime, which implemented this decree, did so without debate. Had there been any permissible public response, the policy would have evinced a bitter reaction. In the much more liberal environment of 1991, the anger of many people came through uncensored.

The presidential decree, "On Ceasing Acceptance for Payment of USSR Gosbank 50- and 100-Ruble Bank Notes Issued in 1961 and Limiting Cash Withdrawals from Citizens' Deposits," was issued on January 22, 1991. It stipulated that 50- and 100-ruble notes would no longer be accepted as currency but that they could be exchanged for ruble notes of other denominations. The decree further stated that, for the first six months of 1991, starting on January 23, ordinary citizens could withdraw only 500 rubles a month from savings banks.[187] The ruble exchange was to take place only during the period from January 23 to January 25. The amount that could be exchanged could not exceed the average monthly wage during an individual's last year of work, up to 1,000 rubles.[188]

Formally termed a "ruble exchange," the ruble confiscation had the overriding purpose of wiping out the illegally earned cash holdings of those in the second economy, in some cases reputed to be enormous sums.[189] More than one-third of the cash in the hands of the population was made up of 50- and 100-ruble notes; most significantly, these denominations were of great importance in the second economy, where they were used much more than in the legal economy.[190] In addition, there were an estimated 7 billion rubles abroad as a result of smuggling operations.[191] While the stated purpose of the ruble exchange was to penalize illegal economic activity—a purpose that would make such an action acceptable to the general population—it may be argued that the confiscation was also intended to diminish some of the inflationary pressure embedded in the huge "ruble overhang," the enormous amounts in involuntary savings that had accumulated over the past several years because of the chronic goods shortages.

In essence, the logistics of the exchange were as follows: Individuals would take their 50- and 100-ruble notes to designated exchange points and immediately get a ruble exchange for an amount equal to their monthly salary. If an individual had 50- and 100-ruble notes in amounts that exceeded his or her salary, that excess was recorded, along with the owner's explanation of its source. This record and the extra money was sent to special commissions that had been created under the raion and city executive committees, who determined whether the individual had come by the money honestly. On the basis of that decision, the person was either allowed or denied the right to exchange his extra 50- and 100-ruble notes.[192]

What was at stake was the confiscation of 48.2 billion rubles of the roughly 136 billion rubles in circulation at the beginning of 1991.[193] But the ruble confiscation was doomed from the beginning, if only because rumors about it had existed perhaps as early as November. Several newspapers even reported it.[194] Second-economy currency dealers unloaded a substantial amount of their 50- and 100-ruble notes the month before the Gorbachev decree, after they had received information that one of the state's money-printing factories had been instructed to print a new currency.[195] In Stavropol', large numbers of people rushed to deposit rubles in the savings bank branches. The rush had been triggered by a rumor that the banks had been notified that existing rubles were to be exchanged on a one-to-one basis, provided that an individual's savings account did not exceed 3,000 rubles. In a period of three days, 5 million rubles were deposited, and state bonds, which were not usually in great demand, suddenly became a hot item.[196] The large sums deposited in this one city alone suggest the substantial hoarding by Soviet citizens, a pattern which, once confiscation began, would leave the population in the very circumstances it was attempting to avoid.

The total amount confiscated was reported to be 41.2 billion rubles, or about 85 percent of the old 50- and 100-ruble notes, leaving some 7 billion rubles unaccounted for.[197] However, these had been effectively confiscated because they were rubles that members of the second economy would presumably never be able to use.[198] Given the mammoth size of the second economy, it is doubtful that the confiscation really did much harm to its intended victims. There is also evidence that when enterprises, organizations, and cooperatives surrendered their 50- and 100-ruble notes on the first day, in many instances the sums were quite a bit larger than had been anticipated, suggesting that illegal earnings were being laundered through those places.[199] The *Tashkomisintorg* (the trade commission in Tashkent), for example, brought in about 900,000 rubles, which it said was office cash in hand, when in fact petty cash was supposed to be no more than 1,000 rubles.[200] This was not an isolated instance, although it was certainly an egregious one.[201]

There were a number of other ways people found to get around the confiscation. In Moscow, some bought airline tickets, which were easy to resell because they were ordinarily so difficult to come by. Others bought money orders which they could cash in at a later date for acceptable currency. Still others paid off their debts in 50- and 100-ruble notes.[202]

But many people did not have institutional connections or the power or the guile to minimize or even avoid the pain imposed by the confiscation. These were often ordinary people, such as pensioners who suffered because of their savings habits. Pensioners were entitled to exchange up to a maximum of 200 rubles for new banknotes, but many did not trust state banks and kept their money at home.[203] Any savings that they had under the mattress in addition to the allowed 200 rubles would be gone if that extra money was in 50- and 100-ruble notes. With no way to prove that this money had simply been saved over a period of time, and unable to claim that it was a lump-sum bonus payment or an honorarium or that they had received it for any of the other acceptable reasons, they were simply not allowed to exchange these unexplained rubles. The confiscation was therefore a small disaster for those who had saved for a long time and held their savings in cash.[204] This was especially so because so many pensioners were poor; roughly 70 percent received minimum pensions and lived below the poverty line.[205]

The decree also raised special problems in some of the non-

Russian republics. It collided with the cultural traditions of the Uzbeks. By custom, the Uzbeks save money for special occasions such as weddings and funerals, as well as for buying a house. Bank savings accounts and cash in hand in the republic were each equal to 3.5 billion rubles, with much of the latter in large denominations. In order to accommodate a very worried constituency, the president of Uzbekistan, Karimov, signed a decree extending the deadline for exchanging ruble notes until February 1, 1991.[206] Although this was contrary to the Gorbachev decree and in direct defiance of the state bank's announcement that no extensions were to be allowed,[207] the Supreme Soviet gave Uzbekistan a special dispensation, extending the republic's exchange to January 29.[208] Much the same was true of the Turkmen population. In Turkmenistan, the people have a strong preference for keeping a great deal of cash at home, mostly in large denominations.[209] In Latvia, an official reaction opposed the confiscation as a matter of principle. The presidium of the republic's Supreme Council described the process as "degrading" because it implicitly accused everyone of possessing illegally earned rubles. The Latvian council also found fault with the ad hoc commissions selected to decide whether rubles held above prescribed limits were legally earned.[210]

However, public opinion was strongly in support of the confiscation's goal of hurting the second economy; of the 1,000 people polled shortly after the ruble exchange began, 50 percent approved of confiscating second economy earnings. But public opinion polls also showed that 41 percent did not believe that those in the second economy had actually suffered at all from the confiscation. The same percentage thought that "they have suffered, but not much." When asked about whether they believed that honestly earned income would not be affected, as promised by the decree, only about 33 percent of the respondents thought that "honest working people" had not suffered as a consequence of the confiscation. Indeed, 20 percent thought that they had suffered a great deal.[211]

The ruble exchange also caused a great deal of anxiety within the general population about future monetary moves. Rumors quickly flew that either savings banks deposits would be completely frozen or deposits limited to some amount (3,000 to 4,000 rubles were the most frequently mentioned figures) and the rest exchanged at a ratio of 3 : 1 or 4 : 1.[212] There were also rumors that 10-ruble and 25-ruble bank notes would be next. Although officials continued to say that no such exchanges were planned, only 27 percent of poll respondents believed this.[213] If the ruble confiscation successfully dealt a serious blow to the second economy, it also alienated large numbers of the population, who saw it as another blow to their well-being and more evidence that Gorbachev's perestroika was a disaster.

The ruble confiscation action was followed almost immediately by a January 26 decree, "On Measures to Combat Economic Sabotage and Other Crimes in the Economic Sphere." This decree brought the heavy hand of the law into play, giving the police and the KGB the right to enter the premises of any economic organization (and the decree went out of its way to mention specifically individual entrepreneurs) and search places of business with or without the presence or permission of owners. Moreover, every business was required to hand over any records that the authorities requested and provide written explanations of activities if they were demanded. Every producer was now a potential enemy of the people. Indeed, in one place the decree said: "[C]hecks on the observation of norms and regulations guaranteeing the protection of consumer rights in the manufacture, storage, transportation, and sale of consumer goods and of produce intended for foodstuffs, and also in the performance of services to the population, are to be carried out. . . ."[214] Gorbachev's strategy was now clear. If he could not increase the real supply of goods, then he would try to convince the population that he was attacking those who were to blame for the difficulties in their lives. Gorbachev the democrat disappeared temporarily as an expedient to bring order where both he and large numbers of the Soviet population believed chaos reigned.

Conclusion

In an almost desperate way, the country kept looking for scapegoats to blame for the disappearance of food and other consumer
goods. In what sometimes appeared to be a frenetic effort to stem
the tide of the underground economy's growth, the implicit message was that the second economy was the cause of shortages,
when it was never anything more than a symptom and reflection
of them. Blame also fell on the shoulders of the economic and
party bureaucracies. But the real causes of the shortages were the
excessive increases in money incomes, which far outstripped the
production of goods, and the breakdown in the delivery of goods.
When the links created by central planning fell apart, a vacuum
was created and nothing came in to fill it. In an environment of
uncertainty and anxiety, regional protectionism emerged as a policy of good politics but bad economics. As conditions deteriorated, the population's frustration crossed over the line into anger
and sometimes violence. Gorbachev tried to divert the anger,
with measures such as the ruble confiscation, but he misread the
population's sensibilities. The general result was that the welfare
of the Soviet people suffered. In the following chapter, we examine how the standard of living, which was not high when
Gorbachev came to power, actually fell during the years of perestroika.

Notes

1. Economists define the standard of living in terms of real per-capita
output, that is, the nominal value of gross national product deflated either by a
cost-of-living index for consumer goods or an economy-wide price index. In a
more general sense, a nation's standard of living is comprised of four vari-
ables: the availability of goods, the general level of prices, per-capita income,
and a number of intangibles such as the quality of the environment, the crime
rate, and a people's state of health.
2. In the way that Soviet humor has always had of sharply focusing discontent, people sarcastically joked, "This place would really have been paradise if
only the Bolsheviks had managed to create people who don't need to eat." *The
Wall Street Journal* (December 7, 1990), A8.

3. *Komsomol'skaia pravda* (November 24, 1990), 1.

4. *Sovetskaia Rossiia* (October 22, 1998), 1.

5. Karl-Eugen Waedekin, "Soviet Agriculture in 1989: A Third Year of Near Stagnation," *Report on the USSR* (February 16, 1990), 6.

6. *Sel'skaia zhizn'* (October 12, 1990), 2.

7. *The New York Times* (October 4, 1991), A4.

8. *Ogonek*, no. 5 (1990), 1.

9. *Komsomol'skaia pravda* (November 24, 1990), 1.

10. Ibid.

11. Mark Rhodes, "Food Supply in the USSR," *Report on the USSR* (October 11, 1991), 11.

12. *Rabochaia tribuna* (November 30, 1990), 1–2.

13. *Literaturnaia gazeta*, no. 41 (October 10, 1990), 2.

14. *Trud* (October 22, 1989), 1.

15. *Trud* (September 5, 1990), 1.

16. *Sovetskaia Rossiia* (September 5, 1990), 6.

17. Ibid.

18. *Report on the USSR* (September 14, 1990), 36.

19. *Izvestiia* (September 4, 1990), 1.

20. *Sovetskaia Rossiia* (September 5, 1990), 6.

21. *Izvestiia* (September 4, 1990), 1.

22. Moscow Television Service in Russian (September 3, 1990). From FBIS-SOV–90–176 (September 11, 1990), 82–83.

23. *Izvestiia* (November 25, 1990), 2.

24. *Pravda* (November 30, 1990), 6.

25. *Izvestiia* (November 25, 1990), 2.

26. Ibid. (December 8, 1990), 2.

27. Moscow Television Service in Russian (September 24, 1990). From FBIS-SOV-90-188 (September 27, 1990), 24.

28. *Izvestiia* (October 20, 1990), 2.

29. Moscow Domestic Service in Russian (November 26, 1990). From FBIS-SOV-90-228 (November 27, 1990), 79.

30. *Pravda* (August 30, 1990), 1.

31. *Sel'skaia zhizn'* (September 30, 1990), 1.

32. *Sovetskaia Rossiia* (October 19, 1990), 3.

33. *Pravda* (November 14, 1990), 2. From FBIS-SOV-90-225 (November 21, 1990), 82.

34. Moscow Domestic Service in Russian (November 22, 1990). From FBIS-SOV-90-227 (November 26, 1990), 93.

35. Moscow *Ian Press Release* in English (December 11, 1990). From FBIS-SOV-90-243 (December 18, 1990), 52.

36. *Pravda* (September 17, 1990), 1.

37. *Komsomol'skaia pravda* (September 9, 1990), 1.

38. *Pravda* (September 17, 1990), 1.

39. Moscow Domestic Service in Russian (October 11, 1990). From FBIS-SOV-90-197 (October 11, 1990), 103.

40. Moscow Television Service in Russian (September 29, 1990). From FBIS-SOV-90-190 (October 1, 1990), 36.

41. *Sovetskaia Rossiia* (September 20, 1990), 1.

42. *Report on the USSR* (April 5, 1991), 30.

43. *Glasnost'*, no. 7 (February 14, 1991), 1.

44. *Izvestiia* (November 26, 1990), 1.

45. *Sel'skaia zhizn'* (October 1, 1990), 1.

46. Moscow Television Service in Russian (September 21, 1990). From FBIS-SOV-90-188 (September 27, 1990), 64.

47. Hong Kong AFP in English. From FBIS-SOV-90-243 (December 18, 1990), 103.

48. *Izvestiia* (September 21, 1990), 2.

49. *Report on the USSR* (October 19, 1990), 17.

50. Moscow Television Service in Russian (September 20, 1990). From FBIS-SOV-90-185 (September 24, 1990), 71.

51. *Izvestiia* (August 4, 1990), 1.

52. Ibid.

53. *Pravda* (September 29, 1990), 1.

54. Elizabeth Teague, "New Incentives Lure Townspeople into the Fields," *Report on the USSR* (October 19, 1990), 17.

55. *Krasnaia zvezda* (June 27, 1991), 1; and *Izvestiia* (August 5, 1990), 1.

56. Only about one-fourth of the military vehicles were actually driven by army conscripts; the others were driven by local citizens in the region being harvested. *Sel'skaia zhizn'* (September 4, 1990), 2.

57. *Krasnaia zvezda* (June 27, 1991), 1.

58. *Pravda* (August 3, 1990), 1–2.

59. *Izvestiia* (June 22, 1989), 1.

60. Ibid. (June 21, 1990), 2.

61. *Pravda* (September 24, 1990), 1.

62. Ibid. (August 20, 1990).

63. *Izvestiia* (May 4, 1985), 2.

64. Moscow Television Service in Russian (September 19, 1990). From FBIS-SOV-90-184 (September 21, 1990), 61.

65. Moscow Television Service in Russian (December 8, 1990). From FBIS-SOV-90-240 (December 13, 1990), 83–84.

66. *Report on the USSR* (July 21, 1989), 47–48.

67. *Pravda* (January 10, 1991), 2.

68. *Ogonek*, no. 5 (1990), 1.

69. Moscow Interfax (October 24, 1991). From FBIS-SOV-91-209 (October 29, 1991), 36.

70. *Pravda* (May 23, 1989), 3.

71. *Sotsialisticheskaia industriia* (November 15, 1989), 3.

72. Leningrad Maritime Press Service (May 30, 1990). In FBIS-SOV-90-107 (June 4, 1990), 98.

73. *Moscow News*, no. 13 (1991), 11.

74. *Rabochaia tribuna* (April 16, 1991), 2.

75. *Rabochaia tribuna* (April 16, 1991), 2. What one does not know is what household food inventories were during "normal" times. Even in the absence of such information, it is clear that people held stocks above usual inventories.

76. *Krasnaia zvezda* (May 13, 1990), 1; and *Sovetskaia Latviia* (June 2, 1990), 2.

77. *Sovetskaia Rossiia* (June 5, 1990), 6.

78. *Trud* (October 5, 1991), 1.

79. *Izvestiia* (August 23, 1989), 1.

80. Ibid. (May 26, 1990), 2.

81. Moscow Domestic Service in Russian (June 5, 1990). From FBIS-SOV-90-114 (June 13, 1990), 114. The card was issued to all citizens over the age of fourteen. The reason for replacing the passport system was that it was inconvenient, with certificates and other reference documents coming into use along with passports. See Moscow Domestic Service in Russian (June 2, 1990). From FBIS-SOV-90-129 (July 5, 1990), 91.

82. *Izvestiia* (February 9, 1991), 1.

83. Ibid. (May 29, 1990), 3.

84. Ibid. (June 1, 1990), 3.

85. The system was actually less rigid in practice than it was in principle. Many sales clerks were embarrassed to ask shoppers for their passports, and in some places salespeople allowed outside visitors to shop in Moscow stores. See *Argumenty i fakty*, no. 22 (June 1990), 1.

86. Moscow Television Service in Russian (June 2, 1990). From FBIS-SOV-90-109 (June 6, 1990), 96.

87. *Izvestiia* (July 7, 1990), 1.

88. Ibid. (July 24, 1990), 2.

89. Moscow Domestic Service in Russian (October 22, 1990). From FBIS-SOV–90 (October 23, 1990), 95; Moscow in English to Great Britain and Ireland (October 22, 1990). From FBIS-SOV-90-205 (October 23, 1990), 69.

90. *Report on the USSR* (February 1, 1991), 52.

91. *Trud* (October 31, 1990), 2.

92. *Izvestiia* (September 7, 1990), 2.

93. Ibid. (September 21, 1990), 2.

94. The discussion of the basics of the Ukrainian coupon system is drawn from *Trud* (October 31, 1990), 2; *Pravda Ukrainy* (October 28, 1990), 1 and 3; Joint Publications Research Service (JPRS-UEA-90-046) (December 20, 1990), 15–16; and *Trud* (November 3, 1990), 1. The cards were also issued to pensioners, invalids, students, and vocational-technical school institution trainees.

95. *Trud* (November 3, 1990), 1.

96. *Pravda* (November 13, 1990), 2. This was not the only manifestation of native cynicism. The local population called the coupons issued by the government "perestroika money."

97. *Izvestiia* (December 26, 1990), 7.

98. *Report on the USSR* (July 12, 1991), 28.

99. Ibid. (August 23, 1991), 25.

100. *Komsomol'skaia pravda* (January 13, 1990), 2.

101. Ibid. (January 19, 1990), 1.

102. *Izvestiia* (September 5, 1990), 2.

103. *Pravda* (November 18, 1990), 3. The city had actually imposed rationing earlier, on July 1, for liquor and wine. Any purchases above the monthly allowance were also priced at 75 percent above the basic price. See Moscow Maritime Service in Russian (June 30, 1990). From FBIS-SOV-90-128 (July 3, 1990), 91. Some 44 percent were in favor of rationing and 42 percent were against. See *Moscow News*, no. 49 (1990), 4.

104. *Moscow News*, no. 49 (1990), 4.

105. Dmitri V. Pavlov, *Leningrad 1941, The Blockade*, trans. John Clinton Adams (Chicago: The University of Chicago Press, 1965), 79.

106. Moscow Television Service in Russian (October 21, 1989). From FBIS-SOV-89-204 (October 24, 1989), 89.

107. Moscow TASS in English (November 12, 1990). From FBIS-SOV-90-219 (November 13, 1990), 88.

108. *Izvestiia* (March 5, 1990), 3.

109. *Pravda* (September 27, 1990), 1.

110. *Report on the USSR* (November 9, 1990), 36 (R3); and *Izvestiia* (December 5, 1990), 2.

111. Gorbachev sent a note to the Lithuanian Supreme Soviet and the Council of Ministers on April 13 warning that there would be economic consequences to their actions. A week later, the central government completely cut Lithuania off from its supply of oil and decreased the gas supply from 18 million to 3.5 million cubic meters a day. It was then that Lithuania began to prepare for rationing. See *Pravda* (April 20, 1990), 1 and 2.

112. Ibid.

113. *Izvestiia* (May 3, 1990), 2.

114. A discussion of the Lithuanian ration program can be found in *Izvestiia* (January 8, 1991), 1.

115. Vilnius Radio (July 18, 1991). From FBIS-SOV-91-139 (July 19, 1991), 67.

116. *Izvestiia* (February 1, 1991), 2; and *Sovetskaia Rossiia* (February 8, 1991), 1. Krasnodar claimed that it stood in fortieth place in the republic in meat consumption, in spite of the fact that it was one of the republic's largest producers of meat.

117. *Izvestiia* (February 1, 1991), 2.

118. Ibid. (March 8, 1990), 2.

119. *Report on the USSR* (April 19, 1991), 35.

120. *Pravda* (April 30, 1985), 1.

121. Ibid. (October 1, 1985), 1–2; and Ibid (October 9, 1985), 2.

122. *Pravitel'stvennyi vestnik*, no. 7 (February 1990), 4–5.

123. *Moscow News*, no. 13 (1991), 11.

124. *Planovoe khoziaistvo*, no. 11 (November 1990), 55.

125. Ibid.

126. *Sovetskaia Rossiia* (July 28, 1989), 1–2.

127. *Ekonomika i zhizn'*, no. 17 (April 1991), 7.

128. *Planovoe khoziaistvo*, no. 11 (November 1990), 56. When shortages actually occurred and times became tougher for so many people, a number of these buyers turned from being prudent consumers to participating in the black market, selling the clothes they had bought because prices had risen so much.

129. *Planovoe khoziaistvo*, no. 11 (November 1990), 56.

130. *Pravitel'stvennyi vestnik*, no. 7 (February 1990), 4.

131. *Pravda* (May 23, 1989), 3.

132. *Planovoe khoziaistvo*, no. 11 (November 1990), 58.

133. *Trud* (October 28, 1989), 2.

134. *Izvestiia* (February 25, 1990), 2.

135. Moscow Television Service in Russian (June 2, 1990). From FBIS-SOV-90-118 (June 19, 1990), 119.

136. *Report on the USSR* (January 13, 1989), 25.

137. Ibid. (January 20, 1989), 24.

138. Ibid. (July 28, 1989), 45.

139. *Izvestiia* (December 23, 1989), 2.

140. Ibid. (March 31, 1990), 7.

141. Ibid. (January 26, 1990), 2.

142. Moscow Television Service in Russian (September 6, 1990). From FBIS-SOV-90-178 (September 13, 1990), 63.

143. *Izvestiia* (January 26, 1990), 2.

144. Moscow Television Service in Russian (September 3, 1990). From FBIS-SOV-90-174 (September 7, 1990), 40–41. By September 1990, trade-related debts to the West were about $3.5 billion. While a 5 billion Deutsche mark credit eased the Soviet obligation to Germany, its many other unpaid bills forced Western and Japanese firms to halt shipments to the USSR, placing a burden on Soviet enterprises and consumers. See *Pravda* (September 29, 1990), 2; and *The Wall Street Journal* (October 10, 1990), A17.

145. *Sovetskaia Rossiia* (February 22, 1989), 1.

146. *Report on the USSR* (April 28, 1989), 28. It was not made clear whether these ruble valuations were in domestic retail prices or in the so-called *valiuta*, or hard currency rubles.

147. *Argumenty i fakty*, no. 15 (April 1989), 8.

148. *Report on the USSR* (July 28, 1989), 43.

149. *Moscow News*, no. 29 (1990), 10. The Moscow City Council decided that it would have to find ways on its own to earn the hard currency it needed by engaging in joint projects with foreign firms.

150. Moscow Television Service in Russian (October 6, 1990). From FBIS-SOV-90-196 (October 10, 1990), 81.

151. *Izvestiia* (July 20, 1990), 7.

152. Moscow Television Service in Russian (October 6, 1990). From FBIS-SOV-90-196 (October 10, 1990), 81.

153. *Izvestiia* (September 10, 1990), 2.

154. Moscow World Service in Russian (August 30, 1990). From FBIS-SOV-90-170 (August 31, 1990), 47.

155. *Izvestiia* (September 20, 1990), 2.

156. *Pravda* (September 6, 1990), 2.

157. Ibid. (August 30, 1990), 6.

158. Moscow World Service in English (August 29, 1990). From FBIS-SOV-90-169 (August 30, 1990), 49.

159. *Pravda* (September 10, 1989), 1.

160. Ibid. (September 27, 1989), 2.

161. *Moskovskaia pravda* (September 26, 1989), 4.

162. *Izvestiia* (September 26, 1990), 3.

163. *Report on the USSR* (January 11, 1991), 29–30.

164. *Moscow News*, no. 13 (1991), 11.

165. *Ekonomika i zhizn'*, no. 48 (November 1990), 5.

166. *Trud* (October 17, 1989), 2.

167. *Pravda* (December 3, 1985), 2.

168. *Ekonomika i zhizn'*, no. 48 (November 1990), 5.

169. *Izvestiia* (March 15, 1991), 3.

170. Ibid. (April 1, 1990), 2.

171. T. Koriagina, "Tenevaia ekonomika v SSSR," *Voprosy ekonomiki*, no. 3 (1990), 117.

172. Iu. Kozlov, "Tenevaia ekonomika i prestupnost'," *Voprosy ekonomiki*, no. 3 (1990), 121; and *Komsomol'skaia pravda* (January 7, 1990).

173. Moscow All-Union Radio Mayak Network (July 9, 1991). From FBIS-SOV-91-132 (July 10, 1991), 56.

174. *Ekonomika i zhizn'*, no. 12 (March 1991), 16.

175. Ibid., no. 47 (November 1990), 8.

176. *Trud* (November 23, 1990), 4.

177. *Sovetskaia Rossiia* (September 25, 1990), 4.

178. *Trud* (November 29, 1989), 2.

179. TASS (December 25, 1990). From *Report on the USSR* (January 4, 1991), 63.

180. Moscow TASS in English (September 25, 1990). From FBIS-SOV-90-190 (October 1, 1990), 53.

181. Moscow Television Service in Russian (November 22, 1990). From FBIS-SOV-90-228 (November 27, 1990), 62.

182. *Sovetskaia Rossiia* (September 25, 1990), 4.

183. *Pravda* (December 6, 1990), 1 and 2; and *The New York Times* (December 5, 1990), A9.

184. *Pravda* (December 19, 1990), 6.

185. See William Moskoff, *The Bread of Affliction: The Food Supply in the USSR During World War II* (New York: Cambridge University Press, 1990).

186. Harry Schwartz, ed., *Russia's Soviet Economy*. 2nd ed. (New York: Prentice-Hall, 1954), 479–480.

187. *Pravda* (January 23, 1991), 1. In March, it was announced that this limit was to be removed. See *Izvestiia* (March 8, 1991), 1.

188. *Pravda* (January 23, 1991), 2.

189. *Pravda* (January 24, 1991), 1.

190. According to Prime Minister Pavlov: Moscow Central Television (January 22, 1991). From FBIS-SOV-91-015 (January 23, 1991), 52–53.

191. Moscow Central Television (January 22, 1991). From FBIS-SOV-91-015 (January 23, 1991), 52.

192. *Argumenty i fakty*, no. 4 (January 1991), 1 and 4.

193. Ibid., 1; and *Izvestiia* (February 1, 1991), 1.

194. *Argumenty i fakty*, no. 4 (January 1991), 1 and 4.

195. Moscow TASS in English (January 28, 1991). From FBIS-SOV-91-019 (January 29, 1991), 40. The black market in 100-ruble notes sent their price plummeting to 10 rubles by late evening of January 23 with expectations that their price might fall as low as three rubles the following day: Moscow Central Television (January 24, 1991). From FBIS-SOV-91-017 (January 25, 1991), 42.

196. *Komsomol'skaia pravda* (December 18, 1990), 1.

197. *Report on the USSR* (February 22, 1991), 31.

198. V.V. Gerashchenko, the chairman of Gosbank, thought it was possible that the final count turned in to the banks could even go as high as 43–45 billion rubles. See *Trud* (February 1, 1991), 1.

199. *Izvestiia* (January 29, 1991), 2.

200. Ibid. (February 1, 1991), 1.

201. See, for example, *Trud* (February 1, 1991), 1.

202. Conversation with Anthony Jones (February 10, 1991).

203. Moscow Central Television (January 23, 1991). From FBIS-SOV-91-017 (January 25, 1991), 42–43. There was a provision in the decree whereby pensioners could hand in 50- and 100-ruble bank notes over the monthly limit by applying to the regional executive committee or city executive committee of the party for exchange of these "extra" rubles. See *Pravda* (January 23, 1991), 2.

204. Moscow Domestic Service in Russian (January 23, 1991). From FBIS-SOV-91-016 (January 24, 1991), 66–67.

205. *Argumenty i fakty*, no. 29 (1990), 4.

206. *Izvestiia* (January 25, 1991), 1.

207. Moscow Central Television (January 24, 1991). From FBIS-SOV-91-017 (January 25, 1991), 41.

208. *Izvestiia* (January 29, 1991), 2.

209. Ibid. (January 25, 1991), 1.

210. Riga Domestic Service in Russian (January 25, 1991). From FBIS-SOV-91-017 (January 25, 1991), 63.

211. *Izvestiia* (February 13, 1991), 2.

212. Moscow Central Television in Russian (February 8, 1991). From FBIS-SOV-91-028 (February 11, 1991), 52.

213. *Izvestiia* (February 13, 1991), 2.

214. Ibid. (January 28, 1991), 1.

3

Prices, Income, and the Falling Standard of Living

Among the most striking changes for the Soviet population during the perestroika period was the precipitous decline in the standard of living. In a relatively few years, the prices that people had to pay for goods rose at extremely rapid rates, adding to the woes imposed by goods shortages. Not since World War II had they experienced so much hardship. All this happened at the very same time as the government was trying to reform the economic system, albeit haltingly. Not surprisingly, a population that was already in pain insisted that the government not introduce such changes as price reform that would bring even more pain. The simple truth is that the population's experience of inflation and a falling standard of living was in conflict with the government's policies of reform. Ultimately, the government's efforts to obtain both economic reform and popular peace by raising both prices and wages, resulted in the worst of all possible worlds—an inevitable, self-perpetuating, downward spiral of the economy.

Inflation

The rate of inflation increased dramatically through the perestroika years, eroding both the value of income and the Soviet people's confidence in the government, in the ruble, and in the new economic freedom. After years during which nominal prices had been held constant by administrative fiat and open inflation was therefore extremely low, a combination of a very bad monetary policy, changes in pricing policy, and structural changes in the goods markets led to increased open inflation and eventually to frighteningly high rates of inflation. The people's experience of years of steady prices on a day-to-day basis was replaced by extreme uncertainty and fear about future inflation. Almost all the people believed they were victims, a view that was not without some justice. The corrosive nature of inflation not only demonstrably lowered almost everyone's standard of living, it also engendered anger toward the government in general and toward Gorbachev and the entrepreneurs in particular.

Throughout the Soviet period, prices had been set by one of the many branches of the state bureaucracy, the State Committee on Prices. In principle, retail prices were supposed to have been set to clear the market; but because these prices had often been fixed for long periods, they seldom actually represented equilibrium prices. Neither consumers nor managers had played a role in determining the prices that had prevailed in the Soviet market. And prices themselves, instead of having served a role in the allocation of resources, had actually served an administrative function. While the Soviets could legitimately claim that there was little open inflation, in fact there had always been a great deal of repressed inflation because macrodemand had always exceeded macrosupply, a situation that manifested itself in chronic shortages and long lines. Thus, as long as there was no concomitant increase in the supply of goods, any policy of price-decontrol was bound to lead to a rise in prices.

Although there was a substantial amount of inflation during the Gorbachev era, it was much different from the kind of inflation one would find in an economy like that of the United States. Soviet prices, artificially held below equilibrium for so long, were climbing upward in an effort to find their equilibrium level—that is, the point at which demand and supply were equal.

Table 3.1

**Estimates of Soviet Retail Price Increases, in Percent
1981–1991**

	CIA	Soviet
1981–1985	2.2	5.7
1986	4.4	6.2
1987	2.2	7.3
1988	3.1	8.4
1989	6.0	10.5
1990	—	53.6
1991 (Jan–June)	—	90.0
1991 (entire year)	—	650–700

Sources: 1981–1989: "The Soviet Economy Stumbles Badly in 1989," Central Intelligence Agency (April 20, 1990), 7; 1990: Philip Hanson, "Pavlov's Price Increases," *Report on the USSR* (March 22, 1991), 9; 1991: TASS (July 17, 1991); from *Report on the USSR* (July 26, 1991), 39; Moscow TASS (November 18, 1991), citing *Kommersant*, FBIS-SOV-91-223 (November 19, 1991), 36.

The United States, on the other hand, experienced inflation problems because of such supply shocks as the oil embargo. In principle, a large one-time upward adjustment in prices could reduce or even eliminate underlying inflationary pressure in the Soviet economy. But as it turned out, such a one-time correction was unacceptable to the population, and prices and wages kept climbing.

As Table 3.1 shows, the rate of inflation accelerated during the perestroika years. From 1981 to 1985, it was at most one percent a year, according to both Soviet and CIA data. But beginning with 1986, it began to rise and simply took off in 1990.

Much of the inflationary pressure was due to misguided economic policy. A great deal of it was caused by increases in wages, which far outstripped productivity growth (see Table 3.2). This was especially true beginning in 1988. As a consequence of this imbalance, household savings kept rising. Some of these savings were probably voluntary, money put away perhaps to buy an expensive scarce item like an automobile, either from the state or on the black market. But most of the population's in-

Table 3.2

Money Income and Labor Productivity Changes, USSR, in Percent

	Money Income	Labor Productivity
1986	3.9	—
1987	3.9	—
1988	9.2	5.5
1989	12.9	2.3
1990	14.7	−3.0

Source: Ekonomika i zhizn', no. 9 (February 1991), 12; and no. 6 (1990), 15; Moscow TASS (January 26, 1991); from FBIS-SOV-91-018 (January 28, 1991), 37.

creased money holdings at the end of the 1980s and into the 1990s constituted forced savings: the goods people hoped to buy with their increased incomes did not exist. For example, from April 1, 1989, to April 1, 1990, savings increased in the USSR by 21.9 percent.[1] No matter how high incomes climbed, the increasing demand they represented could not bring forth more goods.

The worst form of excessive increases in wages came in the form of indexation—tying wage increases to price increases. Below, we look at indexation policies in some detail. Suffice to say here that indexation has never been an intelligent economic policy. Rather, it has always been political policy; in Gorbachev's Soviet Union, it came about partly as a well-intentioned expression of sympathy for a beleaguered population and partly to keep an angry population at bay. Whatever the government's motives, indexation by its very nature led to persistent inflation and increased expectations of continual protection. All of this was especially dangerous for a Soviet economy so desperately in need of a sound stabilization policy. There could never be a question of whether indexation would be harmful, only how much more damage would be done to an economy that was rapidly sinking.

Other policies fueled the mounting inflation. The Law on the State Enterprise, which went into effect on January 1, 1988, gave managers considerably more freedom to set the prices of the goods they produced. This occasionally led to excessive over-pricing of goods that manufacturers were producing in the same way they always had or with only minor changes. In one case, the Ukrainian State Committee on Prices rolled back the newly set prices on 236 items. More than a million rubles of what it termed "unlawfully obtained profits" were confiscated and put into the republic's budget.[2] There were other ways by which managers increased their profits. One was to change the structure of a product line, reducing the production of low-priced items and increasing the output of high-priced ones.[3]

Yet another Gorbachev policy that had an inflationary impact was his antialcohol campaign. On June 1, 1985, two months after he took office, a strict antialcohol policy went into effect with the intention of refocusing the energies of the people on work, productivity, and sobriety and away from the excessive drinking and slovenly work that had characterized the earlier period.[4] Prices were raised on all alcoholic beverages and the hours for buying them were restricted.[5] Noble as Gorbachev's aims were, they led to disastrous results. Not only was the policy deeply resented by the public, it also had unintended economic side effects. Although alcohol production fell during the 1985–1987 period by 37 billion rubles, which was roughly equal to 25 percent of food sales, there was no compensatory production of other goods on which people could spend the money that formerly went to alcohol; and this placed even more pressure on price levels.[6]

A decline in earnings from the sale of Soviet products abroad also added to the empty shelves, the inflationary pressure, and popular unhappiness. When the Soviets began to experience a shortfall in export earnings, in part because their oil revenues declined, they responded by decreasing their imports by 8 billion rubles' worth of nonfood consumer goods, or roughly the equivalent of 5 percent of their 1985 sales of these items.[7]

Another factor leading to rising prices was the increased role of free enterprise. The prices charged by cooperatives in particular were wholly determined by supply and demand. In an economy with massive shortages, entrepreneurs in the new cooperatives were able to charge "high" prices. In July 1988, for example, meat prices in the cooperative cafes all across the country were 3.5 to 5 times higher than they were in state cafes and 1.3 to 2.1 times higher than the prices in state restaurants.[8] Charges of price gouging were leveled against the cooperatives. Similar charges were made against the collective farm markets that had operated for decades and toward which there had always been urban antipathy over their allegedly excessive prices. The charge of price-gouging was not altogether without merit. The so-called trading cooperatives were in many instances little more than legalized speculators, with selling prices bearing little if any relationship to actual value.[9] It was estimated that the trading cooperatives' markups over the prices in the state retail and wholesale trade organizations represented 50 to 60 percent of their revenues.[10] Popular resentment toward the new entrepreneurs was strong and criticism of them was sharp. People had a real fear of a possible tyranny of private entrepreneurs, of the high prices they could charge in a shortage economy. They were regarded as nothing short of parasitic, if not downright evil for taking advantage of the population's vulnerability in a time of economic stress.

Yet the role that cooperatives played in generating higher prices should be kept in perspective. Although they were a handy and visible scapegoat for the public, the cooperatives were never a dominant factor in the retail market.

The public's hostility toward rising prices was at least equal to its antipathy to shortages. Protests took several forms. In July 1989, for instance, there was a Saturday morning boycott at a number of food markets as a way of fighting the so-called market mafia.[11] In that same year, in a more dramatic instance of anger against "profiteers," a crowd of mostly young, unemployed men in the Turkmen city of Nebit-Dag set fire to a large number of cooperatives and assaulted the owners.[12]

Price Reform

Over the entire course of the Gorbachev era, the government waffled over the formulation of a price reform that would undo the long-standing policy of heavy subsidies which had created shortages and distorted relative prices and the allocation of resources. The state faced a serious dilemma—which it never did resolve during the era of perestroika—of whether to adopt economically sensible policies that would allow prices to be determined freely and thereby lead to more efficiency, or to make the purely political decision to keep prices as artificially low as possible and thereby keep the population from railing against high prices. And if there was to be price decontrol, how rapid should it be? Should the prices of some goods remain under the absolute control of the state and remain subsidized? These were questions to which there were only hesitant and inconstant answers. The government never established a consistent policy, and the public never understood the problem.

Most reformers understood that revising prices was an absolute prerequisite for creating an efficient economic system. They knew that there could never be a thriving Soviet Union without the elimination of both the subsidies and the fixed prices that had distorted economic outcomes and kept prices well below the equilibrium level. Subsidies on manufactured consumer goods, for example, which were 90 billion rubles in 1990, were scheduled to rise to 140 to 150 billion rubles in 1991; and the cost of production was at least 25 percent higher than the revenues from the sale of these goods.[13] According to the head of the USSR State Committee for Prices, at the beginning of 1991, for every ruble of food products sold (excluding alcohol), there were 1.37 rubles in subsidies.[14]

But the ordinary citizen had absolutely no understanding of the economic issues involved: that huge subsidies created budget deficits and inflationary pressure and distorted resource allocation and the distribution of income. Nor was there any realization by the man on the street that below-equilibrium prices led to excess demand and thereby resulted in shortages and the ubiquitous and eternally long lines for food and consumer goods. Instead, everyone expected a cornucopia of goods at low prices.

Resistance to the kind of price reform that would eliminate the system's structural anomalies was virtually universal. A public opinion poll taken in December 1988 by the All-Union Center for the Study of Public Opinion examined the population's views on the forthcoming retail price reform. Sixty-one percent of those interviewed were against the reform, and those in the lowest income groups were almost unanimously against any policy that would raise food prices. However, the results also suggested Soviet citizens were willing to endure higher prices if their lives would be better as a result, if the assortment and quantity of food products also increased. But there was no faith in the idea that rising food prices would eliminate the food shortage, and only 15 percent of the people polled believed that the state would fully compensate the population for price increases.[15] Indeed, when prices for virtually all goods were rising rapidly, and when hardly any goods could be found at all, why should the people trust a government which told them that the prices of such consumer goods as textiles and household appliances would go down as much as 30 percent during 1990 and that senior citizens would be able to buy boots and shoes and shirts at quite low prices?[16] In part, this climate of public suspicion, if not outright hostility, contributed to the government's decision in 1989 to postpone increases in food prices for at least two years.[17] However, tabling price increases temporarily did nothing to diminish the urban population's great pessimism over future inflation. In an October 1989 survey, 57 percent said they did not believe that the rapid rise in prices could be stopped in the next one to two years, and only 15 percent said they thought inflation could be halted at all.[18]

Perhaps there was nothing that could have diminished the gut fear that people had about the fall in their standard of living. For them, there was no redeeming value in any economic policy that made their lives worse in the short run.

The May 1990 Price Reform Proposal

In May 1990, Leonid Abalkin, the deputy prime minister in charge of economic reform under Nikolai Ryzhkov, submitted a comprehensive economic reform proposal that included a major initiative on prices. The Abalkin plan proposed abolishing central control over most prices and allowing most buyers and producers in the economy to negotiate prices. But to contain the expected price increases, prices of a number of basic commodities, such as oil, gas, coal, and electricity, would remain fixed. It was believed that the Abalkin reforms would increase prices on consumer goods by 150 to 200 percent. In order to calm the expected protest against such a policy, Abalkin proposed indexing all incomes, using a market basket of basic goods that would be specified by the government and taking additional measures to protect such vulnerable groups as pensioners. The government's estimates were that the proposed social safety net would mitigate 90 percent of the expected inflation.[19] Perhaps the most threatening aspect of this broadly-based, state-administered plan for price increases was the proposal to triple the heavily subsidized price of bread in July and to raise the prices of other foods the following January. The idea of tripling bread prices bordered on heresy; they had not changed in thirty years, and now the cost of bread, which was the staple of the limited Soviet diet, was about to rise dramatically.[20] There was an instantaneous outcry against the proposal, and it died amidst a storm of protests.

Burned by the hostility of the popular response, the central government decided that prices should be frozen until the following year. However, there were local initiatives to raise prices. These decisions, usually taken at the republic level and occasionally at the city level, reflected the underlying conflict between the center and its periphery over who was sovereign in the realm of food prices. In several instances in the Baltic republics, already embattled over the issue of political independence, prices were raised; Leningrad and Moscow also pursued an independent price policy. Some of these measures were self-protective. Leningrad, for example, raised the prices of all alcoholic beverages by 20 percent on July 5, but only after Estonia had raised alcohol prices in late May, inducing Estonians to buy the now relatively inexpensive Leningrad liquor and resell it in Estonia.[21] Disturbed by the encroachments on what it believed was its turf, the central government intervened several times. The city of Moscow, for example, was forbidden to sell tobacco at market prices during the tobacco shortage.[22] Still, the challenge to traditional central authority in determining prices continued. In November 1990, Lithuania introduced new prices on a number of food and non-food luxury items and required that all income from the price increase remain in the republic.[23] The battle lines between the center and the republics and cities had been drawn.

About the same time, the central government made a second, albeit quite modest, attempt at price reform. The USSR Council of Ministers said that prices for luxury and certain other goods deemed nonessential to the population's well-being would be determined by the market as of November 15. These items included jewelry, fur goods for adults, rugs and carpeting, high-quality porcelain, crystal, high-quality electronic goods, certain high-quality furniture, spare parts for automobiles, seafood delicacies, and some meat products.[24] While this was an effort to reduce the enormous burden of the subsidies, its impact was insignificant; these were not the kinds of goods purchased by most people and their value amounted to only about 6 percent of total retail turnover.[25]

In spite of its relatively benign impact on overall consumption, price reform continued to generate a great deal of displeasure. The Russian republic almost immediately denounced the center's new pricing policy as a violation of the republic's sovereignty and as an effort "to undermine the authority of its leaders."[26] Kazakhstan also rejected the center's decision.[27] These responses raised the danger of asymmetrical pricing polices among the different republics. Moldavia, fearing an outflow of scarce goods if neighboring Ukraine raised its prices, called for a coordinated policy.[28] The General Confederation of USSR Trade Unions, rather than demanding a rollback of the policy, asked for monetary compensation for the price increases.[29] Less than two weeks later, the storm of controversy caused by the price increases forced the Supreme Soviet to announce that it would re-evaluate its decision.[30] But by then a re-evaluation was moot. By mid-

December, all the republics, with the exception of Armenia, had decided to switch to market prices for luxury goods, mostly following the central government's original list. As a result, the prices for nonstaple goods doubled in Moldavia, Latvia, and Kazakhstan and increased by 60 percent in Ukraine and 20 percent in Belorussia.[31]

Taken together, the responses to the proposed increases in the price of bread—the commodity that went right to the heart of the ordinary citizen's sense of well-being—and in luxury goods provided all the evidence that one might probably need for the hopelessness of national price reform under existing political and social circumstances, which included inter-republican jealousies and a general mistrust of the central government.

In the Baltic states, there was a complicated mixture of nationalism, different economic policies, ethnic rivalries, and general distaste for price increases. A 1990 survey in Estonia examined the attitudes of Estonians and ethnic Russians about the government's proposal to eliminate subsidies and allow the prices of meat and dairy products to increase. The results showed that while 50 percent of the Estonians supported such a policy, only 16 percent of the ethnic Russians did. One possible reason for the difference in attitudes was that while Estonians wanted their own nation and were willing to make sacrifices to achieve this goal, the Russian-speaking population had no such incentive. As well, urban Estonians, unlike the republic's ethnic Russians, had friends and relatives in rural areas who provided them with access to food.[32] But ethnic pride aside, Estonians revolted against price increases in January 1991. In several cities, demonstrations and leaflets published in both Estonian and Russian demanded a halt to price increases and even called on the government to decrease prices.[33]

A whole set of policies was adopted during this period of reform, in response to the population's assumption that low prices were an entitlement. These policies also demonstrated how much the national or the republican governments felt the need to allay public anger and frustration over inflation. In February

1989, reacting to the anger of factory managers over stipulations in the new enterprise law, the USSR Council of Ministers imposed the requirement that the production of inexpensive goods in consumer goods industries would be part of state orders. Enterprises were forbidden to raise the prices of goods on which they had made no significant changes and were also prohibited from raising the prices of goods produced for children and the elderly. Moreover, price increases for new or high-fashion goods could not exceed 15 percent.[34] Estonia raised the price of meat and milk and several other goods, and in October 1990, also increased taxes by 10 percent, which created a backlash of protest.[35] To reduce the consequent public tensions, the Estonian government responded by freezing prices on January 15, 1991, until the central government decided on price reforms. In early 1991, the USSR's Main Administration for Price Control proudly announced that it had expropriated some 300 million rubles of "illegal profit" nationwide which had been gained through "unjustifiable price increases."[36] The central government was clearly trying to find a balance, as tenuous as it was, between rational prices and political peace.

But the population demanded more. As inflation worsened in 1991, governments intervened to provide price relief. In February, Lithuania directed both its state enterprises and state joint enterprises to use their own funds to reduce the prices of workers' meals in their eating facilities by at least 50 percent.[37] Inexpensive (and heavily subsidized) factory meals served as a kind of buffer against the high food prices that workers and their families had to endure. Thus, the central government responded: in April, Gosplan and the USSR Ministry of Finance adopted a resolution that allowed state enterprises to reimburse their own cafeterias out of their profits. As an incentive to the enterprises the income they used to reduce prices for factory meals would not be taxed.[38]

Individual republics instituted even further price reform. At the beginning of 1991, Latvia increased prices 3 to 3.2 times on several key foods, including bread, meat, and milk, simply by removing their subsidies.[39] This followed on the heels of a survey taken the previous summer by the Latvian Association of Sociologists which had asked, "Are price increases permissible?" Of those who had been surveyed, 69 percent assented to price increases for alcohol and tobacco and 56 percent supported an increase in the price of bread. However, most objected to a rise in the price of meat, milk, consumer services, transportation, and clothing.[40] When prices went up in January, the Latvian government itself offered compensation for the increases to a minority of the population, instead placing the burden of compensation onto state enterprises.[41] It was obvious that the Latvian government should have paid better attention to its pollsters. The price increases immediately evoked mass demonstrations in opposition to the new policy. The trade unions argued that enterprises did not have the resources to provide the 66-ruble compensation proposed by the government.[42] Even if they had had the money, the Latvian standard of living would have fallen by about 60 percent.[43] In order to placate the population, Prime Minister Godmanis pledged to reassess the four- to fivefold increase in prices at worker cafeterias. It was estimated that after the new prices went into effect, Latvians would require 243 rubles a month for subsistence at a time when two-thirds of them had monthly incomes of less than 200 rubles.[44]

After the central government raised prices on April 2, 1991, Latvia, which had already increased its prices, indicated that it would review whether the prices of bread, meat, and milk needed to be increased again.[45] The Latvian government decided to raise the prices of all dairy and meat products on May 2, 1991, but backed off from the decision when workers in a number of enterprises threatened to go on strike.[46]

The effort to reform prices spread through the Baltics. On January 7, Lithuania increased the price of foods by 100 to 200 percent and in some instances by as much as 500 percent. The price increases were something of a surprise to Lithuanians who a little more than a week before had been promised a delay in the price reform. As compensation, the government offered a package that would at least double wages.[47] The day after the government announced its decision on price increases, protest demonstrations forced the government to withdraw them.[48] Six months later, a new government under Prime Minister Gediminas Vagnorius announced price increases on the average of 50 percent, with bread prices rising 20 percent and prices for dairy products, 26 percent. Ironically, this was precisely the level of increase that had been proposed by the previous government, but now nominal incomes had tripled, to an average of 600 rubles a month in industry. The compensation package offered by the Vagnorius government was substantial, far greater than the one the central government had offered in April 1991 to the entire USSR. The Lithuanian government's compensation amounted to at least 135 rubles a month to industrial workers, a raise of 22.5 percent. To make it easier for enterprises to pay the higher wages, the enterprise tax was reduced from 35 percent to 29 percent. The republic's budget also provided allowances of 80 rubles a month for children and 250 rubles a month for nursing mothers.[49] Thus the Lithuanian government was able to secure a more peaceful response to price increases, but only by sweetening the pot so substantially that, in effect, it bought price reform with a large financial commitment both in terms of lost tax revenues and additional expenditures—and a virtual guarantee of higher inflation in the future.

On July 1, 1991, Estonia also introduced free-market prices for all food except for bread and milk whose prices the government retained the right to set. A step in this direction had already been taken in 1990 when the republic's government had rescinded subsidies for milk and meat, potatoes and other vegetables, and grain.[50]

Mounting budget deficits forced other republics and cities to consider price increases. Georgia, with a deficit of more than one billion rubles, raised the prices on all their main food products in January 1991. Because it imported virtually all of its grain, three-fourths of its milk, and about half its meat, the Georgian government felt that it was no longer capable of continuing to subsidize the retail prices of imported goods.[51] Leningrad, faced with losses amounting to 100 million rubles in the food and processing industries, as well as the central and the Russian government's unwillingness to undertake price reform, decided in February to increase the prices of food staples and, at the same time, to introduce a plan for social protection in the form of cash compensation for the price increases.[52]

The April 1991 Price Reform

The most important single national price reform initiative during the Gorbachev era took place on April 2, 1991, and was accompanied by a compensation plan, albeit incomplete, to protect the population from the new, higher prices. In many ways, it was like the May 1990 proposal put forward by Abalkin, except that the legislation came at a time when prices were beginning to explode out of control. During the first four months of 1991, personal money income rose by 56.8 billion rubles, even though output fell by 3 percent relative to the same period in 1990. There was only one way for Soviet goods markets to achieve balance, and that was with a rise in prices. But what made economic sense meant only more misery and pain from the people's point of view.

The reform was based on two principles, put forward in March: Prices were to be raised in stages and were to reflect the cost of production and supply and demand; and the ceilings on price increases were to be the same all over the USSR. This was far from the complete liberalization of prices that the most radical economic reformers had prescribed; price determination still involved state intervention. The rise in prices was also to be coordinated with the introduction of compensation measures such as wage increases and pensions, as well as other social expenditures. The prices of certain goods and commodities, such as medicine, toys, fur goods, and home-heating energies, were to be kept at their existing levels; and subsidies for meat, dairy and fish products, medicines, and some other goods were to be partly retained in 1991. It was predicted that, as a direct consequence of the reform, the price level would rise, on average, 60 percent.[53] The principles of social protection provided for increases of 60 to 80 percent in allowances for families with children as well as for a monthly 65-ruble increase for pensioners.[54]

With the introduction of the April 1991 price reform, there were now three categories of prices: fixed prices, which applied to goods whose prices could be no higher than the level set by the state; so-called regulated prices, which were negotiated but had an upper limit and applied to about 15 percent of all goods, mostly expensive items; and free-market prices, which applied to about 30 percent of all goods.[55] All the basic foods were covered by fixed state prices. Such items as cars, televisions, wines and liqueurs, beer, timber, and woollens had regulated prices. The goods for which free prices would be allowed included stereo equipment, all foreign-made fashion clothing, and other of the most expensive goods. The three-tier system of prices was designed with two goals in mind—equity and progress toward decontrolling prices. Thus, because the most expensive goods were not covered by compensation, the burden of higher prices fell most heavily on the middle- and upper-income groups.

The goal of moving from price controls to free-market prices was to be accomplished by diminishing the importance of subsidies. The April price reform was supposed to eliminate 125 billion of the estimated 225 billion rubles in 1991 subsidies. Moreover, it was supposed to decrease the quantity of goods demanded by 15 to 20 percent and thereby reduce some of the excess demand, which was estimated at 160 to 200 billion rubles.[56] As Table 3.3 illustrates, the new reform resulted in dramatic increases in the prices of food and other vital consumer goods. Overall, the prices of consumer goods rose 175 percent and food prices increased by 240 percent.[57]

Reactions to the price reform proposal were predictably hostile and included popular protests. There were meetings in Kaliningrad and Volgograd, and on March 24, a week before the new prices were established, a Leningrad rally petitioned the USSR Supreme Soviet not to increase prices but to stabilize the economy, as if these

Table 3.3

Percentage Increase in Retail Prices, April 2, 1991

Meat and meat products	200
Milk and dairy products	130
Eggs and egg products	100
Bread, flour, groats, and pasta	200
Sugar	135
Tea	100
Fish commodities	30
Salt	240
Vegetable oil, margarine, and mayonnaise	100
Household and toilet soap	100
Food concentrates, including baby food	200
Certain domestically produced tobacco products	50
Underwear, popular types of fabrics, clothing, and footwear	135
Goods for children	195
Cultural, consumer, and household goods	75
Passenger transport tariffs:	
Rail	70
Air	80
Sea	140
Consumer communications services	20

Source: Pravda (March 20, 1991), 2.

were entirely separate issues.[58] Likewise, in a meeting with Prime Minister Valentin Pavlov, the Moscow Federation of Trade Unions demanded that there be no price increases until a law on indexation was adopted and even threatened a general strike in the city if their demands went unmet.[59] The Kiev Council of Trade Unions also asked the Ukrainian government to approve a law on indexation of incomes immediately.[60]

The day after the price increases went into effect, workers in a number of factories around the country held brief strikes for higher wages.[61] One of the areas struck was Ukraine, where transport drivers and workers in Kiev's major enterprises carried out work stoppages for limited periods over the issue of the price increases. There were also spontaneous demonstrations on April 16 in the city's central square. The insistence of the protesters and of a number of deputies was enough to elicit a response from Ukrainian Prime Minister Vitold Fokin. While describing the price reform as "an operation without anesthesia," he said that prices could not be lowered in Ukraine because it would lead to an outflow of goods into other republics, where prices were higher. The best alternative, he insisted, was adequate compensation and public assistance.[62] On April 17, demonstrators in Lvov demanded that the government either rescind the five-percent sales tax or introduce a "rational" policy on prices. The rally's call for the government to stop experimenting with economic policy and find a sensible path toward reform reflected the general impatience and skepticism of the population.[63]

In some places, public animosity was so strong that local authorities did rescind the price increases. In Moscow, there were many complaints about the rise in the price of *osobaia*, small cheese products which children got in their school lunches. The long-time price was 51 kopeks, but after the reform it shot up to 3.07 rubles. After hearing a number of complaints, the Moscow City Political Committee agreed to lower the price to 1.30 rubles. While this move no doubt pleased Moscow parents, it did not please the manufacturer, who stopped delivering the cheese.[64] Retrenchment also occurred in Uzbekistan, where the decision was made to lower prices and thereafter to introduce price ceilings on all meat and dairy products.[65] In Belorussia, the republican government reduced the price of children's clothing by up to 50 percent, and city authorities in Minsk issued instructions to lower prices in school and factory dining rooms.[66] Kirgizia lowered retail flour prices to their prereform levels as of April 15 and returned to the prices previously charged in school and student cafeterias. It also eliminated the five-percent sales tax on bread, grains, children's meals, and school uniforms. Simultaneously, in an effort to soften the impact of the price increases, it decided to raise the pay of workers in education, health care, social security, and culture and to eliminate certain restrictions on child allowances.[67] In May, the Tadzhik government decided to lower prices on locally produced goods by 5 to 50 percent. The anticipated loss of 300 to 350 million rubles in government revenues was to be covered by raising the retail prices of vodka, brandy, champagne, and wine by an average of 70 percent.[68] Governments all over the USSR were forced to find the right mixture of price reform and popular appeasement.

As a major part of this effort, the compensation issue loomed large for both the government and the population. People did not want their standard of living to deteriorate any more than it already had, and the government not only felt an obligation to moderate the impact of the price increase, but also recognized that its only chance to gain support for price reform was to assure the population that monetary compensation would minimize the damage. In early February, Ivan Silaev, chairman of the RSFSR Council of Ministers, defined full compensation as compensation for the entire increase in state-sector retail prices, but acknowledged that the state could not compensate the population for the increase in private-sector prices.[69]

The central government's plan for increased wages and social assistance was intended to offset the impact of price increases. The centerpiece of the compensation package was the rise in state wages and salaries by a minimum of 60 rubles a month. State enterprises, which were given the right to determine their own wage and salary schedules, could raise wages and salaries above that level, but they could not offer less. In order to give enterprises the capacity to raise wages and salaries, the tax rate on enterprise income was cut to 35 percent;[70] retirees received an additional 65 rubles a month and families received another 40 rubles a month for each child.[71] In mid-May the Gorbachev government again increased the compensation for families with children, after prices for school uniforms and other children's clothing had doubled and sometimes tripled.[72] Families received an annual allowance of 200 rubles for each child under the age of thirteen and 250 rubles for each child over thirteen. The entire compensation program was supposed to return 85 percent of the price increase to the public, thereby significantly reducing the sting of the reform.[73] However, it only covered the increases in the state retail prices of 296 types of goods and services that were part of the state's "consumer basket"; it did not compensate for the rising prices in collective farm markets or in the cooperatives where free-market prices reigned.

The central government's policy of damage control, as noble as its intentions were, minimized the virtue of reform: the state had now formally adopted the ludicrous policy of trying to fight shortages by raising prices *and* incomes.

Other efforts to cushion the impact of price increases were also half measures. About a week before the price reform went into effect, Gorbachev issued a decree which increased bank deposits held as of March 1 by 40 percent, a one-time-only provision which was intended to compensate the public for the loss in real value of their savings that would result from the price reform. The decree also repealed the restriction on cash withdrawals which had been imposed by the January ruble confiscation policy.[74] However, there was a catch to this measure. If a savings account was greater than 500 rubles, the 40-percent addition to it would be placed into a special account and frozen until 1993. In other words, the population would not really be able to touch their additional nominal rubles for nearly two years.[75] Given the trajectory of events, by the time 1993 rolled around, inflation would have eroded the real value of the compensation. The savings compensation decree was therefore something of an illusion.

Although the consumption funds of the enterprises where individuals worked were the chief source of compensation money, the complete compensation program was expensive to the state.[76] The USSR State Committee for Prices and the USSR Ministry of Finance estimated that the total cost would be about 240 billion rubles, of which an estimated 203 billion would go directly to the population; the remainder was to be spent in other areas where expenditures were needed to relieve pressures of rising prices, such as law enforcement, health care, and student and public food catering.[77] No more than about one-fourth of the total expenditures were to be covered by the central budget, with the rest to come from the republics. The central government estimated that the republics would still wind up 66 billion rubles in the black, because price increases would lead to profits exceeding compensation by that amount.[78]

Attendant to the protection package was the creation of a new bureaucracy, a network of price control bodies whose more than 6,000 inspectors had the responsibility to ensure that the ceilings on new state prices were being observed. They were deemed to be necessary because the combination of chronic shortages and the new economic freedoms for entrepreneurs had created pressure for market prices that were in many instances well above state price ceilings.[79] Illegal pricing was found in 248 state retail stores investigated in Moscow from April 3 to 5; goods were being sold in those stores at prices negotiated right on the spot, and in certain instances, sales workers were pocketing the difference between what they actually charged customers and what they were supposed to charge.[80]

For ordinary people, the price increases seemed brutal. Some three weeks after the reform, the promised compensation had not come. Pensioners and families with several children were the worst off, but no one escaped unscathed. In one of a number of letters to the chief trade union newspaper, *Trud*, a man with a wife and five children said he and his family were able to survive only because of the help they received from their church and the charity of friends at work. Another letter from a man with a wife and two children said that the 700 rubles he and his wife earned went entirely to feed his family.[81] Even if we discount some of the claims and allow for a certain amount of hyperbole, we are left with the fundamental conclusion that workers were hurting very badly.

If one of the justifications for the price increases was that producers would then have an incentive to increase their output, it failed. No additional goods showed up on the shelves, and food shortages continued everywhere.[82] In fact, in constant prices the volume of retail trade in April 1991 was only 68.7 percent of the April 1990 level. That is, output had dropped by about one-third in that period.[83]

Indeed, there were a number of problems with the price reform, but the central one was that its premise was flawed. The very idea that price reform could be achieved via administrative controls was a contradiction in terms. In fact, the reform was merely a compromise. On the one hand, there was a recognition that prices were well below equilibrium, that they were the cause of a substantial part of the budget deficit and of inflation, and that the goal of eventually moving to a market economy could never be achieved without prices that reflected the forces of supply and demand. On the other hand, considerations had to be made for popular feelings, which would be inflamed when the new and much higher prices further damaged the standard of living. A confused government was trying to protect its population against the consequences of reform at the very same time that it was instituting reform.

Moreover, the center was trying to implement a nationwide policy at a time when its political hegemony had ceased to exist. Just as republican independence adversely affected the movement of resources, so it brought inconsistency and confusion to price reform. The central government acted as if it could introduce a uniform policy when the USSR was already in a state of partial dissolution. Republics and several cities simply went their own ways on a number of occasions. They did so for several reasons. First, reforming prices on their own was another way of asserting their independence from the central government. Second, they recognized that although price reform was economically rational, they, too, had to face a popular backlash. Third, they were also facing a budget crisis and needed to rid themselves of the burden of subsidies. Fourth, nationalist governments appealing to nationalistic sentiments could introduce policies that addressed their specific economic problems but did not necessarily apply to the entire USSR.

The price reform did not succeed in saving the economy in the perestroika era. First, the central government had no sizable bloc of support. Its largest constituency, the working class, felt belea-guered, if not betrayed. A government not popularly elected had elected to impose an unpopular policy.

The other shortcomings of the economy could not be over-come by price reform, certainly not in the short run. There was no economic mechanism to replace central planning; paranoia and petty jealousies reigned in inter-republic relations; there were great deficiencies in resources—all this was too over-whelming for price reform to fix all by itself. And in the mind of the population, the price reform policy was just further evidence of the fundamental ineptitude and cruelty of government policy. However bad life had been before, it had not been worse than this; and it was going to get worse, they were sure. And they were right.

Poverty

Before Gorbachev came to power, the very idea of undertaking discussions on such issues as poverty and welfare was impossi-ble. They were not part of the public debate because they came dangerously close to revealing the rotten parts of the economic and social system. But after Gorbachev opened up discussion with his policy of glasnost in 1988, candor and good intentions provided outsiders with a great deal of information about the standard of living in the USSR, even if that information was not always systematic or of the highest quality. At a minimum, we have a reasonably reliable general picture of what happened to the standard of living of the Soviet population during the per-estroika years. The information that emerged as a result of glasnost shows us clearly that if anything is true about changes in the standard of living of the population during this period, it is that many more people became poor. Poverty, once righteously declared by the Soviets to be one of the chief products of capital-ism, enrolled millions of additional Soviet citizens in its ranks during the Gorbachev years.

The level of income in the USSR below which individuals

could be said to be living in poverty is elusive. In part, this is due to the fact that the poverty line kept shifting because of rapid increases in both nominal income and inflation and in part it is due to the absence of consensus on what amount of income constituted the "poverty line." In 1988, the USSR State Committee on Labor and Social Questions and *Goskomstat*, the state's official statistics agency, proposed different definitions of the poverty level. The former said that 105 rubles a month was the minimum acceptable level, and the latter said it was 75 rubles. The figure finally chosen, for no obvious methodological reason, was 78 rubles a month.[84] Under this definition, 41 million people, or 14.5 percent of the population, lived in poverty.[85] One suspects that the figure of 78 rubles was chosen because, at the higher figure of 105 rubles, 90 million people or about one-third of the population would have been categorized as living in poverty.[86] That would have implied a huge financial burden for the state's assistance programs; moreover, a public admission that 90 million people were living in poverty would have been a bitter pill for the government to swallow. A mid-October article in *Izvestiia* argued that a more accurate definition of the poverty line was 100 rubles, a figure estimated to encompass 70.9 million people.[87] Indeed, at the end of 1990, the official poverty line was raised to 93.3 rubles a month; then, in 1991, in response to the continued escalation of prices, it was raised again to 180–200 rubles.

Although the official poverty line kept going up, many believed that the actual poverty line was much higher than the official definition—in April and May 1991, it was variously estimated to be 200 rubles (*Komsomol'skaia pravda*), 227 rubles (USSR Ministry of Labor and Social Questions), and 270 rubles (General Confederation of Trade Unions).[88] Using the International Labour Organization's rule of thumb, that poverty is equivalent to two-thirds the average wage, this would have been 165 rubles in late 1990, placing about 56 percent of the country in poverty.[89] Parenthetically, it is interesting to note that when the population was asked in August 1991 what they believed the subsistence minimum to be, their estimate was 328 rubles, a figure which would have meant that 84 percent of the population lived below the poverty line![90] Even with a recognition that subjective assessments of economic conditions tend to exaggerate objective conditions, it is hard to escape the conclusion that almost everyone in the USSR felt that things were going badly.

Some groups were more vulnerable to poverty than others. Large families were quite vulnerable, with 75 percent living at the poverty level.[91] These families tended to be concentrated in Central Asia, Kazakhstan, and Azerbaidzhan.[92] Family allowances from the state were inadequate in the face of the increased cost of living; for example, the monthly stipend of 4 rubles for a fourth child, 6 rubles for a fifth, and 12.5 rubles for a tenth child made almost no dent in the real costs of providing for a family. Moreover these stipends were allowed only for children from age one to age five. In general, the central government's allocation to children in poor families declined during the years of perestroika. While the percentage of the central budget that went to support poor children had been 0.56 percent at its peak in 1975, that allocation fell to 0.20 of the budget by 1988, an absolute decline of 300 million rubles. A new law, amending the 1974 allowances to extend the period of coverage for children, was to take effect on October 1, 1989; but it was delayed until at least 1991.[93] The postponement put more children at risk; by 1991, one-third of all children were estimated to be living in poverty.[94]

In Central Asia and elsewhere, children were especially threatened. In 1990, it was reported that some Turkmen women and children suffered outright starvation. As many as 60 percent of Turkmen women were said to have a protein deficiency, which contributed to the generally weak and undernourished condition of their newborn infants. In Ashkhabad, 33 percent of the babies were born with symptoms of intrauterine malnutrition.[95] Children also suffered when the price of school lunches tripled in April 1991. In Nizhnii Tagil, near the Urals, a number of children were reported to have fainted in school because they were skipping lunch.[96] Reports that 75 percent of Moscow's school children were going without lunch raised more fears of malnutrition.

A second group hit by poverty was women, in large part because they were disproportionately at the low end of the pay scale. In 1989, when the average monthly wage was 240 rubles, 11.5 percent of the state labor force earned 100 rubles a month or less. Of this group, 75 percent were women. But at the other end of the income scale, of those who earned 300 rubles or more, only 22 percent were women.[97] Two of the poorest groups of women were nursing mothers who had left the labor force and were receiving the small state allowance instead of their regular salaries and single mothers.[98] When the state gave its citizens a supplement to compensate for the dramatic price increases in 1991, the Committee of Soviet Women protested because women who were not in the labor force were left out and therefore unable to provide adequately for themselves and their children.[99]

A third group mired in poverty were the aged of the Soviet Union. In 1989, when the rule of thumb was that pensions should constitute 60–70 percent of the average wage, a pension should have been 140–165 rubles a month, considerably higher than the less than 100 rubles a month that two-thirds of the pensioners received. Roughly 60 percent of Soviet old-age pensioners, or 35 million people, were living in poverty.[100]

The homeless, once hidden behind the veil of secrecy that marked the Soviet period, were extremely vulnerable to the deteriorating conditions. Popularly referred to as *bomzhi*, the police acronym for "without a definite place of residence," they were everywhere present, but of unknown number. A 1988 estimate speculated that there were several hundred thousand homeless in the country.[101] The *bomzhi* were often associated with temporary or seasonal work. In 1989, in the far east city of Khabarovsk where people came to work in the seasonal fishing industry, there were an estimated 10,000 homeless out of a total population of 600,000.[102] In the city of Leningrad, the number of homeless may have been as high as 100,000 people by 1991.[103] The number of homeless increased when a very unlikely group, servicemen and their families, returned from duty abroad. One estimate in the fall of 1991 was that 292,000 such families were without an apartment. It was also reported that 9,000 military families in Moscow moved like vagabonds from one place to another, paying rents that were well above their housing allowances.[104]

There were also substantial differences among the republics in the amount of poverty. As of April 1991, only 3 percent of the Estonian population had an income below 100 rubles a month; that figure was 7 percent in Belorussia and 11 percent in both Ukraine and Russia. But in Kirgizia, 47 percent lived in poverty; in both Turkmenistan and Azerbaidzhan, 49 percent; in Uzbekistan 57 percent; and in Tadzhikistan, 69 percent.[105] However, even in the relatively better off republics, the standard of living fell during the years of perestroika. In Estonia, for example, where poverty had a minimal presence, the standard of living fell by more than 40 percent in 1990, caused by a price increase of 70 to 75 percent against a wage increase of only 28 percent.[106] There were also differences among the cities, even among cities within the same republic. For example, the minimum subsistence income at the beginning of 1991 was 202 rubles in Moscow, 173 rubles in Vladivostok (October 1990), and 154 rubles in Togliatti, located on the Volga River near Kuibyshev, at a time when it was 177 rubles for the RSFSR as a whole.[107]

The central government first officially admitted that poverty was an issue in May 1991, at the Fourth Congress of USSR People's Deputies. Gorbachev signed a decree, to be implemented on July 1 of that year, which introduced the concept of a minimum consumer budget to show the cost of a market basket of goods and services. Minimum consumer budgets were to be developed for the country as a whole, and for the republics and the various regions. The budgets were to be used for forecasting the standard of living and formulating social policy in such areas as state pensions and state spending on a variety of social services.[108] (See Appendix to this chapter.)

The high price of food forced Soviet families to spend a substantial percentage of their income on day-to-day sustenance.

Table 3.4

Expenditures of Gross Family Income, 1988, in Percent

	Average Monthly Per Capita Income, in Rubles				
	All Families	Below 75	75–100	100–150	150–200	Above 200
Food	34.3	51.5	42.7	35.8	31.9	28.4
Non–food goods	30.4	27.4	29.2	30.3	32.0	29.7
Services	9.6	8.0	9.8	10.3	9.1	7.9
Taxes, collections, and payments	8.1	3.8	5.7	7.8	8.6	8.9
Other expenses	8.8	8.6	8.5	8.5	9.7	12.0
Savings	8.8	0.7	4.1	7.3	8.7	13.1

Source: Ekonomicheskaia gazeta, no. 25 (June 1989), 11.

Table 3.4 shows that, overall, more than one-third of household income was spent on food in 1988. For low-income families, the situation was even worse. At a time when the official poverty line was 75 rubles, more than half of family income went to buy food. Moreover, those families with the lowest incomes were able to save little if anything at all.

Overall, however, Soviet citizens saved more than 8 percent of their incomes, well up from the one percent they had saved at the beginning of the 1950s. In 1951, the average savings deposit was 124 rubles; in 1989, 1,514 rubles.[109] While the high savings rate reflected an improvement in the material situation of Soviet lives over almost a fifty-year period, it also reflected the serious shortage of consumer goods, which caused people to channel a great deal of involuntary savings into banks. Data from Moscow show the deleterious impact of inflation on the standard of living. In Table 3.5, we see that in the period from 1985 to 1990, income rose by 33.5 percent, but expenses rose by 34.6 percent. What stands out is that Muscovites were able to spend within their limita-

Table 3.5

Average Per Capita Income and Expenses, Moscow Industrial Worker and Employee Families, in Rubles per Month

	1985	1988	1989	1990
Income	161	170	193	215
Expenses	153	170	184	206
Food Expenses	58	62	65	70

Source: Moscow News, no. 51 (1990), 10.

tions only by reducing their consumption of food (Table 3.6). In every food category, monthly per capita consumption fell.

There is some reason for believing that the data which suggest that Muscovites were spending roughly one-third of their income on food were fictitious, at least in 1991. The Director of the Center for Price and Market Research Policy said that, as of June 1991, people in Moscow with average incomes were spending as much as 70 percent of their income on food, and the poor were spending perhaps 85 percent of their income just to eat.[110]

What did people themselves think about their material situations? In a May–June 1991 survey of 1,255 people in both urban and rural areas, the National Public Opinion Center found that only 21 percent of those it interviewed said that their cost of living was less than 300 rubles a month, a figure considerably higher than many people's wages. Some 20 percent said that 300–400 rubles was needed for an "adequate" life and about 33 percent said that a per-capita income of more than 500 rubles a month was needed for a "comfortable life."[111] An August 1991 poll conducted by the same organization asked 3,000 citizens what they thought might lead to a fall in their standard of living. Twenty-three percent feared a cut in salaries, 16 percent thought their income might fall after retirement, and 26 percent worried about the loss of a job.[112] In another poll at the same time, 64 percent said they feared their income might fall below the poverty line, while only 17 percent believed their income would not

Table 3.6

Average Per Capita Food Consumption, Moscow Industrial Worker and Employee Families, in Kilograms per Month

	1975	1985	1988	1989	1990
Bakery products	7.5	6.3	6.2	5.9	5.8
Potatoes	8.9	6.9	6.7	6.4	5.9
Fruits	4.6	4.8	4.8	4.6	3.6
Meat products	9.25	8.7	8.8	9.0	8.9
Dairy products	36	32	31	31	31
Butter	0.7	0.7	0.65	0.6	0.6
Eggs (in units)	23	20	20	20	19

Source: Moscow News, no. 51 (1990), 10.

fall to this level. It is striking that those who worked for the state were most apprehensive about poverty. While only 14 percent of those who worked for joint-stock societies and 25 percent of workers in the cooperatives feared a future in which they would be poor, 69 percent of those who worked in state enterprises feared a future of poverty.[113] The state, upon which most people relied for their livelihood, inspired little confidence in its workers. The evidence from this survey indicated, as well, that workers had no faith in the state's traditional commitment to full employment and the guaranteed income that accompanied a guaranteed job.

As the standard of living fell and the likelihood of a market economy increased, the Soviet citizenry became increasingly unnerved by the prospect of living in poverty. The social protections which had once been taken for granted now became dubious. No one knew with certainty, either in the halls of government or on the street, what it was that should be done to ensure citizens' protection from the anticipated ravages of inflation, unemployment, and the market economy. The socialist regime had created many entitlement programs, and the popular belief was that these social welfare measures should exist forever. In the world of the ordinary Soviet citizen, there seemed nothing incompatible between creating a market economy that would bring forth the surfeit of goods they had never enjoyed and sustaining a secure public welfare system.

Public officials were thus faced with a terrible predicament. Should they choose to respond to most of the demands for social protection and thereby do the politically safe thing, they risked escalating the already mounting rate of inflation as wage increases and budgetary expenditures produced the predictably vicious wage-price spiral. On the other hand, if they ignored the pleas of the population, they would not only be ignoring the genuine suffering of their citizens, but they would also risk raising popular ire and perhaps open rebellion.

Pressures mounted on both the central and the republican governments to protect the population through indexation of incomes. The first piece of legislation to try to protect the population against inflation was passed in Belorussia late in 1990. The general outline of the plan was to index incomes after each 5-percent increase in the consumer price index, starting in January 1991. All wages, pensions, benefits, grants, and savings would be indexed.[114] In February 1991, the Belorussian Supreme Soviet passed a revised law on income indexation. Part of it indexed the minimum wage retroactively to the beginning of the year, starting at 125 rubles a month. For those living below the poverty level, there would be a one-percent increase in their salaries for every one-percent increase in prices. For those with a poverty-level income to those earning twice that amount, there would be an increase in salaries of 0.8 percent for a one-percent increase in prices, an increase of 0.5 percent for those earning four times the subsistence level, and no indexation for anyone earning in excess of four times the subsistence level.[115] In January 1991, the Kirgiz government introduced a procedure for indexing both income and savings once the cost of livng rose by more than 5 percent.[116] In April 1991, the RSFSR Supreme Soviet passed a law which provided for a minimum wage of 180 rubles a month as of October 1, to rise to 195 rubles on January 1, 1992. This included a 60-ruble compensation for the large price increases.[117] In May 1991, the Ukrainian government signed an agreement with the Ukrainian Trade Union Federation that called for a higher minimum wage, wage indexation, and guarantees that the republic would establish a rationing plan should supplies decline seriously.[118] In that same month, the Moldavian government, which had initially signed an agreement with the republic's Trade Union Council on April 15, signed a supplementary accord whereby it would raise the minimum wage as well as increase its expenditures on state-subsidized meals in educational and social institutions to correspond with the level of inflation.[119] Finally, in June 1991, the USSR itself passed legislation to index incomes. The law provided for the central budget to index pensions, stipends, certain other transfer payments, and the salaries of nonprofit state organizations. Indexation for state enterprises would be part of collective bargaining agreements. The legislation said that once the rise in consumer goods prices exceeded 5 percent, incomes would be indexed within three months.[120] The potential cost was staggering, an estimated 3.55 billion rubles for every one percentage point increase in the index of retail prices.[121]

The public coffer was not the only source of protection, although it was admittedly the most important. For the first time in Soviet history, in a remarkable turnabout, the USSR openly acknowledged and accepted private charity. The Soviet Charity and Health Fund, possibly the largest of the private charity organizations, began its work in 1988. In 1988 and 1989 it collected more than 46 million rubles. An accounting of its operations, reported in *Pravda*, shows both the sources of its income and the recipients of its largesse. As of January 1, 1990, the organization had collected 16.6 million rubles from industrial enterprises, 14.7 million rubles from public and state organizations, 7.6 million rubles from various groups, 3.5 million rubles from individual citizens, and another 3.5 million from the fundraising activities. In 1989, among other things, the Fund gave monetary assistance to 45,000 pensioners and disabled persons and to 15,000 disabled Afghan war veterans and the families of soldiers who had died in that war; it provided free food for 17,500 people, clothing and bedding for 4,000, home repairs for 1,200 families of pensioners and disabled people; and it helped 11,000 people to get medical assistance.[122] In October 1989, the Moscow Charity Bank opened its doors with 58 million rubles in capital. It was established by a coalition of the Ministry of Social Security, the Ministry of the Health of the RSFSR, the USSR State Committee for Public Education, the Credit and Finance Institute of Soviet Banks, and the foreign economic association Interservis. The bank defined its roles as those of financing social programs and providing credit, and its plans included raising money from industrial enterprises, public and religious organizations, and individuals in the USSR and abroad. It also planned to start joint ventures both in the Soviet Union and abroad, with profits going to charitable purposes.[123]

Soup kitchens also began to appear for the first time in the USSR's history. A special cafeteria was opened in April 1989 in Leningrad to feed the elderly poor, providing free dinners for those who received a pension of less than 70 rubles a month. The food was regarded as ordinary—soup, a fish-based dish, stewed fruit—"the food of old people," as one social worker put it. The soup kitchen was the brainchild of *Miloserdie*, a private organization that raised funds from Soviet enterprises. The initial requirement of 25,000 rubles to start the cafeteria was raised from the contributions of more than fifty enterprises, including 12,000 rubles from a single cooperative.[124] In October 1989, the RSFSR Red Cross Society also opened a soup kitchen to feed those who were approved by the organization's central committee.[125] Generous as these organizations were, however, their resources were but a drop in the bucket of the population's mounting impoverishment.

The 1991 Sales Tax

To add to the woes of the citizenry, a sales tax of 5 percent was imposed on the entire Soviet population on January 1, 1991, for the announced purposes of funding social security benefits, increasing the salaries of some public employees, and reducing the budget deficit. About 70 percent of the sales-tax revenues were earmarked for the republics, the remaining 30 percent for the central government.[126] It was a despised tax, coming at a time when the economic situation for Soviet families was already deteriorating rapidly and when the population lived in fear of higher prices as the idea of price reform was resurrected. Opposition to the tax came almost immediately, with particularly strong distaste for the tax on food. After withstanding the pressures for a number of weeks, the central government and the republican governments both began to yield to the popular opposition. On April 5, Gorbachev modified the original decree, recommending that both the Union and republican governments decrease the number of goods subject to the tax; but at the same time he warned that reducing sales-tax revenues would substantially reduce public spending options.[127]

In due course, the republics revised their tax laws. In early April, Kazakhstan canceled its tax on several important foods and a few manufactured goods.[128] Later that same month, the Belorussian government, under pressure from striking workers and an angry population, abolished the sales tax on certain foods, including confectionaries, fish products, oil, margarine, tea, beer, and potatoes and vegetables.[129] The following month, the Ukrainian Supreme Soviet voted to remove the 5-percent sales tax on some food items and basic consumer goods.[130] Russia had actually removed its tax on a number of items even before the recommendations in early April. On February 20, the RSFSR Council of Ministers had issued a long list of items that would not be subject to the tax, including many basic foods, children's clothing and other consumer goods for children, and medical supplies.[131] In mid-May, the Russian republic went even further, eliminating the tax on irtually all foods.[132]

The torrent of pressure on the central government to get rid of the hated sales tax came to a head when Gorbachev and the heads of nine of the republics agreed in late May to eliminate the tax on meat, milk, bread, pasta, fruit, vegetables, beer, baby food, coal, gas, gasoline, and telephone and postal services. It remained in force on wine, restaurants, and luxury goods.[133]

The sales tax, which came to be known as the "presidential tax," only served to fuel the flames of anger and the sense of injustice that people felt. Justified or not, Gorbachev suffered the fate of politicians everywhere who introduce taxes at a time of economic hardship: he became the focus of popular outrage and resentment.

Conclusion

Goods shortages had been a constant factor throughout the Soviet period, but the increasing shortages during the Gorbachev era widened the gap between the promise and the deed. As a consequence, the Soviet population rejected both Gorbachev and perestroika. Compounding the misery for the citizenry was significant open inflation, a phenomenon which had not existed during the entire sixty-year period of central planning, with the exception of the World War II years. In addition, after the major accomplishments of the system, the absolute decline in the standard of living, and the concomitant impoverishment of large numbers of the population, was an entirely new phenomenon in peacetime. There were many understandable responses—resignation, despair, black humor, and passivity, to name but a few—all of which had been part of the people's survival mechanisms of the past. But, mostly, their responses were anger and disillusionment.

We have examined the events and issues that led the Soviet population to lose faith in perestroika in their role as consumers. Next, we examine the issue that turned the Soviet population against perestroika in their role as producers, namely, the rise of unemployment.

Appendix

A market basket of goods and services in a Western nation typically reflects the consumption pattern of the population in order to measure the cost of living regularly. Because the Soviet Union never had a true measure for it, officials faced many pitfalls in setting about to determine the Soviet cost of living. Although there were systematic studies of what people consumed, state retail prices, ordinarily held constant for long periods of time, were accepted as the true measure of prices, and therefore there was never a meaningful measure of inflation. Few ever actually accepted the state's assertion that its prices reflected true price movements in the country, but there was no other measure to counter the state's economic information. It was really only at the end of the 1980s that the Soviets began to collect and process economic data that would enable them to develop worthwhile economic statistics. Even so, their primitive methods of data collection, their lack of personnel to collect data, and their late entrance into this effort meant that data on the standard of living of the population were imperfect, to say the least. *Goskomstat's* original method for calculating the standard household budget was to provide 62,000 families with notebooks in which they wrote down every household expenditure, right down to the last kopek.[134]

Beginning in 1990, *Goskomstat* again calculated an index of prices of consumer goods and services, this time employing a new methodology. The new procedure used actual prices, including market prices and temporary prices, rather than the state's price list or the average price of roughly the same group of goods. The new methodology incorporated retail prices, collective farm market prices, and the prices of services and resulted in a new market basket that included 650 consumer goods, 50 agricultural products, about 21,000 types of industrial goods, and more than 100 types of services.[135]

Notes

1. *Ekonomika i zhizn'*, no. 21 (May 1990), 2.
2. Moscow Domestic Service in Russian (July 18, 1988). From FBIS-SOV-88-138 (July 19, 1988), 69.
3. Philip Hanson, "Inflation versus Reform," *Report on the USSR* (April 21, 1989), 14.
4. See *Izvestiia* (March 20, 1985), 3; and *Pravda* (March 23, 1985), 3.
5. *Izvestiia* (August 27, 1985), 2.
6. *Ekonomicheskaia gazeta*, no. 1 (1989), 10. The prospect of a shortfall in expenditures was in fact predicted at the time. See, for example, *Pravda* (September 4, 1985), 2.
7. Ibid.
8. *Izvestiia* (October 7, 1988), 3.
9. See, for example, *Trud* (August 26, 1989), 6; and *Pravda* (August 29, 1989), 2.
10. *Pravda* (September 29, 1989), 1.
11. *Sotsialisticheskaia industriia* (July 22, 1989), 4.
12. *Izvestiia* (July 10, 1989), 2.
13. *Pravda* (January 2, 1991), 2.
14. *Argumenty i fakty*, no. 2 (January 1991), 5.
15. *Ekonomicheskie nauki*, no. 11 (November 1989), 71–78.
16. *Argumenty i fakty*, no. 52 (1989).
17. Moscow Domestic Service in Russian (August 4, 1989). From FBIS-SOV-88-150 (August 7, 1989), 100.
18. *Ogonek*, no. 48 (November 1989), 3.
19. *Izvestiia* (May 25, 1990), 1.
20. *The New York Times* (May 23, 1990), A1.
21. *Pravda* (July 16, 1990), 2.
22. Moscow TASS (September 7, 1990). From FBIS-SOV-88-174 (September 7, 1990), 48.
23. *Izvestiia* (November 26, 1990), 2.
24. *Pravda* (November 15, 1990), 1.
25. Ibid. (January 2, 1991), 2.
26. Ibid. (November 15, 1990), 2.
27. *Izvestiia* (November 16, 1990), 1.
28. Moscow Television Service in Russian (November 15, 1990). From FBIS-SOV-88-222 (November 16, 1990), 77.
29. *Trud* (November 20, 1990), 1.
30. *Pravda* (November 27, 1990), 1.
31. *Izvestiia* (December 13, 1990), 1.
32. *Rabochaia tribuna* (December 9, 1990), 2.
33. Tallinn Domestic Service in Estonian (January 11, 1991). From FBIS-SOV-88-009 (January 14, 1991), 102–103.
34. Moscow TASS (February 3, 1989). From FBIS-SOV-88-022 (February 3, 1989), 65.

35. Paris AFP in English (January 15, 1991). From FBIS-SOV-88-010 (January 15, 1991), 85.

36. *Sel'skaia zhizn'* (February 5, 1991), 2.

37. Vilnius Radio (March 22, 1991). From FBIS-SOV-88-058 (March 26, 1991), 71.

38. *Trud* (April 5, 1991), 1.

39. *Sovetskaia Rossiia* (January 3, 1991), 1.

40. *Izvestiia* (February 15, 1991), 4.

41. *Sovetskaia Rossiia* (January 3, 1991), 1.

42. Moscow TASS (January 11, 1991). From FBIS-SOV-88-009 (January 14, 1991), 108–109.

43. Assuming a 300-ruble-a-month income, a tripling of prices would mean that, all other things being equal, people would be able to buy only one-third of what they previously had purchased. A 66-ruble supplement would still leave roughly a 60-percent decline in the standard of living.

44. Moscow TASS (January 10, 1991). From FBIS-SOV-88-008 (January 11, 1991), 55.

45. Riga Radio (April 3, 1991). From *Joint Publications Research Service–Soviet Union–Economic Affairs*, JPRS-UEA-91-019 (April 19, 1991), 54–55.

46. Moscow Radio (May 1, 1991). From FBIS-SOV-88-086 (May 3, 1991), 37.

47. Moscow TASS (January 7, 1991). From FBIS-SOV-88-004 (January 7, 1991), 44.

48. Moscow Central Television and TASS International Service (January 8, 1991). From FBIS-SOV-88-006 (January 9, 1991), 52–53.

49. *Baltfax* in English (June 28, 1991). From FBIS-SOV-88-127, (July 2, 1991), 70.

50. *Izvestiia* (June 25, 1991), 2.

51. Moscow TASS (January 4, 1991). From FBIS-SOV-88-004 (January 7, 1991), 59.

52. Moscow Domestic Service in Russian (February 10, 1991). From FBIS-SOV-88-028 (February 11, 1991), 56.

53. *Izvestiia* (February 20, 1991), 1.

54. *Pravda* (March 21, 1991), 1–2.

55. *Argumenty i fakty*, no. 12 (March 1991), 4.

56. *Komsomol'skaia pravda* (March 19, 1991), 1; and *Argumenty i fakty*, no. 11 (March 1991), 5.

57. Moscow TASS (April 3, 1991). From FBIS-SOV-88-065 (April 4, 1991), 42. For a more detailed breakdown of price increases, see *Rabochaia tribuna* (March 22, 1991), 2.

58. Moscow All-Union Radio (March 24, 1991). From FBIS-SOV-88-057 (March 25, 1991), 68.

59. Moscow Domestic Service in Russian (March 7, 1991). From FBIS-SOV-88-045 (March 7, 1991), 40.

60. Kiev International Service in English (April 17, 1991). From FBIS-SOV-88-076 (April 19, 1991), 63.

61. Moscow TASS (April 3, 1991). From FBIS-SOV-88-065 (April 4, 1991), 42.

62. Moscow Radio (April 16, 1991). From FBIS-SOV-88-074 (April 17, 1991), 84.

63. Moscow Central Television (April 17, 1991). From FBIS-SOV-88-075 (April 18, 1991), 44–45.

64. *Trud* (April 10, 1991), 1.

65. Moscow All-Union Mayak Network (April 5, 1991). From FBIS-SOV-88-066 (April 5, 1991), 75.

66. *Izvestiia* (April 9, 1991), 2.

67. Moscow All-Union Radio Mayak (April 10, 1991). From FBIS-SOV-88-071 (April 12, 1991), 75.

68. Moscow All-Union Radio (May 12, 1991). From FBIS-SOV-88-092 (May 13, 1991), 76; and Radio Moscow (April 20, 1991). From *Report on the USSR* (May 3, 1991), 29–30.

69. Moscow Domestic Service in Russian (February 8, 1991). From FBIS-SOV-88-028 (February 11, 1991), 86.

70. Moscow TASS (February 14, 1991). From FBIS-SOV-88-032 (February 15, 1991), 51–52.

71. *Argumenty i fakty*, no. 11 (March 1991), 5. The Ukrainian government allocated an additional 3.1 billion rubles in order to provide compensation somewhat above the levels specified by the Union government. Everyone received 5 rubles a month more than Moscow had specified. Thus, workers and employees received 65 rubles a month, and pensioners received 70 rubles a month. Kiev International Service in English (March 29, 1991). From FBIS-SOV-88-063-S (April 2, 1991), 13.

72. *Vremia* (May 14, 1991). From *Report on the USSR* (May 24, 1991), 32. This was actually the level of compensation for children that had been proposed in the original compensation package. See *Pravda* (February 15, 1991), 2.

73. *Argumenty i fakty*, no. 11 (March 1991), 5.

74. Moscow Central Television (March 23, 1991). From FBIS-SOV-88-057 (March 25, 1991), 40.

75. Moscow Central Television (March 24, 1991). From FBIS-SOV-88-058 (March 26, 1991), 51.

76. *Argumenty i fakty*, no. 11 (March 1991), 5.

77. *Izvestiia* (April 30, 1991), 1–2.

78. *Argumenty i fakty*, no. 12 (March 1991), 4.

79. Moscow Central Television (February 19, 1991). From FBIS-SOV-88-036 (February 22, 1991), 53.

80. *Rabochaia tribuna* (April 10, 1991), 1.

81. *Trud* (April 24, 1991), 1.

82. *Pravda* (May 20, 1991), 2.

83. *Izvestiia* (June 3, 1991), 2.

84. *Moscow News*, no. 17 (1991), 10.

85. *Pravitel'stvennyi vestnik*, no. 17 (August 1989), 12.

86. Ibid., 12.
87. *Izvestiia* (October 17, 1990).
88. Moscow All-Union Radio (May 1, 1991). From FBIS-SOV-88-085 (May 2, 1991), 38; *Izvestiia* (May 23, 1991), 1; *Trud* (May 9, 1991), 1, 2.
89. *Trud* (October 18, 1990), 1.
90. Moscow *Interfax* (November 22, 1991). From FBIS-SOV-88-229 (November 27, 1991), 28.
91. *Literaturnaia gazeta*, no. 49 (December 1989), 12. The number of people in a "large family" was not defined.
92. *Ekonomicheskaia gazeta*, no. 25 (June 1989), 11.
93. *Literaturnaia gazeta*, no. 49 (December 1989), 12.
94. *Rabochaia tribuna* (May 1, 1991), 1.
95. *Komsomol'skaia pravda* (April 25, 1990), 2.
96. TASS (April 22, 1991). From *Report on the USSR* (May 3, 1991), 33.
97. JPRS-UEA-90-019 (June 7, 1990), 110.
98. *Sotsialisticheskaia industriia* (June 1, 1988), 3.
99. *Report on the USSR* (April 19, 1991), 21.
100. Aaron Trehub, "The Congress of People's Deputies on Poverty," *Report on the USSR*, no. 24 (1989), 6.
101. *Current Digest of the Soviet Press* 40, no. 11 (1988), 19.
102. *Moscow News*, no. 10 (1989), 15.
103. Ibid. no. 30 (1991), 8.
104. Moscow Central Television (October 23, 1991). From FBIS-SOV-88-207 (October 25, 1991), 26.
105. *Izvestiia* (May 23, 1991), 1.
106. Moscow TASS (November 23, 1990). From FBIS-SOV-88-243-S (December 18, 1990), 20.
107. *Trud* (March 19, 1991), 2.
108. *Izvestiia* (May 22, 1991), 1.
109. *Sel'skaia zhizn'* (November 26, 1989), 4.
110. *Moskovskie novosti* (July 29, 1991). From *Report on the USSR* (August 9, 1991), 28.
111. Moscow *Interfax* (June 21, 1991). From FBIS-SOV-88-121 (June 24, 1991), 61.
112. Ibid. (October 26, 1991). From FBIS-SOV-88-208 (October 28, 1991), 41–42.
113. Ibid. (November 22, 1991). From FBIS-SOV-88-229 (November 27, 1991), 28.
114. Moscow TASS (December 22, 1990). From FBIS-SOV-88-247 (December 24, 1990), 97.
115. *Ekonomika i zhizn'*, no. 8 (February 1991), 20.
116. *Sovetskaia Kirgiziia* (January 22, 1991), 1. From JPRS-UEA-91-016 (April 2, 1991), 55.
117. *Report on the USSR* (April 26, 1991), 42.
118. Ibid. (May 10, 1991), 34–35.
119. Ibid.

120. Moscow *Interfax* (May 28, 1991). From FBIS-SOV-88-103 (May 29, 1991), 52.

121. TASS (June 25, 1991). From FBIS-SOV-88-123 (June 23, 1991), 31.

122. *Pravda* (April 20, 1990), 1.

123. Moscow TASS (October 20, 1989). From FBIS-SOV-88-207 (October 27, 1989), 96.

124. *Sotsialisticheskaia industriia* (July 2, 1989), 4. A more complete description of the soup kitchen can be found in William Moskoff, "The Aged in the USSR," *Report on the USSR* (September, 15, 1989), 8.

125. *Pravda* (October 12, 1989), 2.

126. TASS (December 29, 1990). From *Report on the USSR* (January 11, 1991), 24.

127. Moscow Central Television in Russian (April 5, 1991). From FBIS-SOV-88-067 (April 8, 1991), 48.

128. Moscow All-Union Radio (April 4, 1991). From FBIS-SOV-88-066 (April 5, 1991), 74.

129. Minsk Domestic Service in Belorussian (April 21, 1991). From FBIS-SOV-88-078 (April 23, 1991), 65.

130. *Report on the USSR* (May 10, 1991), 32.

131. *Sovetskaia Rossiia* (March 7, 1991), 3.

132. Moscow TASS in English (May 16, 1991). From FBIS-SOV-88-096 (May 17, 1991), 41. The only food items still subject to the sales tax were alcohol and tobacco products, coffee, and chocolate. It should also be noted that as the largest republic in the country, Russia's decision to eliminate the sales tax so early on so many items diminished much of the tax's revenue-enhancing intentions.

133. TASS (May 21, 1991). From *Report on the USSR* (May 31, 1991), 31.

134. See *Sotsialisticheskaia industriia* (June 1, 1988), 3.

135. *Izvestiia* (January 11, 1990), 1.

4

Unemployment

Perhaps the most important principle of social and economic justice that the postrevolutionary leaderships had honored was that of providing a job for all those who wanted to work. Although there had been unemployment in the 1920s, by the end of 1930 unemployment was officially declared eliminated in the Soviet Union, and the labor exchanges in Moscow and Leningrad were closed.[1] For more than half a century since, full employment, in principle and to a very substantial degree in practice, became a fact of daily life.[2] That changed under perestroika. The anger and anxiety of the Gorbachev years was strengthened by the growth of unemployment and by fears that it would soon mushroom out of control. Unemployment was a new concept in the psyche of the Soviet citizen.

How Many Employed?

Trying to secure dependable estimates of the number of unemployed in the country has been futile. The basic reason for this is that for more than fifty years, full employment had been the ideologically established reality; there was no need to count what did not exist. Once unemployment became a reality and it was readily apparent that there would be even more of it, a mechanism to count the unemployed should have been established, for all the reasons that it is done in capitalist economies. But in fact, as unemployment increased in 1988, 1989, and on into 1990, no official measure of the number of unemployed was available; and the lack of such a measure hampered the country's ability to define the extent of unemployment, its sources, and how much and what kind of assistance had to be provided for those without jobs.

One of the ambiguities of creating such a measure is that there is a difference between the standard western definition of the unemployed—that is, those who are without work but seek work—and the old Soviet definition which put all those who were able-bodied and not in school among the ranks of the unemployed, even if they did not want to work. The underlying ideological principle in the Soviet Union was that every potentially productive member of society should be involved in what used to be called "social production." Using the Soviet definition of "unemployment," it was not possible to distinguish between a person who was involuntarily unemployed and one who did not care to work, such as a woman choosing to stay at home to take care of young children. Under the Soviet definition, they both were "unemployed."

The confusion in the effort to estimate the number of unemployed can be seen in the variety and range of figures produced. In 1988, after having never talked about an unemployment problem, the government estimated that unemployment had risen by one million, including 700,000 in industry, at a time when total employment was just over 117 million and industrial employment was 37.4 million.[3] Then, in the summer of 1989, Aleksei Lebedev, chairman of the International Association for Studying Unemployment and Homelessness, estimated that there were 4.5 million unemployed in the country, an unemployment rate of about 3.8 percent.[4] An April 1990 report said that there were 2 million unemployed,[5] while a June 1991 report estimated unemployment as between 1.5 and 2 million.[6] A month later, the RSFSR classified only 3,000 people as unemployed, hardly consistent with a nationwide estimate of up to two million.[7] A 1991 article by V. Vidiapin, rector of the Plekhanov Institute, claimed that perhaps 5–6 million had been "unemployed" for a number of years.[8] The report issued in August 1990 by the working group appointed by Gorbachev and Boris Yeltsin to develop a plan of economic reform, the so-called 500-Day Plan, used the figure of 6 million unemployed.[9]

It was not until the fall of 1990 that the State Committee for Statistics, *Goskomstat*, issued official unemployment figures, setting the total at 2 million. *Goskomstat* used the International Labor Organization's definition of unemployment—that a person must be without remunerative employment, must be looking for work, and must be willing to start working at once.[10] The official nature of this figure notwithstanding, throughout perestroika, the Soviet Union was without a method for counting the unemployed. In the halls of government, where it mattered most, they were really still in the dark as to how to come up with a reliable figure for unemployment.

Among the reformers, the conceptualization of unemployment became more sophisticated in 1990. The 500-Day-Plan group made a distinction between permanent unemployment and frictional unemployment. Of the estimated 6 million unemployed on January 1, 1990, 4.5 million were considered to be permanently unemployed, and 1.5 million were categorized as frictionally unemployed.[11] These figures are at striking odds with figures produced less than a year later by Anatolii Kapustin, a people's deputy and head of the All-Union Fund for the Protection of the Unemployed. He maintained that there were 8 million unemployed, 2 million of whom were unemployed for the long term and 6 million of whom were frictionally unemployed.[12] The most noticeable thing about these two estimates is the difference in the relationship between permanent and frictional unemployment, which only served to add to the confusion over the question of how many were actually unemployed.

Types of Unemployment

Economists distinguish three general categories of unemployment: cyclical unemployment, which occurs when the level of total demand for goods and services in the economy is inadequate to support full employment; structural unemployment, which occurs when the job vacancies that exist in the economy do not match the skills that are available; and frictional unemployment, which occurs because of normal turnover in the labor force, as when people change jobs.

From the beginning of the five-year plans until 1985, cyclical unemployment had not been an issue in the Soviet Union. Frictional unemployment, however, was recognized. It occurred, first, because of the extraordinarily high labor turnover that was voluntarily engaged in by as many as 25 million people a year;[13] and, second and of considerably less importance, because of the short-term variations in the demand for labor due to seasonal fluctuations in the economic activity of certain industries.

During the perestroika era, two new types of unemployment became discernible in the Soviet economy. The myriad changes, intended and unintended alike, that took place in the functioning of the economy gave rise to the first sizable amount of involuntary unemployment since central planning had been introduced. This was structural unemployment—that is, the growth of unemployment with the simultaneous presence of an allegedly large number of job vacancies. But at the same time, a second type of unemployment was also emerging in the Soviet Union, what I call involuntary frictional unemployment. It resulted from the breakdown in central planning and the frequent interruptions in the flow of capital into production.

Structural Unemployment

There were a variety of causes of the new structural unemployment. One was the impact of self-financing in Soviet enterprises. Among other things, the Law on the State Enterprise that went into effect on January 1, 1988, required Soviet enterprises to draw their investment funds from their profits. This was a new responsibility for Soviet enterprises, which had previously relied on the state budget for their funding, and it had an immediate impact on employment. From 1987 to 1989, 1.6 million people lost their jobs because of the closings of failing enterprises.[14] For example, a fall in profitability led to a decline in the ability of Leningrad enterprises to buy machine tools, which in turn led to the loss of 8,000 industrial jobs in the city. An even higher level of unemployment in the city was avoided only by the creation of a second shift and the more intense use of the existing stock of machine tools.[15]

Further, as part of the restructuring of investment policies, about 26,000 major construction projects, representing 500 billion rubles in spending, were closed down by the fall of 1990;[16] the result was that a sizable but unknown number of construction workers lost their jobs, among them, those building pipelines and power stations in Siberia.[17]

After Gorbachev announced the first substantial cuts in defense spending in his United Nations speech of December 1988, the Soviets began to convert defense-related production facilities to civilian production. By mid-1991, about half the output from the enterprises in the former military-industrial sector was civilian goods.[18] The shift to nonmilitary production had an appreciable effect on employment. Of the 300,000 workers who had to leave their jobs in defense plants in 1990, only 76 percent found jobs in civilian production.[19] That is, about 75,000 people lost their jobs in the process of implementing the shift away from defense spending.

The Russian republic was disproportionately affected by the conversion process because 82 percent of the Soviet military-industrial complex was located there.[20] About 8 million people were employed in Russia's defense sector and, when their families are counted in, some 30 million people were dependent on the Russian military-industrial sector.[21] The city of Glazov, located in the Urals, was heavily dependent on two large defense plants and felt the sting of conversion. The situation in the city became so serious that its officials sought outside advice on how to cope with the conversion's negative economic impacts, including unemployment. Turning for help to the Scientific Research Institute of Labor in Moscow, city officials put together a package that included a municipal employment agency and an unemployment compensation fund and discussed ways for local enterprises to slow down the layoff process.[22]

One problem related to the structural unemployment caused by the conversion of defense industries was the need to find domestic employment for military personnel then stationed in Eastern Europe and former East Germany. With the end of the cold war, the Soviet government had committed itself to the withdrawal of troops from these areas. Their demobilization meant finding civilian jobs for these people. As one of the ways to deal with this eventuality, the USSR and the Federal Republic of Germany agreed to establish five centers for retraining former Soviet armed forces personnel.[23]

Workers in defense industries themselves tried to meet the impact of conversion on their lives as an organized group. A Congress of the Armed Forces Workers and Employees Trade Unions met in October 1990, at a time when the Supreme Soviet was still debating legislation on social protections for the population. The tone of the Congress was rather mild. It took the limited stand that all trade unions, including those associated with the army, should be watchful and do nothing that would "deliberately support unemployment."[24]

The vocal and articulate environmental movement that emerged under the protection of glasnost also had an impact on unemployment. In the wake of the April 1986 Chernobyl disaster, an unrelenting antinuclear drive sprang up in many places. Some functioning nuclear power plants were simply closed down, the construction of others was put on hold, and still others were converted to non-nuclear purposes. By the spring of 1991, four years of environmentalist opposition resulted in the stoppage of construction and design work on 60 nuclear power plants whose total capacity would have been about 100 million kilowatts.[25] There is no doubt that the movement's efforts had an effect on employment, as several examples show: At the Rostov Nuclear Power Station, workers picketed in protest against the loss of their jobs when construction of the facility was halted in the fall of 1990.[26] The construction of the Crimean Atomic Power Station led to a two-year dispute with environmentalists; when construction was finally halted. Early in 1991, about 17,000 people in the Crimean town of Shchelkino, who had depended on the nuclear plant coming into operation, were without their hoped-for livelihood.[27]

Involuntary Frictional Unemployment

A second major cause of unemployment came at the end of the 1980s with the breakdown in the discipline of central planning. While the USSR floundered in a state of limbo because of Gorbachev's hamletic approach to economic reform, the republics and their constituent enterprises lost faith in the central planning system. The shortfalls in supplies led to unemployment in a number of areas of the economy, including both light and heavy industries. At the end of 1990, the weaving and textile divisions in about 40 clothing factories shut down because of the shortfall in inputs. In the association *Roslegprom* alone, 77,000 clothing workers were laid off. And by late 1990, almost 33,000 home workers, mostly mothers with young children, were also laid off, in all cases because suppliers had not sent supplies to the producing enterprises.[28]

Factory closings kept mounting; by the spring of 1991, more than 400 light-industry plants were reported shut down because of a lack of raw materials.[29] The absence of raw material inputs put 340,000 out of 770,000 Russian republic textile workers and another 100,000 leather, shoe, and sewing industry workers out of work. A great deal of the supply problem arose from the fact that, while it had increased raw material prices, the government had not raised the prices on finished goods. Consequently, enterprises in the textile and other consumer goods industries had been losing enormous sums of money. They were supposed to finance the purchase of their inputs out of their profits, but without raised prices they were unable to afford the purchase of supplies.[30]

Workers in heavy industry were also affected. In the city of Donetsk in eastern Ukraine, 800 of the workers at a plant producing large-diameter pipe were let go at the end of 1990 because their factory had been unable to acquire crucial inputs from either domestic or foreign sources during the last six months of the year.[31]

Who Are the Unemployed?

We can get some sense of who was hit by unemployment by looking at the 1991 figures for the registered unemployed in the Russian republic. Of the 25,000 people who signed up in the first month after Russian workers could register as unemployed, 43 percent were blue-collar workers, 33 percent were white-collar workers, and 8 percent were young people. Women made up an unspecified but "significant" portion of those registered.[32] However, in the city of Moscow alone, the social composition was quite different. Of the first 37,600 unemployed who registered at the city's labor exchange, 90 percent were either office workers or specialists with a secondary or higher education. Perversely, 85 percent of the 96,000 job openings in the city were for blue-collar workers.[33]

By early 1988, the Soviet economic bureaucracy—a major target of those carrying the banner of economic reform—employed nearly 14 million people in more than 800 all-Union and republican ministries and departments. Early expectations were that the personnel in these ministries and departments would be reduced by about 33 percent, or about five million people.[34] At least in the early stages of the shakeout process, however, the evidence is that those in the bureaucracy seemed to emerge relatively unscathed.

On the other hand, certain groups were especially in danger of becoming casualties of unemployment, particularly women and young people. Unfortunately, there are no systematic national data on the gender of the unemployed. At a plenary session of the Soviet Women's Committee in October 1988, just about the time when the economy began to dip severely, the mood was quite pessimistic. In the aftermath of the meeting, *Izvestiia* essayist Marina Lebedeva predicted that of the 16 million people who would become unemployed in the ensuing ten years, 15 million would be women. While this number is surely an exaggeration, it reveals the deeply felt sense of Lebedeva's comment, "Words to the effect that women have achieved equality with men hide a contemptuous attitude toward us."[35] The city of Moscow's unemployment figures show that of the first 60,000 who registered as unemployed in the first six months after the unemployment offices opened in mid-1991, 70 percent were women.[36] Moreover, data from the first two months after the office's opening show that women were disproportionately the victims of job loss, whether they were blue-collar or white-collar workers. That women comprised 80 percent of laid-off white-collar workers can perhaps be explained by the fact that low-level positions were occupied predominately by women. But this does not explain why 75 percent of the blue-collar workers laid off in the city were women.[37] It does not seem imprudent to suggest that sex discrimination was a cause of this pattern; Lebedeva's fears may have been exaggerated in degree, but not in kind.

Young people also began to comprise a disproportionate share of the unemployed in the country. The employment situation for young people changed for two broad reasons. First, the *vuzi*, or higher educational institutions, were taking a smaller percentage of secondary-school graduates; second, the demand for secondary-school graduates in the labor market was declining. As to the first issue, while 60.6 percent of the secondary school graduates in 1985 went on to full-time study at *vuzi*, by 1989 that figure had fallen to 57 percent. However, applications to higher educational institutions kept rising, perhaps in part because of the declining prospects for young people in the labor market. In 1985, 23,600 secondary-school graduates failed to get jobs, a number that grew to 36,200 in 1987 and to 90,500 in 1989. In the same 1985–1989 period, the number of youths who did not go to school after the eighth year and wound up unemployed quadrupled. Young people in some republics were especially hard hit. In Kirgizia, Uzbekistan, and Ukraine, the number of unemployed school-leavers went up sixfold, in Azerbaidzhan by eight times, and in Moldavia, there was a staggering twentyfold increase.[38]

The youth organization Komsomol predicted that the number of unemployed young would exceed 2 million by the end of 1991. While this figure is excessively high, it was reasonable to be alarmed over the status of unemployed young people. As a means of dealing with the problem, Komsomol jointly created a Youth Employment Society with USSR *Goskomtrud* (the State Committee on Labor), in essence, a labor exchange. The organization's main role was to develop a data bank on job vacancies.[39]

Before the employment legislation that permitted people to choose *not* to work, Soviet law could officially designate anyone eighteen years or older as a "parasite" or "vagrant" if they were not gainfully employed. In 1988 and 1989, 221,600 and 168,000 people, respectively, were officially warned to stop leading lives as "parasites." Of the 1989 group, 28.6 percent were aged eighteen to twenty-nine. About 120,000 of that group who had received warnings found jobs; 17,000 refused to take a job; and 22,900 were sent to labor dispensaries. The number of people accused of vagrancy and begging was somewhat lower than it was for those accused of parasitism. In 1988, there were 142,400 vagrants and beggars, and in 1989, 140,000. Almost 93 percent of the vagrants were of working age, and they were young— about thirty-three percent were between the ages of eighteen and thirty.[40] This was a change from the pattern of the late 1960s and early 1970s, when it was the middle-aged who predominated among the Soviet vagrant population.[41]

When they did work, the "bums" in Soviet society often took seasonal or temporary or scavenging jobs, working in lumbering or fishing, or collecting bottles and scrap. But there were many others who had come to big cities, often leaving their families behind, and found it difficult to surmount the complexities of job registration and housing. The authorities often would not even assign dormitory space to a man with a family, for fear that he would bring them along and create crowded conditions. Many men were thus forced to live like vagrants without a job or housing.[42]

Central Asia suffered from great impoverishment and higher levels of unemployment than the rest of the country, a fact that had both national and local import. The region became a hotbed of tension; as unemployment rose, there was more and more open resentment on the part of indigenous ethnic groups against "outsiders." And while labor mobility in Central Asia had not been as high as in other parts of the country, some observers began to fear that massive unemployment could force Central Asian workers to spill into other areas of the country in search of scarce jobs. What follows is an examination of the unemployment situation in Uzbekistan, Tadzhikistan, and Kirgizia during the perestroika years.

In Uzbekistan, with a population just under 20 million, perhaps 9 million lived below the poverty line in 1990.[43] As elsewhere, the republican government really did not know the true number of unemployed.[44] By one estimate, unemployment was between 800,000 and one million in mid-1990.[45] However, a large number of these people, such as nonworking mothers of large families and seasonal agricultural workers, were probably not unemployed in the Western sense of the term. Less than a month after registration of the unemployed began in mid-1991, 600,000 people signed up in Uzbekistan.[46] With an able-bodied labor force estimated at 9 million,[47] that would make the unemployment rate 6.7 percent, certainly among the highest in the USSR. The problem was aggravated by the low level of mobility. Migration from the rural to urban areas in Uzbekistan was 9 per 1,000 population, compared to 45 per 1,000 in the RSFSR and 33 per 1,000 in the USSR as a whole.[48]

The causes of the high unemployment can be identified for several Uzbek regions. In the Fergana Valley, the key causes were high population density and the dependence on a single crop, cotton. The narrowness of Uzbekistan's economic base was compounded by the fact that only 8 percent of the cotton was processed in the republic. The spinning, weaving, and sewing of cotton goods was done mainly in other republics.[49] In the region of Karakalpakia, there was a second set of reasons for high unemployment. Ecological disasters had become a serious problem in this area because the waters from the Aral Sea that once irrigated this land had dissipated, and the waters from the Syr-Darya and the Amu-Darya Rivers were wasted because of the excessive use of water for irrigation. The land had become a semidesert.[50]

The Uzbek republican government belatedly tried to solve its own unemployment problems. In the Fergana Valley, an economic recovery plan enunciated near the end of 1989 centered on expediting the construction of several light-industry enterprises, including a cotton-wadding factory, a knitwear factory, and a knitted outerwear plant. But these aspirations were inadequate to absorb the large number of unemployed. Some 65,000 to 70,000 people were expected to find jobs elsewhere, in enterprises in the regions.[51] Moreover, many of the unemployed could not find work because they were so unskilled. A newspaper in the capital city of Tashkent, describing the local population in the Namangan Oblast, said that the majority "do not have . . . anything to offer."[52] While there were jobs for stone workers, plasterers, welders, secretaries, and bookkeepers, no one had the skills either to fill these positions or to train others in them.[53] Also absent was the financial capacity of the republic to aid the unemployed.[54]

In Tadzhikistan, the unemployment situation in April 1991 was described as a "crisis."[55] The Tadzhik population of 5,300,000 was about 70 percent rural; only about 20 percent were employed in industry. Several problems created unemployment there. The skills that available jobs demanded and the capacities of the labor force were mismatched.[56] At the same time, the economy was not able to absorb the graduates of higher education institutions, technical schools, or even secondary schools, because jobs for the educated were in short supply.[57] As elsewhere, estimates of unemployment were not totally reliable. In the capital city of Dushanbe, about 70,000 were reported to be without work in 1990.[58] A little more than a year later, unemployment estimates were quite a bit higher. It was thought that, throughout the republic, between 230,000 and 600,000 were unemployed and that another 47,000 soon would become unemployed.[59] The effect of this dire situation was the creation of a class of severely underemployed people, mostly quite young. Toward the end of 1989, it was believed that more than 130,000 young people, or about 10 percent of the republic's youth, were neither employed nor in school.[60] At the beginning of 1990, it was estimated that another 117,000 young people were only partially employed, doing seasonal work.[61] The consequences were socially calamitous, as embittered unemployed youth took to vandalism and rioting.[62]

The threat to civil order that resulted from high unemployment in Tadzhikistan was also present in Kirgizia, whose population of 4,500,000 is more than 60 percent rural. In early 1990, at a time when there were an estimated 100,000 unemployed in Kirgizia, there were spontaneous demonstrations in the capital city of Frunze. The main participants were young and unemployed, some of the many unemployed young people who had come to the city from the countryside in search of jobs and were poorly housed in semibasements, barracks, and crowded dormitories. They took to the streets when a rumor spread that thousands of Armenian refugees from Azerbaidzhan were coming to the city and that they would immediately receive apartments.[63] These demonstrations not only showed the intensity of anti-outsider sentiment, they also reflected the volatile feelings over the issues of employment and housing.

The ramifications of unemployment were vividly demonstrated in 1989 and 1990 in the Osh region of Tadzhikistan, where there was fighting between the Kirgiz on one side and Tadzhiks and Uzbeks on the other. Of the estimated 100,000 unemployed in all of Tadzhikistan, about 60 percent came from the Osh Oblast. With tension high because of unemployment, armed battles over land and water rights involving thousands of villagers took place between Tadzhiks and the Kirgiz in June

1989.[64] Then, in June 1990, there was another clash in Osh between the Kirgiz and Uzbeks, in which 35 people died. The precipitating event on this occasion was the Kirghiz seizure of a piece of land to build housing that Uzbeks claimed belonged to them.[65] What overlaid the issue was the immense frustration associated with massive rural unemployment, the absence of jobs in cities, and the pitiful supply of amenities. The worst part was that there was no obvious solution to what was a long-standing problem that had exploded into public view with horrifying consequences.

Refugees and Unemployment

A special variant of the unemployment problem was caused by the interethnic tensions in a number of republics, especially in Central Asia, the Caucasus, and the Baltics. The targets of the indigenous groups' anger were typically ethnic Russians, who subsequently left these areas in large numbers because of the discomfort and sometimes danger they felt living in a hostile environment. Ethnic tension was not the only cause of internal migration, however. Disasters such as the nuclear accident in Chernobyl, the earthquake in Armenia in December 1988, and such ecological tragedies like the drying up of the Aral Sea also forced people to leave the places where they had always lived and worked—nearly a million in the case of Chernobyl.[66] Our present focus, however, is on the refugee problems caused by the ethnic tensions, because such tensions were endemic to the country whereas disasters are not typical.

The refugee problem made losers of everyone. The economies of the republics whose people were leaving in large numbers were damaged, seriously in certain sectors. The lives of the refugees were turned upside down, at least temporarily. By the spring of 1990, there were about 600,000 refugees in the USSR: in Armenia there were 230,000, in Azerbaidzhan, 210,000, and in the RSFSR, more than 150,000.[67]

There were a variety of reasons why Russians were the victims of nativist campaigns in the non-Russian republics. Principally, ethnic Russians were handy scapegoats at a time when national-ism became a great force within many republics; they repre-sented the resented imperial policies pursued by the central government over decades of rule. We may use as an example events in Uzbekistan, where the nationalist *Erk* ("Will") Party adopted a strong nativist stance: "The Erk Democratic Party is the first party in Uzbekistan and in Central Asia that gives pride of place to the interest of the indigenous nationality. . . . Power should be in the hands of representatives of the local nationality. Who works at the plants, what language specialists use, in what language films are shown in the movie theaters—all this should be decided by representatives of the local nationality."[68] After the riots in Fergana in June 1989, about 177,000 Russians, many of whom were highly skilled specialists, left Uzbekistan "under duress." The migration of Russians continued in 1990,[69] as ten-sions mounted in the Central Asian republics and in the ethnic conflicts in the Caucasus.[70] Indeed, in Uzbekistan, Caucasians as well as Russians were the focus of xenophobia. Rumors abounded that Azeris were going to be resettled in the republic, anti-Armenian leaflets were discovered, and anti-Russian leaflets appeared in the mailboxes of some Russians in Tashkent, order-ing them to leave by March 1.[71] In fact, the Russians did not need such threats. So desperate were they to leave the republic, that the Tashkent newspaper was filled with advertisements by Rus-sians trying to exchange their apartments in Uzbekistan for ones in *any* Russian city.[72]

We can see similar attitudes and processes in other republics. In Tadzhikistan there were interethnic clashes in February 1990, and that summer, a law was passed which made Tadzhik the state language.[73] In the first seven months of 1990, some 23,000 Rus-sians left the republic. These included not only workers in the construction industry and the Ministry of Light Industry, but per-sonnel seen as absolutely vital to running the local economy. There was concern that it would be difficult to replace the em-ployees who were leaving the Dushanbe Heat and Electric Power Plant and therefore that the city's winter heat supply would be jeopardized. Doctors, lawyers, teachers, and engineers also left. Much the same was happening in Kirgizia, where 34,000 people left the republic in the first six months of 1990, many of them skilled construction workers and engineers.[74] In Estonia, Russians were regarded as the "least welcome," literally regarded as a fifth column in the republic.[75]

Nevertheless, some people recognized how much harm was done to the local economy by the departure of the Russians. In late 1990, the Uzbek popular front, known as *Birlik*, was strongly encouraging Russians to stay in the republic.[76] But a great many Russians felt threatened by the situation in Central Asia. One estimate was that as many as 130,000 Russians were prepared to leave Uzbekistan, more than 50,000 were ready to leave Tadzhikistan, and about 20,000 would depart from Kirgizia if they felt their safety threatened.[77] This raised the specter in the Russian republic of large numbers of unemployed Russians wandering the country in search of a home and a job.

The refugee problem was extremely costly to the USSR. Over one billion rubles had been spent on dealing with Transcaucasus refugees by January 1990, with an anticipated expenditure of at least an equal amount to provide them with housing and jobs. A large number of refugees went to Moscow seeking help. The newspaper *Trud* estimated that 41,000 refugees were in the city in 1990, living mainly in suburban guest houses.[78] While the city government provided some help, it was of a very limited nature—a one-time only relief payment of 100 rubles. In view of the shortages in the city, it is obvious that Moscow did not have much to offer refugees. On May 15, 1990, the capital's diminished capacity to support social services was felt when it stopped paying anything for refugee housing or providing them with food.[79] It was clearly the city's intent to do everything possible to ensure that large numbers of refugees would not converge there, and that there would be no permanent settlement of refugees in the Moscow area.[80]

The combination of mounting numbers of Russian refugees and limited state funds reached a point where private parties stepped in to form a Committee for Russian Refugees.[81] It was private charity that provided help beyond the state's limited largesse. As of the fall of 1990, the committee had collected 200,000 rubles to assist refugees. At the time, it said it was helping 3,500 Russian refugees who were registered in the city of Moscow and the Moscow Oblast, along with 1,700 Armenians and 200 Azerbaidzhanis. Many of these people were living in hotels, where conditions were described in less than glowing terms.[82] These were small numbers relative to the number of Russians who had left Central Asia in the previous two years. Most likely, the number whom the committee helped reflects the fact that the aid was extremely limited and few could be cared for. A fund of 200,000 rubles for the 5,400 refugees registered with the committee amounted to only 37 rubles a person, hardly enough to do much good.

In contrast, a couple of republics put up barriers to entry by anyone, including of course refugees. Fearful of refugees coming into their republics, both Estonia and Moldavia erected immigration quotas. In 1991, Moldavia allowed immigration equal to 0.05 percent of the population, which meant a quota of about 2,000 people.[83] The Estonian parliament imposed an immigration quota of 2,290 people at the beginning of the same year.[84]

Unemployment was an obvious consequence of the refugee phenomenon. Regrettably, there does not seem to have been any follow-up on the problem and, consequently, it is not known how many of the refugees experienced only short-term unemployment, how many were victims of long-term unemployment, or how many may never have found a job.

Unemployed Youth and Crime

Another major social problem associated with unemployment was the rise in crime. Particularly after 1987, crime rose throughout the perestroika era in both magnitude and severity.[85] In 1988, crime was reported up by 9.5 percent.[86] In 1989, nearly 2.5 million crimes were reported, a 31.8 percent increase over 1988, with serious crimes up by 15 percent.[87] In the first half of 1990, the number of crimes committed by minors rose by 9.7 percent.[88] Of the minors who committed crimes, about 17 percent were either unemployed or not in school.[89] This was consistent with the 1987 figures, which showed that while there was only one crime for every 24–26 working adolescents, there was one crime for every 5–6 unemployed adolescents.[90] The anger and frustration of youth had become a time bomb waiting to go off. In 1990, about 70 percent of school graduates in Central Asia could not find a job, and, in 1991, it appeared that of the graduates from higher educational institutions, only those who had degrees in the medical field or in education were assured of employment.[91] In Leningrad, about 33 percent of all young workers applying for their first jobs could not find work. Most did not receive explanations when they were turned down, but of those who did, 15 percent were turned down because of financial pressures and another 15 percent, because there were no openings.[92]

There has been substantial agreement among observers that unemployment led to the rise in crime in the country. In early 1988, for example, it was asserted that the unemployed committed 20 percent of the crime in the Kabardino-Balkaria Autonomous Republic in the northern Caucasus region.[93] And when the crime rate rose by 37 percent in Turkmenia in the first four months of 1989, authorities claimed that one explanation was the increase in unemployment. At the time, 200,000 workers, including 50,000 adult males, were not working because of a "lack of jobs in the republic."[94] The most alarming figures on the connection between unemployed youth and crime came from the Leningrad procurator's office at the end of 1989: one-fourth of all crimes in the city were committed by unemployed youths, and they were the ones committing the most serious crimes.[95]

Unemployment Legislation and Benefits

There were two important pieces of legislation on the unemployment question during the Gorbachev era. The first came in January 1988, when unemployment was first emerging as an issue. The second was signed into law three years later, in January 1991, when there were many more unemployed and a recognition that the problem was growing. The 1988 legislation was a joint resolution originating with the old party and government hierarchy; the second was a law that came out of the Supreme Soviet, the parliament. The first was a dose of mild medicine by a timid establishment for an ailment not fully developed; the second was radical surgery performed by popular will on a patient who had become much worse after three years.

The first legislative action, in 1988, "On Ensuring Effective Employment of the Population, Improving the System of Job Placement, and Reinforcing Working People's Social Guarantees," was a joint resolution of the CPSU Central Committee, the USSR Council of Ministers, and the All-Union Central Council of Trade Unions (AUCCTU), the official trade union organization. The text of the resolution reflected the ambivalence of the political and economic leadership toward the issue of unemployment. On the one hand, there was the long-standing socialist commitment to everyone's right to have a job, and, on the other, there was recognition of the need for economic reform and greater efficiency. Thus, the resolution said: "All working people . . . should be confident that their right to work is really guaranteed. At the same time, every worker, specialist and office employee must work properly, at peak efficiency. . . ."[96] The issue of efficiency versus equity, which every market economy had struggled with in the twentieth century, now became part of the Soviet agenda, but perestroika was walking a tightrope high above the ground, and the net below had many holes.

The resolution considered the retraining, job placement, and dismissal of workers. The first two were merely desiderata without the commitment of additional resources to deal with them. For the time being, the leadership had sidestepped some of the tough issues. The failure to confront emerging joblessness was reflected in the resolution's statement that the first line of defense against unemployment was to find released workers jobs within the enterprises that had just fired them. The substantive heart of the resolution was its effort to protect workers' rights. The dismissal procedure required management to give workers two months' notice. A person losing his job was also entitled to a severance allowance equal to one month's pay, an increase over the two weeks' severance pay previously allowed. In addition, if a person did not find a job, the former employer was required to give the worker another two weeks' wages.[97] These provisions show that at the level of official policy-making, there was no real understanding of what it meant to fight unemployment.

Three years of experience with unemployment was a great teacher. The January 1991 legislation was a serious document that took great pains to define the problem and to establish a framework for ameliorating it.[98] There was also a second important dimension that distinguished this legislation from the 1988 document. The changed political landscape had accorded the republics new status: the new division of power and responsibility between the center and the republics was explicitly recognized in the new law.

The new legislation had two key changes in the rights of citizens to work. The first was spelled out in Article 5, "State Guarantees of the Right to Work": the state guaranteed free education and retraining, freedom to choose one's job, free assistance in finding a job, protection against job discrimination, and the promise of a job for at least three years to specialists graduating from state schools. But no longer was there a universal guarantee of a job. Section IV, "Social Welfare Guarantees in Case of Loss of Employment," detailed the benefits for someone who lost a job. But again, just as there was no guarantee of a job at the end of a retraining period, there was no guarantee of one when unemployment benefits ended.

The second crucial change made by the law was in the definition of employment and unemployment. Working was now a voluntary act; under Article 4, able-bodied people who did not work could no longer automatically be candidates for the pejorative category of "parasite" or "vagrant." Article 2 defined the unemployed "as able-bodied citizens of working age who for reasons that do not depend on themselves do not have work and earnings (income from work), who are registered with the state employment service as persons seeking work, who are able and ready to work, and to whom that service has not made offers of a suitable job." Suitable work, defined in Article 3, meant jobs that matched people's education, age, length of job experience, and the distance they would have to travel to work.

The national legislation "recommended" that the republics bring their legislation into compliance with the new law. Actually, only a minority of the republics, including Ukraine, Moldavia, and Kazakhstan, passed separate pieces of unemployment legislation to accord with their own vision of how to deal with unemployment.[99] In the main, the republican documents closely resembled the national legislation. But each had its own flavor and favored different areas of interest. For example, the Moldavian law devoted an entire article to the organization of public works projects as a means of employing people who were having difficulty finding a job. The Kazakh law required enterprises to both "guarantee efficient use of labor resources and create jobs for persons in need of social protection." The exact number of such jobs was to be determined by the local soviets of people's deputies and could be as high as 3 percent of the number of workers in a given enterprise (Article 18). The Ukrainian law promised undefined benefits to those employers who created jobs in areas where there was high unemployment or surplus labor, or in mining regions (Article 16).

To coordinate efforts to deal with unemployment at the national and republic levels, a protocol was signed on May 5, 1991, between the central government, represented by the USSR Committee on Labor and Social Problems, and the republic ministries of labor and social problems. It defined for 1991 a coordination of efforts in such areas as retraining, job information, and the financing of unemployment benefits, and it was signed by all the republics except Georgia and the three Baltic republics, although these four in fact took part in drafting the document. Armenia and Moldavia signed only the item dealing with international cooperation on unemployment issues.[100] For the first time in sixty years, unemployment benefits became part of the government's responsibility, with both philosophical and practical repercussions. Not only were such benefits ideologically alien, but the state was now faced with another large social assistance program at the very time that its capacity to finance such programs was shrinking.

Except for the payment of unemployment benefits, which were to begin on July 1, the January 1991 employment legislation went into effect immediately. The basic terms of the unemployment provisions entitled people who lost their jobs to continue to receive their average wages for a period of three months, provided that they registered with the employment service within ten days after they had been laid off. If at the end of this three-month period they did not find "suitable work," they were then classified as unemployed and were eligible for unemployment benefits from the state. While the actual length of time one could receive benefits was determined by the republics, the minimum period was specified as twenty-six calendar weeks during a twelve-month period for people who had lost their jobs and thirteen calendar weeks for people trying to find jobs for the first time. Funding for the new unemployment benefits was a problem at both the central and republican levels, as the six-month delay in the payment of unemployment benefits demonstrated.[101] Even then, because of funding problems, only eleven of the republics agreed to begin paying unemployment benefits on July 1.[102]

There was some concern that, as unemployment benefits were paid, workers would become fussier about taking a new job and would prefer to remain unemployed.[103] But this has not seemed to be a problem; the dramatic decline in living standards made it impractical for people to afford the luxury of unemployment. The minimum unemployment benefit was 50 percent of the base wage earned at one's previous job, so long as that payment did not amount to less than the officially established minimum wage. For first-time job seekers, the unemployment benefit was to be at least 75 percent of the minimum wage.[104] These conditions were a compromise between what the unions wanted and what the state was willing to give. The unions wanted to base benefits on the higher average wage, while the state wanted to use the lower base wage; and the state had wanted benefits to last only six months, while the unions had wanted them for one year.[105]

Several republics established benefit levels different from the basic legislation, as was their right. Russia offered 75 percent of one's *average* wage at the last place of employment (which is higher than the basic wage) for the first three months, 60 percent for the next four months, and 45 percent for the last five months.[106] Belorussia decided to pay benefits based on how long an unemployed person had worked, but the amount could not exceed twice the minimum wage.[107] Estonia started paying unemployment benefits on April 1, 1991, earlier than the other republics, in an amount equal to about 80 percent of basic pay, with the stipulation that the sum could not be less than the "physiological minimum for subsistence."[108]

There were great differences in the capacities of the different republics to fund unemployment benefits. As of mid-1991, when the terms of the employment legislation took effect, the RSFSR had set aside one billion rubles for unemployment benefits, and Ukraine had allocated 200 million rubles with the promise to increase this amount to two billion before the end of 1991. But the Central Asian republics, beset by great poverty, had not allocated a single ruble for unemployment benefits.[109] The city of Moscow had a similar difficulty: Igor Zaslavsky, the newly named Director General of Moscow's labor exchange, said that, as Moscow would not be able to contribute funds for unemployment benefits, the central and republic governments would have to provide them all.[110] Nevertheless, unemployed Muscovites were the beneficiaries of a relatively generous benefit package. When the benefits legislation went into effect on July 1, Muscovites who had not worked since February 1 could receive between 45 and 75 percent of their previous pay for up to one year. The money came from the city's employment fund, which was made up of 1 percent of the wage fund of the capital's state enterprises and organizations.[111]

Not all funds to assist the unemployed came from the state. Some monies were privately donated, although the sums were so inconsequential that at best they represented the honorable intentions of concerned citizens. The most well-known of these was the Unemployment Protection Foundation whose chairman, Anatolii Yurkov, was editor of the newspaper *Rabochaia tribuna*, which had spearheaded the foundation's organization.[112] In Ukraine, the Lvov Oblast's committee of textile and light industry workers' unions established a charitable fund for unemployed workers with money from the social development funds of the various enterprises involved. As of November 1990, 100,000 rubles had been collected. The committee could also channel unused funds into this new charity under rights granted by the Ukrainian trade union congress.[113] Other groups formed to raise money to assist the unemployed, many of which used a mixture of public and private resources. In February 1991, the All-Union Social Fund for Protection from Unemployment was established, with the first contribution of two million rubles coming from a membership that included some of the coal-miner organizations within the Ministry of the Coal Industry, the USSR Union of Composers, and several state enterprises and organizations.[114] In April, the Moscow city executive committee set up an account for a labor solidarity fund (*fond trudovoi solidarnosti*) in the Commercial People's Bank, which would be the repository of voluntary contributions from organizations and individuals as well as income from charity events and *subbotniki* (the "voluntary" unpaid work done on one's day off).[115] The fund was to supplement the legislatively mandated fund into which the government and state enterprises paid.[116] In the Kazakh city of Dzhezkazgan, a knitted goods factory started a so-called *fond riska* ("risk fund"); initially intended to assist low-income families, it was used to help the unemployed as of April 1991.[117]

Everyone agreed that the expenditures to implement the 1991 legislation—for retraining, unemployment benefits, and a job placement system—would be high. But the newness of the problem and the lack of certainty about its proportions made it difficult to arrive at a firm figure for the total tab. An early estimate of the costs in Russia alone was 12–13 billion rubles.[118] Labor Minister Vladimir Shcherbakov thought that the central government would need 4–6 billion rubles to finance the program just for 1991.[119] What those reckoning the costs of dealing with unemployment did not grasp was that a substantial part of retraining expenses would be offset by savings in wages to the "hidden unemployed," those workers and staff members who were on the payrolls at enterprises or ministries but who did no work much of the time. The state had been paying these people a salary with essentially no return, but after retraining, these workers could produce real goods and services.

The New Labor Market and Employment Services

The labor market under central planning had consisted of two main segments. In one, which was much like that of a market economy, workers were free to find their own jobs and enterprises were free to hire whomever they wished. The high level of voluntary turnover among workers is evidence of how much freedom there was in this segment of the labor market. Alongside the collective farm markets, it was one of the Soviet Union's most enduring institutions resembling a market mechanism. The other segment of the Soviet Union's labor market had been under strong administrative direction whereby workers who graduated from higher educational institutions were assigned their first jobs. These were their state jobs, and, with certain rare exceptions, these individuals were not free to work where they chose, although many doctors, carpenters, tailors, and teachers did sell their labor on the black market. Administrative direction of the centrally controlled segment of the labor market was also evident in the functions of *Orgnabor*, the All-Union Resettlement Committee and the Administration for Organized Recruitment, which, since the 1930s, had played a variety of roles in supplying labor to different parts of the economy.[120]

Employment bureaus (*biora trudoustroistva*) had been established in 1967 to alleviate the labor shortages that were being felt in the country at that time.[121] Opened only in selected Soviet cities, they were intended neither to cast a wide net nor to register the unemployed. Under perestroika, when unemployment became a concern, in fifty-three major oblasts, career guidance centers (*proforientatsionni*) were established. These were augmented by about 2,000 autonomous bureaus which contracted with individual enterprises to help people find jobs, and another 903 job centers (*profpunkti*) which were exclusively to help young workers find jobs were also established.[122] Several major criticisms were levied against these organizations. The first was that the largest enterprises tended to monopolize them and dictate how many employees they wanted. As well, most jobs that people found through these organizations were low-paying, menial positions.[123] And the organizations were located in too few places. In Ukraine, there were employment services in only half of the cities and raions of the republic. Most tended to be located well away from city centers, and only 14 of the 750 bureaus were computerized.[124] There was simply no employment system that covered everyone in all places.

The new involuntary unemployment created a new role for the state in job placement and retraining of the structurally unemployed. When the Supreme Soviet passed legislation on unemployment in January 1991, it did so with the expectation that existing employment services would play a major part in alleviating unemployment. Nikolai Gritsenko, the chairman of the Parliamentary Commission on Labor, Prices and Social Policy, said that 23 million people were expected to enter the labor market in 1991, an estimated 12.7 million of whom would find jobs on their own, but almost 10 million of whom were expected to be helped by the unemployment service after retraining.[125] Even allowing for a certain amount of error in Gritsenko's estimate, there is no mistaking the major role that state placement centers were expected to play as the shape of the labor market changed.

A nationwide job placement system was supposed to have been set up by the end of 1988. Each center was to have been computerized and employ about thirty people—sociologists, psychologists, lawyers, and computer specialists.[126] But such a system was not completed by the time the Gorbachev era ended. It fell to individual republics to pick up the slack when the national placement system failed to materialize. In January 1991, the Ukrainian Council of Ministers decided to set up its own service in order to help the unemployed while the republic was going through its transition to the market.[127] Still, only a few of the republics set up well-functioning state employment services. Along with Ukraine, the RSFSR, Belorussia, and Kirgizia claimed to have good success in placing people in new jobs. In the first ten days after the employment law went into effect, 24,000 people used the Russian state employment service, and 90 percent of them were said to have found new jobs.[128] However, the state employment system did not develop in much of the rest of the country because the 1991 law shifted its financing away from the center to the republics. This was part of the general drive to decentralize control over major areas of the economy and give the republics more autonomy. But because the poorest republics (Azerbaidzhan and those in Central Asia) were the ones with the worst unemployment problems and financial bases that were least able to support a state employment service, it was a counterproductive move. The inadequacy of resources for social services in those republics was demonstrated by the closings of even the small job placement services that had existed.[129]

In 1990, the state's job placement services had applications from 4,143,364 citizens. Some 52 percent of these applicants had voluntarily quit their jobs, while only 3.9 percent, or just over 16,000, had been laid off. Overall, the placement facilities found jobs for 64.8 percent of all applicants and 69.9 percent of those who were previously unemployed.[130] Still, this meant that 30 percent of the unemployed who went to the old placement centers could not find jobs. The claim that the job placement system was inadequate to the purpose of handling the new unemployment seemed fair: a new structure was needed.

To fill the gap, some cities developed their own job placement centers, with varying degrees of success. Ivanovo, about 150 miles northeast of Moscow, opened a data bank, called the *Banka Rezerva Kadrov*, in the city's employment agency. The center, which in 1989 served 27,000 individuals, was developed to serve as a regional center for the unemployed.[131]

In some places, nonofficial agencies emerged, creating a "gray" job market. In the Moldavian city of Tiraspol', a center was organized by a cooperative, that is, by a private concern which employed a computer data bank to match employers with employees. The need for such a service was immediately demonstrated when, on the first day the cooperative opened its doors, 200 unemployed people showed up for assistance. But they were in for a disappointment: the cooperative did not have the support of the government and, after first threatening to close it down, the local bureaucracy finally drove it out of business. The local government had based its objection on an anticipated new Moldavian law that would put the unemployment issue exclusively in the hands of the state.[132] Moscow also had its "gray" labor exchange in the private sector. More than 20 cooperatives functioned as employment agencies, charging job seekers an average of 15 rubles for information about a job vacancy.[133] A black-market unemployment office operated in Tashkent. The people it attracted included those who had criminal records, chronic down-and-outers, as well as ordinary Tashkent citizens, all united by the fact that they did not have a *propiska*, an official registration card, and therefore could not legally get a job in the city. Those who needed day laborers came to this office and hired illegals to work for the day at jobs ranging from digging ditches or painting to doing yard, electrical, or cement work. While the authorities had previously frowned on such black-market activity, they now built a small shelter at this place, giving the operation a *de facto* legal status.[134]

A specialized job placement system for young people, the Labor Exchange Youth Employment Society with headquarters in Moscow, was established in 1990 by 17 organizations, including the Komsomol Central Committee, USSR *Goskomtrud*, the Young People's Commercial Bank, the Central Television main youth program, and the conservative newspaper, *Molodaia gvardiia*. Each of the founding organizations contributed 360,000 rubles, with an additional 350,000 rubles from the Komsomol Central Committee, to assist in the exchange's development. Once it was established, enterprises submitted profiles of the types of workers they were looking for; the exchange interviewed candidates and had the authority to hire suitable job applicants for the enterprises.[135] About 50,000 people used the system in the first year, and about half of these were offered jobs through the exchange.

The Moscow Labor Exchange, bearing the same name as the old exchange that had existed until the end of 1930, was reborn in October 1990, although it did not begin formal operations until 1991. It was placed under the command of Igor Zaslavsky.[136] Although it was organized around a central office, the plan was to decentralize quickly so that each of the ten prefectures of Moscow (with about one million residents in each) would have its own exchange. In turn, each of the 124 municipal districts would have its own social protection service, where people could file for unemployment benefits. This was in contrast to the thirty regional employment bureaus that had existed under the old system and were regarded as too few in number to do a great deal of good.[137] The exchange was to be funded from three sources: a state employment assistance fund, as called for by the 1991 national employment legislation and to which the city of Moscow would also contribute; money that the exchange would make by charging fees to enterprises for finding workers for them; and, contributions from the public.[138] The exchange registered as unemployed and provided retraining only for people with a Moscow residence permit, although there were some early assertions that nonresidents would be allowed to take the most undesired jobs in the city, such as loading and unloading work.[139] The exchange also decided who was eligible for unemployment benefits—and it was only through the exchange that a Muscovite could receive benefits.[140] A job applicant was entitled to turn down a job offered through the exchange once, but if that happened a second time, their unemployment benefits were suspended for three months.[141]

Quite early in 1991, the exchange held job fairs throughout Moscow which Zaslavsky unabashedly described as auctions of workers. The fairs involved both state enterprises and the new cooperatives who were looking for workers. People in search of employment would come to the fairs where enterprises and cooperatives would literally bid for the workers on a competitive basis. Typically, the cooperatives would get the workers they wanted first because they were willing to bid more than the state was. When state enterprises got through bidding for workers and secured the people they wanted, the auction ended. The fairs lasted two to three days and 500 to 700 workers would find jobs. The rest went home, still unemployed.[142]

Originally, Zaslavsky envisioned the Moscow Labor Exchange as much more than simply a place where job placement would be carried out, benefits would be distributed, and retraining would take place. Indeed, his plans were a blueprint for curing every employment problem that could ail a Moscow worker. He had hoped that a center for small businesses and privatization would be developed within the exchange, and that it would provide legal and organizational know-how and act as a guarantor of bank loans for small businesses. The exchange also considered starting up certain businesses for which they believe there was a market and which would employ workers trained by the exchange. Such enterprises, if financially successful, would pay the exchange, which would use the funds to retrain workers, assist the unemployed, and so on. Zaslavsky even wanted to start a social assistance center which would be a combination overnight shelter, distribution point of basic items to the poor, and soup kitchen.[143] He had also wanted the center to be able to help workers find jobs abroad, provide legal advice for those who believed they had been cheated by their employers in concluding a work contract, and institute programs for groups who traditionally had a difficult time finding jobs, such as youth and the handicapped. In Zaslavsky's vision, the exchange would also have offered temporary public works employment, such as "city gardening, road repair, and street vending," until the workers who needed such employment could find permanent work.[144] There was even a thought of having two or three people share a city job so that many individuals could at least have some income from work.[145] This ideal conception of the exchange remained on the drawing board for lack of funds and due to the bureaucratic resistance of the perestroika years.

On July 1, the Moscow exchange opened its doors to the unemployed of the city under the terms of the new employment legislation. During the first 25 days of July, a bit more than 12,000 people showed up at the exchange looking for jobs; only 1,649 of them were officially designated as unemployed and therefore eligible for unemployment benefits.[146] Over the first two months, more than 23,000 Muscovites came to look for jobs, their numbers evenly divided between those with a higher education and those who were unskilled.[147] These 23,000 unemployed were well below the early forecast, which had estimated that there would be 125,000 unemployed in Moscow by the end of 1991.[148] Zaslavsky had expected the appearance of some 35,000 officials in the state bureaucracy alone to make use of the exchange.[149] In fact, by the end of the year, of the 6,000 party people who had lost their jobs in the city, only 466 had looked to the exchange for employment.[150] Indeed, as the Moscow data show, the number of unemployed was well below some of the early projections.

Okun's Law, Job Rights, and Hidden Unemployment

There were many predictions that the number of jobless would skyrocket in the USSR, but the number of unemployed turned out to be relatively small. The official *Goskomstat* figure of two million unemployed was, after all, less than 2 percent of the number employed in the state sector. In fact, it is arguable, that given the collapse of the Soviet economy in 1991, unemployment should have been much higher than it actually was at the end of the year.

Let us apply Okun's Law to the Soviet economy. Arthur Okun demonstrated with data from the United States economy that there is a quantitative relationship between changes in the unemployment rate and the deviation of actual from potential gross national product (GNP). Okun initially found that, in the United States, a 3-percent decline in GNP was associated with a 1-percent increase in unemployment. Later empirical work modified this measure, the most recent showing that a 2.5-percent decrease in GNP is associated with a 1-percent increase in unemployment.[151] If we accept the basic idea of a predictable ratio, the numerical relationship has to be modified in order to apply it to the Soviet Union because labor productivity is so much lower there than in the United States—an estimated 40 percent of the U.S. level.[152] That is, labor productivity in the United States is about 2.5 times higher than it is in the former Soviet Union. Thus, if a fall in GNP in the United States of 2.5 percent is associated with a 1-percent rise in unemployment, then in the former Soviet Union, a 1-percent decline in actual from potential GNP should be associated with a rise in unemployment of about 1 percent.[153] In 1991, from January through September, Soviet GNP fell 12 percent. That means that unemployment should have risen by approximately 12 percent as well. Given a labor force of 115 million in the state sector in 1990,[154] this meant that, according to Okun's law, Soviet unemployment should have risen by roughly 13.8 million in 1991, a far cry from both the official figure of 2 million and the unofficial estimates which ran somewhat higher. Clearly, unemployment at the end of the Gorbachev era was much less than standard economic analysis would have led us to expect. The Soviet economic system seemed almost impervious to unemployment through the end of 1991.

How can we account for this? The primary reason can be found in the jobs rights argument that David Granick proposed—

namely that employees in Soviet state enterprises have a right to keep their jobs.[155] In the Soviet system, everyone was promised a job. There is anecdotal evidence from the perestroika period that in spite of the well-known inefficiencies and unprofitability of Soviet enterprises, workers who were fired from one position managed to find other jobs within their enterprise with relative ease. A 1988 poll of enterprise managers revealed that 82 percent of them believed "that workers should be reassigned within the enterprise."[156] Director Zaslavsky of the Moscow Labor Exchange said in 1991 that he could name "dozens of enterprises" that operated well below capacity but maintained their labor force and still found the money to pay workers.[157] A study in early 1988, when unemployment admittedly had not risen as much as it later would, found that more than 60 percent of the workers who had lost their jobs had stayed at the same enterprise.[158] Others who lost their jobs, particularly managers and members of the economic and planning bureaucracy, also had a soft landing, emerging with new jobs without serious difficulty. For example, when the USSR Ministry of Machine Building for Light and Food Industry and Household Appliances was completely eliminated in 1988, of the 500 people who were laid off in the first round of firings in November 1987, 460 found new jobs.[159]

A second reason why actual unemployment was considerably below what it was calculated to have been may be that, in the face of supply breakdowns, enterprises substituted labor for capital in the production process. Given the fact that Soviet managers frequently engaged in this practice in order to keep production flowing, it is a plausible explanation. In an effort to insulate themselves from the vagaries of supply deliveries, enterprise managers maintained an excessively large roster of workers, many of whom were idle most of the time but all of whom were needed when supplies did arrive, to carry out the feverish production activity known as "storming." This practice, coupled with the promise to provide jobs to everyone, contributed to the long tradition in the Soviet Union of *skrytaia bezrabotitsa* ("hidden unemployment").

One of the costs of full employment was the great inefficiency in Soviet enterprises, many of which were grossly overstaffed. Toward the end of perestroika, estimates of superfluous employment were staggering, one claiming that 8–10 million people were in unessential jobs.[160] A Soviet sociologist suggested that there were 10–16 million people working at *izbytochnye* ("lucrative but unnecessary jobs"), what would be called cushy bureaucratic jobs in the West.[161] At the beginning of 1988, the Vice-Chairman of the USSR Council of Ministers, I. Postiakov, said that there were 17,718,000 employees in the country's entire administrative apparatus and speculated that about 50 percent of the employees in the republic ministries and departments and 30–35 percent of those at the provincial levels would have to be let go.[162] A year later, a high-level *Gosplan* official said that by any conservative estimate, "overemployment" in the economy accounted for at least 10 million persons.[163] In 1991, Labor Minister Shcherbakov sounded an even gloomier note when he said there was a nationwide labor surplus of 15–20 percent, amounting to somewhere in the neighborhood of 28 million persons.[164] Even allowing for defects in the estimation process, the message was clear. There were too many people holding jobs in which they were effectively superfluous. And the message frightened the population.

Soviet citizens were, of course, well aware of hidden unemployment. What they feared was that in the transition, the right to a job would be jettisoned and enterprises would start firing people—bringing unemployment out into the open instead of hiding it. The great fear throughout the country over the possibility of unemployment was confirmed in several polls. In the summer of 1991 a nationwide survey of 5,000 people asked the question: "Do you believe that you may lose your job in the transition to the market?" Forty-six percent said yes, while 40 percent said no.[165] Another survey, conducted in Russia at about the same time, asked the question: "Do you personally consider it probable that you may become unemployed during the next one or two years?" Overall, 27 percent of the Russians who were surveyed thought they would be future victims of unemployment—28 percent of those in urban areas, and 21 percent in rural areas.[166] Even as the economic situation worsened and unemployment was experienced by more and more people, Soviet citizens came to accept the inevitability of unemployment. At least that seems to be the conclusion one can draw from a public opinion poll conducted from 1988 to 1990 by the AUCCTU, the official trade union organization. In December 1988, 58 percent of those who took part in the poll agreed with the statement "unemployment in our country is intolerable," but in November 1989 and December 1990, only 45 percent and 39 percent, respectively, agreed with it.[167]

In addition to the resistance of the system to unemployment and endemic overemployment, there was a great faith that vacancies throughout the country would absorb workers who did lose their jobs. Typical of this opinion was the view of V. Potapov, a Senior Scientific Worker at the Institute for Sociology of the USSR Academy of Sciences. In an August 1990 article in the labor newspaper *Trud*, he wrote that there were 2.8 million job vacancies that could be filled by the unemployed and that in future the second and third shifts in plants could absorb another seven million workers.[168] Indeed, many others believed that the large number of job vacancies in the country was evidence that the unemployment problem was exaggerated. In essence, they took the job openings as proof that, whatever the current level, unemployment could be a great deal less if only the unemployed would fill the vacancies. What was often not understood in these calculations was that the problem was structural in nature: the demand for labor did not match the skills of the available labor supply.

Further, as with the estimates of the level of unemployment and the multiple predictions of future unemployment, the basis for the job vacancy count was shrouded in mystery. The very definition of a job vacancy was obscure, so the numbers varied wildly. In October 1987 and October 1989, for example, it was reported that there were 1.5 million job openings,[169] figures that reflected the number of jobs listed at state placement agencies.[170] But in 1990, the estimated number of job vacancies were variously reported as being 17 million (the AUCCTU's number), or even slightly higher, to between 11 and 16 million.[171] The enormous gap between the lower and upper bounds of the estimates is evidence of the guessing game that existed in this area. The much higher figures also suggest that people believed there were more jobs available than were actually listed by the state placement services.

Goskomstat finally issued official figures for job vacancies at the end of 1990. They showed that, as of July 1, 1990, there were a total of 1,680,100 vacancies, not including positions available for "highly skilled personnel." Of this total, 1,541,100 were for workers and the remaining 139,000 were for "leaders, specialists and other employees."[172] These figures show that job openings, whose numbers were so highly touted as relief for the unemployment problem, were neither highly desired nor matched by local skills. Indeed, the job openings advertised in the fall of 1989 were mostly "low prestige occupations in remote or undesirable locations."[173] In other places, however, such as Minsk, the 13,000 jobs available in the summer of 1991 were mostly all for skilled workers.[174]

Unemployment and Emigration

Despite the long-standing tradition of job rights and the wishful thinking about large numbers of job vacancies, the danger of unemployment led a large number of people to consider leaving the USSR. In the late 1970s and through most of the 1980s, emigration was still looked upon in terms of freedom from political or religious repression, particularly in the cases of Soviet Jews and ethnic Germans; but there is little doubt that economic considerations also affected the decisions of many to leave. During the perestroika era, many individuals expressed a desire to emigrate because of the visible crumbling of the economy. In a 1991 poll, 24 percent of the 3,000 urban and rural residents polled around the country said they were prepared to leave the country because of their fears of even further disintegration of the Soviet economy.[175] Emigration began to be viewed as an escape from a deteriorating standard of living and the growing prospect of unemployment.

Short-term emigration—going abroad temporarily to work—also presented itself as an alternative for solving the country's growing unemployment problems. Much like the situation in the 1960s, when Yugoslavs and Turks became "guest workers" in a number of Western European countries, the Soviets had the possibility of easing a difficult domestic situation by exporting their unemployment problem. The evidence from public opinion polls in 1990 was that as many as two to three million Soviet citizens wanted to go abroad to work on a temporary basis.[176] When asked their "attitude toward someone who decides to emigrate to a capitalist country to work on a temporary basis," 33 percent of poll respondents said they approved and would themselves like to leave.[177] Most of the people who wanted to work abroad were young; only 3 percent of those who expressed a desire for foreign employment were over the age of forty.[178] The government also understood the payoff of temporary emigration. Shcherbakov was frank in stating that temporary employment of Soviet workers abroad could diminish the impact of the shift to a market economy.[179]

There was a great demand for Soviet construction workers on Poland's black market by 1991.[180] Soviet workers began to appear in Poland in January of that year, initially doing low-skilled jobs. Their reputation for hard work and not carping about wages increased their desirability as workers. They were able to earn the equivalent of 2,000–2,500 rubles a month, about half the wages of their Polish counterparts but many times what they could have earned at the time at home.[181] A nationwide poll of 3,000 people revealed that workers expected they could find jobs abroad that were "unskilled and not prestigious" (40 percent), or else that while they might find work abroad in their field, it would demand fewer skills than a similar job at home.[182] But this did not appear to dissuade people from seeking work in other countries. In fact, the thriving black market in the Soviet Union for contracts to work abroad generated profits of 170 million rubles.[183]

Toward the end of the perestroika era, there was great concern in the west that economic refugees would flood the developed European countries. Sweden, Norway, and Finland decided not to allow Soviet citizens to work in their countries, and in 1991, Germany set a quota of 15,000.[184] These restrictions may have been a response to Shcherbakov's 1990 revelation that "thousands" of Soviet citizens were working abroad illegally, primarily in Scandinavia.[185] The anxieties in Western Europe must have been intensified when the head of the Soviet delegation to the Council of Europe Conference on East-West Migration told the group in late January 1991 that he expected 1–1.5 million Soviet citizens to leave the country.[186] But the restrictions also reflected the consensus position of a December 1990 seminar jointly hosted by the Institute for East-West Security Studies and the Refugee Policy Group. In discussions of emigration among the thirteen participating countries, east and west, including the USSR, it was clear that, as a group, the countries outside of the Soviet Union did not desire the emigration of temporary labor from the USSR.[187]

Permanent emigration was a different matter. After clamping down on emigration for most of the 1980s, liberalization of Soviet emigration policy in 1987 led to substantial increases in the numbers of people leaving the country. Permanent emigration rose from 4,000 in 1986 to 29,000 in 1987, 75,000 in 1988, 235,000 in 1989,[188] and to 452,000 in 1990.[189] In the first five months of 1991, however, the number applying for permanent emigration fell by 9 percent compared with 1990, to 138,200.[190]

But in fact, the Soviet Union did not gain anything by encouraging large numbers of its citizens to leave the country. The dangers of looking to permanent emigration to solve the unemployment problem can be seen by examining the professional composition of the Soviet labor force as a whole and of those leaving the country. Sixty-eight percent of the Soviet labor force in 1990 was blue-collar and 32 percent, white-collar.[191] Official figures show that 341,260 of the 452,000 people who emigrated in 1990 had been employed, 40 percent as blue-collar workers and 60 percent as white-collar workers.[192] These figures for all emigres are consistent with the Israeli data which showed that about 55 percent of the more than 180,000 Soviet Jews who emigrated to Israel in 1990 were professionals.[193] Of all the 1990 emigres, blue-collar workers represented 30 percent, white-collar workers represented 35 percent, and retirees and other nonworking persons, 30 percent.

Predictions of Future Unemployment

If estimates of actual unemployment were confusing, the forecasts of future levels of unemployment seem fanciful and, at times, frightening. At both extremes, some predictions appear to have been based on efforts to score political points with a constituency rather than to establish a genuine estimate based on careful reasoning. A number of estimates made between 1988 and 1991, along with the source and date of each, are listed in Table 4.1. There is no apparent rhyme or reason to the predictions. The methodologies employed to arrive at them either are unknown or, at best, were heuristic. There was a spate of forecasts in May and June 1991, just before the Social Welfare Guarantees During Unemployment section of the new employment of the population legislation was to go into effect. Months earlier, on January 15, the Supreme Soviet's decree, "The Bases of Employment Legislation of the Union of Soviet Socialist Republics and the Republics," had been signed into law on January 15 and provided the basic policy framework for both thinking about and coping with the new reality of unemployment.[194] But based on the wide variety of figures in the different unemployment forecasts from 1988 to 1990, the evidence is that there were no solid grounds on which to construct a reliable public policy: the magnitude of the unemployment problem was so uncertain, it could not have been known how much in the way of resources would have to be made available to deal with the problem. Unemployment was a political category, not only a statistical one.

Table 4.1

Predictions of Future Unemployment for the Soviet Union

Amount Forecast	Source of Forecast	Date of Forecast
1. 16 million by the year 2000	Kostin, vice-chairman, Labor Ministry	January 1988
2. 10 million during transition to market	Bunich, deputy chairman, USSR Supreme Soviet Economics Commission	April 1990
3. 10–12 million in the next few months	Shcherbakov, USSR Labor Minister	September 1990
4. 30–40 million: no timetable—apparently for the long term	Shcherbakov	September 1990
5. 6.3 million: no timetable	Gorbachev research group	January 1991
6. 23 million: no timetable	Unspecified independent workers group	January 1991
7. 11.5–18.5 million after transition to market	Plekhanov Institute, Moscow	January 1991
8. 4–5 million in "the next few years"	Narzikulov, kandidat of economic sciences	February 1991
9. 30 million by the start of 1992	*Komsomol'skaia pravda* citing "certain forecasts"	May 1991
10. 20 million within 1–2 years	International Labor Organization	June 1991
11. 30% of able-bodied population	Supreme Soviet experts	June 1991
12. 13 million by July 1, 1991	TASS	June 1991
13. 7–9 million: no timetable	Paulman, USSR Labor Minister	June 1991
14. 10–12 million by the end of 1991	Shokhin, Director of Institute of Employment Problems, USSR Academy of Sciences	June 1991

Sources: (1) *Izvestiia* (January 21, 1988) 3; (2) *Report on the USSR* (April 20, 1990), 37; (3) *Report on the USSR* (September 14, 1990), 39; (4) Moscow TASS in English (September 3, 1990), from FBIS-SOV-90-171 (September 4, 1990; (5) and (6) *Ekonomika i zhizn'*, no. 4 (January 1991), 10; (7) *Sovetskaia Rossiia* (January 5, 1991), 2; (8) *Komsomol'skaia pravda* (February 5,1991), 2; (9) *Komsomol'skaia pravda* (May 6, 1991), 1; (10) *Report on the USSR* (June 21, 1991), 26; (11) Moscow *Interfax* in English (June 27, 1991); from FBIS-SOV-91-126 (July 1, 1991), 28; (12) Moscow TASS in English (June 11, 1991); from FBIS-SOV-91-113 (June 12, 1991), 38–39; (13) Paris AFP in English (June 13, 1991); from FBIS-SOV-91-115 (June 14, 1991), 31; (14) *Argumenty i fakty*, no. 24 (June 1991), 1, 3.

Retraining Workers

As we suggested earlier, structural unemployment during the Gorbachev era accounted for the bulk of the Soviet Union's unemployment. Unemployed workers could not, in principle, find employment even as the economy was expanding. Their status as unemployed implied a need for job retraining, not an entirely new subject to the Soviets. In 1986, 41.7 million workers had upgraded their professional capacities through course work, and another seven million had learned a completely new profession.[195]

As unemployment began to materialize, there was both unofficial and official recognition of the need for a much larger retraining program. One was developed, in two stages. First, in January 1988, a joint resolution, "On Ensuring the Effective Employment of the Population, Improving the System of Job Placement and Increasing Social Guarantees for Working People," was adopted by the CPSU Central Committee, the USSR Council of Ministers, and the All-Union Central Council of Trade Unions. The resolution called for training and retraining workers who had lost their jobs as victims of economic reform.[196] I.I. Gladkii, the chairman of the State Committee for Labor and Social Problems, said that all those who had lost their job could receive retraining through either the educational system or special courses offered at their enterprises. He also said that if laid-off workers signed new work contracts, they could receive the average wage they had earned at their previous jobs during the retraining period.[197] But it soon became evident that the retraining apparatus was not up to the task of handling any significant level of unemployment. By the fall of 1990, *Trud* wrote that of the 4 billion rubles that may be needed for the unemployment fund, only 5–6 percent would be used to pay benefits; the rest would go to setting up a retraining system.[198]

The second stage in developing a retraining program was part of the overall unemployment legislation of January 15, 1991, which set up a state employment assistance fund within the state employment service system at the local, republic, and Union levels. It became the responsibility of the new job placement service to figure out how to finance the costs of unemployment. All producers—including state enterprises, institutions, and organizations—and the private cooperatives made monthly payments into this fund, equal to 1 percent of the wage fund. The fund was to be used to finance retraining, job creation, and benefits to the unemployed.[199] Part of it would be used to pay a stipend to trainees. Ten percent of the fund's financing would come from the Union budget, and the rest from the republican budgets.[200]

The retraining program faced several problems from the start, specifically how actually to pay for the program and how to apportion responsibility among national, republican, and local jurisdictions. The Soviet Union's fiscal crisis had a serious impact on spending plans. In mid-1991, the head of the RSFSR State Committee for Employment announced that the Russian republican government did not have the funds to retrain the unemployed. He said that, at best, the republic could pay unemployment benefits for the rest of the year.[201]

Several models were advanced regarding the issue of who would do the retraining. The first model, embodied in the 1988 resolution, proposed either using an organization's existing training facilities or developing contracts with the vocational-technical schools and the higher and specialized secondary educational institutions.[202] A slight variation on this was proposed three years later by the Plekhanov Institute in Moscow, which suggested that the educational system create special departments to retrain workers in exchange for a fee to be paid by the employment services.[203] Another model was developed in the Kursk Oblast in the RSFSR, where the Trade Union Federation Council and the Kursk Oblast Soviet Executive Committee signed a five-year contract providing for the establishment of retraining and placement centers for workers who were laid off.[204] A third model was represented by the Moscow Labor Exchange, which was itself retraining former members of the planning bureaucracy to be bookkeepers, managers, and computer programmers.[205] A fourth was advanced by the Ukrainian minister of labor in late 1990. He said that once the republic found the positions at which they want people to work, workers would be retrained in their prospective workplaces.[206]

Since the end of perestroika and the breakup of the Soviet Union, there is even more pressure to retrain workers. In the last days of the Soviet Union, A.V. Kapustin, the executive director of the All-Union Public Fund for Protection Against Unemployment, pointed out that it was not difficult to offer an unskilled worker a job that required no special professional preparation; but once unemployment began to affect higher-level professionals, it would be necessary to have a serious retraining program in place.[207] Ukraine expected to develop a retraining system that would handle about 370,000–450,000 workers and 150,000–180,000 specialists annually.[208] But at the time the Gorbachev era came to a close, there was a consensus that the country was ill-prepared to meet the retraining requirements associated with a substantial unemployment problem.[209]

Public Works Projects

The Soviet Union was a country whose national product and unparalleled record of full employment was generated mostly by government spending. So it was not surprising that it should so quickly conclude that one way to deal with unemployment was to prime the pump in hard times. At the end of July 1991, the USSR Cabinet of Ministers adopted a resolution, "On the Organization of Paid Public Service Jobs." The plan was for public works projects using "unskilled work in the construction of roads, hospitals, and schools, area cleaning and landscaping, and planting trees and shrubs along the streets."[210] The jobs were to be voluntary and temporary and would require no special skills.[211]

The use of public works projects to fight unemployment was not new, although there had not been a large-scale public works program in operation, or even thoughts about such a program, until unemployment hit the country in a big way.[212] While the expectations were that more than 1.4 million public works jobs would have to be created by the start of 1992,[213] there is no evidence that anything approaching this number ever actually materialized. In view of the fiscal crisis and the uncertainty concerning who could make decisions about the spending, the general absence of public works programs was not surprising.

Alternative Forms of Employment

Two forms of employment became significant alternatives to working in the state sector during the period of perestroika: working in the new legal private sector, which included the new cooperatives and other small enterprises; and working in the illegal second economy. Both provided the same general benefits—a chance to escape from the stultifying environment of state work and an opportunity to make a great deal more money in the shortage economy than could possibly be earned by working for the state. Moreover, state employment, once a sure thing, was increasingly risky as old jobs disappeared and new ones were not created rapidly enough to absorb all the newly unemployed.

There were plenty of people who wanted to work in the private sector. In a mid-1991 poll in the RSFSR, 20 percent of the 6,000 people who were surveyed said that they would like to become owners or co-owners of an enterprise. But these same people were also very pessimistic about the possibilities of actually getting such an opportunity. Thirty percent said they did not have access to the resources necessary to get their own businesses started, 23 percent said legal guarantees were scant, and 20 percent lacked confidence that in the long run new types of economic activity would succeed. A mere 2 percent thought that all the conditions necessary for a new business to succeed already existed.[214]

The development of legal private enterprises had received its first boost with the passage of the Law on Individual Economic Activity in November 1986. But when the law took effect the following May, there were two conflicting sets of interests. On the one hand was the state, which was quite cautious about who could participate and what activities could be engaged in. On the other hand, there was a great desire on the part of many to try their hand in private business. When it became obvious that the population's ambitions to make money as private businesspeople could not be curbed, new legislation, the Law on Cooperatives, was passed in May 1988, substantially liberalizing the right to work in private business.[215] The subsequent growth of the new cooperatives was staggering. During a period of slightly more than three years, the number of cooperatives grew from 8,000 employing 88,000 people on October 1, 1987, to 245,356 cooperatives employing 6.1 million people by the end of 1990.[216] By the end of September 1991, altogether 6.5 million people were involved in private and individual economic activity.[217]

There is no question that employment in cooperatives was an attractive alternative for many. What is unknown is how many willingly chose cooperatives because they were risk-takers and how many were forced into cooperative work because they were fired or feared the imminent loss of what once had been safe jobs. There is partial evidence that the latter held true for an unspecified number of those who were laid off. The journal *Sovetskaia kul'tura* reported that of the 3 million people who lost their jobs from 1987 to 1989, 600,000 were unable to find other jobs when they were let go. But "many" of them were said to have gone into the service sector and cooperatives.[218]

As regards the second economy, its illegality unfortunately makes it impossible to estimate accurately how many people began to earn their livings from unlawful economic activity. Moreover, even if we could make a reasonable guess at the number of people working in this sphere during the perestroika era, we would have no systematic way to determine the breakdown between full-time and part-time participants. A study done by the Independent Center for Socioeconomic and Criminological Research in the USSR said in 1990 that about 20 million people were working in the black market.[219] An article by Tatiana Koriagina in a leading Soviet journal suggested an even higher level of participation. She stated that at the end of the 1980s, there were 30 million people in the shadow economy, which amounted to more than 20 percent of the total number of employed in the USSR. This is in sharp contrast to the situation in the early 1960s, when it was estimated that less than 10 percent of the labor force (about 8 million people) was in the second economy.[220] According to a western estimate, the amount of labor employed in the second economy seems to have increased during the following decade. Vladimir Treml's study of emigres suggested that in the late 1970s 11.5 percent of the work time of urban adults in the USSR was devoted to activity in the second economy.[221]

The fact that the second economy flourished during the perestroika era, as we discussed in chapter 2, is consistent with the estimate of a massive increase in the number of people employed in these markets. Just as the economic incentive to reap the benefits of dire shortages at a time when state prices were fixed must have been irresistible to many, the incentive of paid work in these illegal enterprises when legitimate employment was threatened may have been seen as a viable solution by many others.

Conclusion

The unemployment experienced under perestroika was the newest phenomenon for the Soviet people. The working class already understood what shortages meant because shortages had been a daily reality for years; and while the standard of living fell during perestroika, it had never really been high anyway. But unemployment was different. Unemployment, along with the prospect of greater joblessness, created considerable apprehension about the future. Loss of income was the most basic material fear. But in the Soviet context, loss of one's job could also mean the loss of access to food, all kinds of consumer goods, and even health care and a place to vacation, because access to these often came through the workplace. The combined loss of all wages and non-wage income stripped citizens of their sense of material security. This background of fear and anger helps to explain the militancy that emerged in the Gorbachev era as a direct response to the failures of perestroika.

Notes

1. *Trud* (January 28, 1988), 1. According to labor exchange data, at the beginning of the planning era in October 1928, unemployment was at 1,365,000; two years later, it had dropped to 240,000 and full employment was declared by the end of the year. *Narodnoe khoziaistvo SSSR za 70 let* (Moscow, 1987), 11.

2. David Granick convincingly argued the principle in his book, *Job Rights in the Soviet Union: Their Consequences* (Cambridge: Cambridge University Press, 1987).

3. Moscow TASS in English (October 28, 1988). From FBIS-SOV-88-210 (October 31, 1988), 72; *Narodnoe khoziaistvo SSSR v 1989*, 48.

4. *Report on the USSR* (August 25, 1989), 40. If the total labor force is the number of employed (115.4 million) plus the unemployed (4.5 million), the unemployed represented 3.75 percent of the labor force.

5. *Ekonomika i zhizn'*, no. 15 (April 1990), 12.

6. Paris AFP in English (June 13, 1991). From FBIS-SOV-91-115 (June 14, 1991), 31.

7. Moscow TASS International Service in Russian (July 9, 1991). From FBIS-SOV-91-134 (July 12, 1991), 92.

8. *Sovetskaia Rossiia* (January 5, 1991), 2.

9. The report, entitled *"Transition to a Market Economy,"* was translated in its entirety in *Joint Publications Research Service-Soviet Union-Economic Affairs*, JPRS-UEA-90-034 (September 28, 1990). The section on unemployment is on pages 42–47.

10. *Ekonomika i zhizn'*, no. 43 (1990).

11. JPRS-UEA-90-034 (September 28, 1990), 42.

12. *Rabochaia tribuna* (April 30, 1991).

13. *Pravda* (April 6, 1990), 2.

14. *Rabochaia tribuna* (April 30, 1991), 2.

15. TASS (March 31, 1988). From FBIS-SOV-88-063 (April 1, 1988), 53.

16. *Trud* (September 25, 1990), 2. Not all of these abandoned projects meant the loss of jobs, however, because so many of them had been lying fallow for a long time.

17. *Izvestiia* (October 16, 1989), 2.

18. *Pravda* (July 25, 1991), 2.

19. TASS (August 16, 1991), 39. From *Report on the USSR* (August 16, 1991), 39. Of the 380,000 people who were to be taken out of military-related production, about 70,000 were expected to become unemployed.

20. Moscow World Service in Russian (April 5, 1991). From FBIS-SOV-91-069 (April 10, 1991), 45.

21. Moscow Television Service in Russian (January 18, 1992). From FBIS-SOV-92-015 (January 23, 1992), 56.

22. *Izvestiia* (June 19, 1990), 2.

23. *Sovetskaia Rossiia* (August 7, 1991), 1.

24. *Krasnaia zvezda* (October 20, 1990), 2.

25. *Izvestiia* (March 23, 1991), 1.

26. Moscow Television Service in Russian (November 12, 1990). From FBIS-SOV-90-220 (November 14, 1990), 45.

27. *Izvestiia* (March 26, 1991), 3

28. *Rabochaia tribuna* (December 23, 1990), 2.

29. *Argumenty i fakty*, no. 14 (April 1991), 6.

30. *Rabochaia tribuna* (January 23, 1991), 1.

31. Ibid. (December 25, 1990), 2.

32. Moscow TASS International Service in Russian (July 9, 1991). From FBIS-SOV-91-134 (July 12, 1991), 92.

33. *Argumenty i fakty*, no. 44 (1991), 3.

34. TASS (March 13, 1988). From FBIS-SOV-88-049 (March 14, 1988), 72.

35. *Izvestiia* (October 23, 1988), 6.

36. Moscow TASS in English (January 24, 1992). From FBIS-SOV-92-018 (January 28, 1992), 50.

37. Elizabeth Teague, "Tackling the Problem of Unemployment," *Report on the USSR* (November 8, 1991), 6.

38. *Sovetskaia kul'tura* (November 10, 1990), 5.

39. *Komsomol'skaia pravda* (March 5, 1991), 2.

40. *Vestnik statistiki*, no. 10 (1990), 47–48. The relative youthfulness of this group may reflect the fact that the low quality of a vagrant life frequently leads to an early death.

41. *Ekonomika i organizatsiia promyshlennogo proizvodstva*, no. 6 (June 1989), 142.

42. Ibid., 141.

43. *Trud* (May 12, 1990), 2.

44. Ibid.

45. Ibid.

46. Moscow All-Union Radio Mayak Network in Russian (July 25, 1991). From FBIS-SOV-91-144 (July 26, 1991), 75.

47. *Stroitel'stvaia gazeta* (October 22, 1989).

48. *Trud* (May 12, 1990), 2.

49. *Pravda* (May 13, 1988), 2.

50. Ibid.

51. *Pravda vostoka* (November 4, 1989), 1.

52. Ibid. (November 15, 1989), 1.

53. Ibid.

54. *Izvestiia* (January 1, 1991), 1. At the beginning of 1991, a private initiative, the Aid Fund for the Unemployed in Fergana, was set up in the Zhilsotsbank.

55. *Trud* (April 30, 1991), 2.

56. Ibid.

57. *Krasnaia zvezda* (September 10, 1989), 1–2.

58. *Pravda* (February 18, 1990), 3.

59. *Trud* (April 30, 1991), 2.

60. *Izvestiia* (September 26, 1989), 2.

61. *Pravda* (February 18, 1990), 3.

62. *Trud* (April 30, 1991), 2.

63. *Komsomol'skaia pravda* (February 13, 1990), 1.

64. An excellent summary of the conflict can be found in *Kommunist Tadzhikistana* (June 28, 1989), 1. From *Current Digest of the Soviet Press* (*CDSP*), 41, no. 28 (1989), 25–26.

65. *Sovetskaia Kirgizia* (June 6, 1990), 1. From *CDSP*, 42, no. 23 (1990), 1.

66. *Moscow News*, no. 41 (1990), 7.

67. *Trud* (May 4, 1990), 2.

68. *Soiuz*, no. 40 (October 1990), 6. From FBIS-SOV-90-203 (October 19, 1990), 103–104.

69. *Report on the USSR* (September 14, 1990), 39.

70. *Izvestiia* (February 13, 1990), 8.

71. *Pravda* (February 17, 1990), 2.

72. *Soiuz*, no. 40 (October 1990), 6. While Russians numerically dominated the group leaving Uzbekistan, Armenians, Jews, and Greeks also left. And while the RSFSR was the principal point of destination, there were those who went to Belorussia and Ukraine, and even some who left the USSR itself. *Izvestiia* (September 12, 1990), 2.

73. *Izvestiia* (August 5, 1990), 2.

74. Ibid. (September 18, 1990), 2. There were an unspecified number of Germans working in agriculture in the group which left.

75. *Pravda* (September 11, 1990), 2.

76. *Report on the USSR* (September 14, 1990), 39.

77. *Moscow News*, no. 5 (1991), 11.

78. *Trud* (May 4, 1990), 2.

79. Moscow Domestic Service in Russian (June 5, 1990). From FBIS-SOV-90-114 (June 13, 1990), 114.

80. Ibid.

81. Ibid. (October 5, 1990). From FBIS-SOV-90-196 (October 10, 1990), 114.

82. Ibid.

83. *Report on the USSR* (April 19, 1991), 33.

84. Moscow World Service in English (January 5, 1991). From FBIS-SOV-91-004 (January 7, 1991), 50.

85. A number of observers point to the coincidence that after the anti-alcohol campaign ended and perestroika began, crime rose. See the remarks by V. Bakatin, the USSR Minister of Internal Affairs in *Izvestiia* (May 23, 1989), 3.

86. *Izvestiia* (February 8, 1989), 6.

87. Ibid. (January 10, 1990), 3.

88. Moscow TASS International Service in Russian (December 11, 1990). From FBIS-SOV-90-243 (December 18, 1990), 60–61.

89. *Pravda* (April 17, 1990), 1.
90. *Izvestiia* (May 23, 1989), 3.
91. *Komsomol'skaia pravda* (May 6, 1991), 1.
92. *Leningradskaia pravda* (December 12, 1989), 3.
93. *Sovetskaia Rossiia* (March 20, 1988), 2.
94. *Izvestiia* (May 12, 1989), 8.
95. *Leningradskaia pravda* (December 12, 1989), 3.
96. *Pravda* (January 19, 1988), 1–2.
97. Ibid.
98. The January 1991 employment legislation was published in *Sovetskaia Rossiia* (January 25, 1991), 1. From JPRS-UEA-91-009 (February 26, 1991), 49–61.
99. For the Ukrainian law, see *Pravda Ukrainy* (March 19, 1991), 2–3. From JPRS-UEA-91-026 (May 24, 1991), 13–23; for the Moldavian law, see *Sovetskaia Moldava* (November 14, 1990), 3. From JPRS-UEA–91–008 (February 15, 1991), 53–58; for the Kazakh law, see *Kazakhstanskaia pravda* (February 8, 1991), 3–4. From JPRS-UEA-91-019 (April 19, 1991), 18–28.
100. *Trud* (May 6, 1991), 1.
101. *Rabochaia tribuna* (January 29, 1991), 1.
102. Moscow All-Union Radio Mayak Network (May 6, 1991). From FBIS-SOV-91-091 (May 10, 1991), 22.
103. *Komsomol'skaia pravda* (February 5, 1991), 2.
104. JPRS-UEA-91-009 (February 26, 1991), 56–57.
105. *Trud* (December 7, 1990), 2.
106. *Argumenty i fakty*, no. 44 (1991), 3.
107. Moscow TASS International Service in Russian (July 19, 1991). From FBIS-SOV-91-141 (July 23, 1991), 63.
108. Moscow TASS in English (December 18, 1990). From FBIS-SOV-90-244 (December 19, 1990).
109. Moscow *Interfax* in English (June 27, 1991). From FBIS-SOV-91-126 (July 1, 1991), 28.
110. Moscow Radio Moscow World Service in English (June 13, 1991). From FBIS-SOV-91-115 (June 14, 1991), 31.
111. *Izvestiia* (July 5, 1991), 3.
112. Moscow Television Service in Russian (September 12, 1990). From FBIS-SOV-90-182 (September 12, 1990), 41. The foundation actually had multiple goals, including job creation, retraining, and the undertaking of a labor market study, as well as the provision of one-time-only benefits for unemployed workers.
113. Moscow TASS International Service (November 29, 1990). From FBIS-SOV-90-236 (December 7, 1990), 95.
114. Moscow Domestic Service in Russian (February 26, 1991). From FBIS-SOV-91-040 (February 28, 1991), 45.
115. Moscow All-Union Radio Mayak Network in Russian (April 23, 1991). From FBIS-SOV-91-079 (April 24, 1991), 50.

116. Moscow Radio Moscow World Service in English (August 30, 1991). From FBIS-SOV-91-172 (September 5, 1991), 48.

117. *Rabochaia tribuna* (April 20, 1991), 1.

118. Moscow TASS International Service in Russian (June 27, 1991). From FBIS-SOV-91-127 (July 2, 1991), 31.

119. Moscow TASS in English (October 11, 1990). From FBIS-SOV-90-198 (October 12, 1990), 78.

120. See Paul R. Gregory and Robert C. Stuart, *Soviet Economic Structure and Performance*, 4th ed. (New York: Harper Collins, 1990), 258–263.

121. Teague, 4.

122. *Trud* (March 29, 1990), 2.

123. Ibid.

124. *Radianska Ukraina* (November 6, 1990), 1, 2. From JPRS-UEA–91–009 (February 26, 1991), 61.

125. Moscow TASS in English (January 15, 1991). From FBIS-SOV-91-011 (January 16, 1991), 35–36.

126. *Izvestiia* (January 21, 1988), 3.

127. Moscow TASS International Service in Russian (January 4, 1991). From FBIS-SOV-91-005 (January 8, 1991), 52.

128. *Sovetskaia Rossiia* (August 7, 1991), 1.

129. *Izvestiia* (February 6, 1991), 3.

130. *Ekonomika i zhizn'*, no. 19 (May 1991), 12.

131. *Rabochaia tribuna* (July 22, 1990), 1.

132. Ibid. (October 13, 1990), 1.

133. *Moscow News*, no. 50, (1990), 10.

134. *Rabochaia tribuna* (February 12, 1991), 1.

135. *Delovoi mir* (July 3, 1991), 1.

136. *Moscow News*, no. 50 (1990), 10.

137. *Sovetskaia Rossiia* (August 7, 1991), 1.

138. *Pravda* (February 1, 1991), 2.

139. Teague, 5; *Pravda* (February 1, 1991), 2.

140. *Izvestiia* (July 5, 1991), 3.

141. *Argumenty i fakty*, no. 44 (1991), 3.

142. *Pravda* (February 1, 1991), 2.

143. Ibid.

144. *Moscow News*, no. 50 (1990), 10.

145. *Izvestiia* (January 19, 1991), 3.

146. *Sovetskaia Rossiia* (August 7, 1991), 1.

147. Moscow Radio Moscow World Service in English (August 30, 1991). From FBIS-SOV-91-172 (September 5, 1991), 48.

148. Moscow Television in Russian (January 4, 1992). From FBIS-SOV-92-005 (January 8, 1992), 57.

149. Moscow Russian Television Network in Russian (May 30, 1991). From FBIS-SOV-91-106 (June 3, 1991), 41.

150. Moscow Television in Russian (January 4, 1992). From FBIS-SOV-92-005 (January 8, 1992), 57.

151. Paul A. Samuelson and William D. Nordhaus, *Economics*, 12th ed. (New York: McGraw-Hill, 1985), 187.

152. John S. Pizer and Andrew P. Baukol, "Recent GNP and Productivity Trends," *Soviet Economy* (January–March 1991), 71.

153. This assumes, of course, that the marginal productivity of labor of Soviet workers relative to the marginal productivity of U.S. workers is .40. The truth is that this is not measurable. The problem is complicated by the fact that there are huge numbers of workers in the former Soviet Union who are regarded as superfluous workers, amounting to perhaps as much as 20 percent of the labor force. These workers have either zero productivity or low productivity and therefore their unemployment does not alter GNP. But, at bottom, it is more reasonable to speak of the ratio of the average productivity of laid-off labor in the two countries as being the same as everyone else's in the respective labor forces.

154. *Rabochaia tribuna* (December 14, 1990), 1.

155. Granick, *Job Rights in the Soviet Union.*

156. Moscow Television Service in Russian (February 12, 1988). From FBIS-SOV-88-033 (February 19, 1988), 78–79.

157. *Sovetskaia Rossiia* (August 7, 1991), 1.

158. *Trud* (January 28, 1988), 1.

159. *Pravda* (March 2, 1988), 1.

160. *Ekonomika i zhizn'*, no. 15 (April 1990), 12.

161. *Rabochaia tribuna* (December 7, 1990), 2.

162. *Pravda* (January 21, 1988), 2.

163. *Izvestiia* (January 11, 1989), 5.

164. JPRS-UEA-91-008 (February 15, 1991), 82.

165. *Moscow News*, no. 31 (1991), 10.

166. Moscow Russian Television Network in Russian (June 29, 1991). From FBIS-SOV-91-127 (July 2, 1991), 79.

167. *Radikal*, no. 22 (June 13, 1991), 6. One indication of the serious ethnic tensions within the various republics was the different level of expectations of future unemployment among the indigenous nationalities and the nonindigenous populations, generally thought of as the large number of Russians found outside the RSFSR. For example, a summer 1990 poll in Latvia asked, "Will the number of unemployed increase in our republic in the immediate future?" While 31.5 percent of the republic's population answered yes to the question, only 25.1 percent of the indigenous Latvians thought there would be more unemployment, compared with 43.8 percent of the nonindigenous residents. *Kommunist Sovetskoi Latvii*, no. 7–8 (July–August 1990), 139–143. From JPRS-UEA-90-043 (December 11, 1990), 121.

168. *Trud* (August 1, 1990), 2.

169. *Trud* (January 28, 1988), 1, 2; *Pravda* (October 31, 1989), 2.

170. *Argumenty i fakty*, no. 45 (October 1989), 4.

171. *Trud* (September 25, 1990), 1; *Trud* (October 12, 1990), 1; *Rabochaia tribuna* (December 7, 1990), 2.

172. *Rabochaia tribuna* (December 14, 1990), 1, 2.

173. *Pravda* (October 31, 1989), 2.

174. Moscow TASS International Service in Russian (July 19, 1991). From FBIS-SOV-91-141 (July 23, 1991), 63.

175. Interfax (May 23, 1991). From FBIS-SOV-91-101 (May 24, 1991), 36.

176. Moscow World Service in Russian (August 8, 1990). From FBIS-SOV-90-154 (August 9, 1990), 36; *Dialog*, no. 5 (March 1990).

177. *Moscow News*, no. 34 (1990), 9. This figure emerges as an average of the results from a number of polls conducted by the All-Union center for the Study of Public Opinion during 1990.

178. *Izvestiia* (August 11, 1990), 7.

179. *Report on the USSR* (June 22, 1990), 35.

180. At least one route to the black labor market in another country begins by obtaining a tourist visa to that country, then finding a job and not going home when the visa expires. *Rabochaia tribuna* (February 6, 1991), 1.

181. *Moscow News*, no. 17 (1991), 13.

182. Moscow Interfax in English (May 20, 1991). From FBIS-SOV-91-099 (May 22, 1991), 28.

183. FBIS-SOV-91-220 (November 14, 1991), 29. The fact that this was actually a scam does not diminish the fundamental reason why people would pay criminals to secure employment for them in another country.

184. *Izvestiia* (October 13, 1990), 2.; Paris AFP in English (June 13, 1991). From FBIS-SOV-91-115 (June 14, 1991), 31.

185. *Moscow News*, no. 25 (1990), 1.

186. Vienna *Kurier* (January 26, 1991), 5. From FBIS-SOV-91-019 (January 29, 1991), 35.

187. See "Ramifications of the USSR Emigration Law," *Meeting Report*, Institute for East-West Security Studies. The fourteen countries attending the seminar were the Czech and Slovak Federal Republic, Finland, Hungary, Poland, (all bordering the Soviet Union), Australia, Austria, Canada, France, Germany, Sweden, Switzerland, the United Kingdom, the United States, and the Soviet Union.

188. Moscow Television Service in Russian (October 26, 1990). From FBIS-SOV-90-209 (October 29, 1990), 50.

189. *Glasnost'* (April 1991). From *Report on the USSR* (April 26, 1991), 41.

190. Moscow TASS in English (June 16, 1991). From FBIS-SOV-91-125 (June 28, 1991), 14.

191. *Narodnoe khoziaistvo SSSR v 1989*, 48.

192. Moscow TASS International Service in Russian (April 18, 1991). From FBIS-SOV-91-075 (April 18, 1991), 19. Almost 60 percent of the emigres went to Israel, 31.3 percent to Germany, 5.3 percent to Greece, and 2.9 percent to the United States.

193. *JWF News* (April 1991), 49.

194. *Sovetskaia Rossiia* (January 25, 1991), 1. From JPRS-UEA–91–009 (February 26, 1991), 49–63.

195. *Soviet Labor Requirements for the Information Era*, Office of Soviet Analysis, Central Intelligence Agency, DCI/ICS 5386-89.

196. *Pravda* (January 19, 1988), 1.

197. *Trud* (January 28, 1988), 1, 2.

198. Ibid. (September 25, 1990), 1.

199. *Pravda* (May 31, 1991), 1.

200. *Argumenty i fakty*, no. 24 (June 1991), 1, 3.

201. *Report on the USSR* (July 19, 1991), 36.

202. *Pravda* (January 19, 1988), 1.

203. *Sovetskaia Rossiia* (January 5, 1991), 2.

204. *Izvestiia* (January 15, 1991), 2.

205. Ibid. (January 19, 1991), 3.

206. *Radianska Ukraina* (November 6, 1990), 1, 2.

207. *Sovetskaia Rossiia* (August 7, 1991), 1.

208. *Radianska Ukraina* (November 6, 1990), 1, 2.

209. See, for example, the statement by E. Afanas'ev, deputy head of the Administration for Labor Resources and Employment of *Goskomtrud*, in *Argumenty i fakty*, no. 45 (October 1989), 4–5.

210. *Argumenty i fakty*, no. 24 (June 1991), 1.

211. *Izvestiia* (July 31, 1991), 6.

212. The Kabardino-Balkaria Autonomous Republic put such a program into operation at the end of 1985. About 20,000 were put to work in a period of three years doing "socially useful work." See *Sovetskaia Rossiia* (March 20, 1988), 2.

213. *Izvestiia* (July 31, 1991), 2.

214. *Sovetskaia Rossiia* (June 19, 1991), 3.

215. A detailed assessment of this early period can be found in Anthony Jones and William Moskoff, *Koops: The Rebirth of Entrepreneurship in the Soviet Union* (Bloomington, IN: Indiana University Press, 1991), chapter 1.

216. *Izvestiia* (November 25, 1987); Moscow INTERFAX in English (May 24, 1991). From JPRS-UEA-91-028 (June 13, 1991), 52.

217. *Ekonomika i zhizn'*, no. 43 (1991), 10.

218. *Report on the USSR* (January 26, 1990), 32.

219. *Rabochaia tribuna* (November 2, 1990), 1.

220. T. Koriagina, "Tenevaia ekonomika v SSSR," *Voprosy ekonomiki*, no. 3 (1990), 117.

221. Vladimir G. Treml, "Study of Employee Theft of Materials from Places of Employment," *Berkeley-Duke Occasional Papers on the Second Economy in the USSR*, no. 20 (June 1990), 21–22.

5

Strikes and the New
Labor Militancy

> Tired cities and settlements, raions and entire oblasts . . . people are
> going out into the squares, sitting down on the warm, summer asphalt
> in front of the big buildings where the local authorities have their of-
> fices. They sit and they sit. Waiting for guarantees of a different life
> from the one allotted to them by the fate of being a miner . . . .
>
> *(Izvestiia*, Story on the Miners' Strike, July 23, 1989, p. 1.)

If any set of events signaled the beginning of the end of the
Gorbachev regime and perestroika, it was the series of coal
miners' strikes that began in July 1989 in the Kuzbass, Donbass,
and Vorkuta and then was renewed with great force again in
March 1991. In 1989, at the end of the strikes, Gorbachev admitted the danger the strikes represented in a speech to the Soviet
parliament: "I must say that we are emerging from a very severe
crisis—a very severe crisis. Perhaps this is the most serious test
our country has ever faced in all four years of perestroika."[1] By
1991, it was clear that Gorbachev had failed the test.

The coal miners' strikes, which affected nearly all of the
nation's 2.5 million miners, revealed the deepest frustrations of
workers with the economic failures of perestroika. These workers
whom the system had given both sustenance and status, were
considered the exemplars *par excellence* of the proletariat. They
were the highest paid workers in the country and their storied toil

was the stuff of legend. What was also remarkable about the miners' strikes was that, for the first time in Soviet history, worker resistance to government policy received prominent public exposure. The entire population was given a daily blow-by-blow description in newspapers and on television. The strikes destroyed every myth about working class harmony and demonstrated that, government rhetoric notwithstanding, blue-collar workers would no longer quietly tolerate their rapidly declining standard of living.

Throughout the Soviet period, the idea that workers would strike was at best inconceivable and at worst anathema. While the structures erected to support the grievances of workers were coated with a democratic patina, they were actually repressive. The determination of wages, the length of the work day, and working conditions were made without the participation of workers and were not subject to dispute. In the official view, there was no need for either participation or dispute, because it was believed that the interests of the party, the state, and the working class were the same. Within an enterprise, any labor disputes were handled by mechanisms that wedded the state's production apparatus to an obedient trade union structure. Worker representation and state authority were so closely bound together that a Soviet publication could claim that "consistent work by state, economic, and public organizations to strengthen legality leads to a considerable reduction of the number (and at some enterprises to a complete elimination) of breaches of labor legislation and, as a result, to the disappearance of labor disputes. In theory we can conclude that labor disputes are not inevitable in the USSR."[2] In the workers' paradise, strikes never needed to take place.

It is well known, however, that in fact, there had been strikes in the past. But the silence of the press and other agencies of the state and the party made it extremely difficult to know how many there were, what they were about, and what their outcome was. From the limited information we did have, we knew only that strikes were few and far between. When one did occur, it was swiftly put down, by force if necessary. In 1962, Soviet soldiers fired on strikers in the southern Russian city of Novocherkassk, and more than twenty people were killed.[3]

While workers in other parts of the country might eventually hear about a strike elsewhere, there was never a labor movement in which strikes played an important role or in which workers were able to support each other with sympathy strikes.[4] Thus, strikes in the postwar period were like tiny islands that appeared every so often and then quickly disappeared underwater again.

A combination of ideology and fear served to keep the proletariat docile. Workers were also relatively quiescent as long as the state kept its part of the social compact, namely guaranteed employment, assured stable prices, and a piece of bread on the kitchen table every day. All these guarantees evaporated as the economy fell apart. And the workers struck back.

The spirit of liberalization that emerged under Gorbachev released the pent-up tensions and put to rest the myth that workers saw their interests as one with those of their bosses. For the first time in the history of the Soviet Union, there was a true proletarian movement whose agenda, particularly beginning in 1989, was set in significant part from below, rather than from above by the Communist Party. The strike became an important weapon for Soviet workers as an unprecedented means of expressing their discontent with politicians and with the deteriorating conditions of their economic situation.

What distinguished the strikes of the Gorbachev era from anything that had occurred previously was that they were no longer isolated and contained events; they occurred frequently, even becoming a routine part of the worker-state relationship. Workers began to collaborate with each other. They formed new independent trade unions that no longer had their primary allegiance to the Communist Party, and these new unions were often significant sources of support for a particular strike.

In certain cases, the economic and political goals of workers had become hard to separate. This was particularly true as workers became frustrated when the regime could not solve its economic demands; economic concerns then became fused with a political agenda. But the focus here is on the cause-effect relationship of economic decline and the strike as an expression of popular anger. The new principle of openness created by Gorbachev coupled with the smoldering anger and frustration of the workers produced just the right formula for the strikes.

The discontent of the working class grew during the era of perestroika as the standard of living fell. It is clear that 1989 was a watershed year for the working class. Economic conditions had begun to deteriorate badly in the second half of 1988 and there was no evidence that they were improving. Yet in spite of the economic problems, there were very few strikes during the first half of 1989 perhaps because there was still no right to strike and no one had proof that strikes would not be met with a harsh response, and perhaps because many workers still wanted to believe that perestroika would succeed.

In mid-January 1989, the Lvov sulfur miners in Ukraine began a two-week warning strike. They stopped delivering their output to customers because their industry was constantly losing money. The miners' debts were equal to about 50 million rubles, attributable to higher costs for fuel, electric power, equipment, and materials, but the miners were not allowed to raise output prices. The workers therefore demanded an increase in the price of sulfur and a minimum of 15 million rubles to construct housing, stores, and other social and cultural facilities.[5] Then in February, a series of strikes by Russian workers in Estonia were set off by the raising of the Estonian national flag on a tower in Tallinn. The growing momentum of the Estonian independence movement caused concern among the Russian minority there. Russians comprised 30 percent of the population and were overwhelmingly opposed to Estonian autonomy.[6] Next, in mid-May, a brief strike by bus drivers in Frunze resulted in a pledge by the Kirghiz government to provide higher pay and better social conditions.[7] During these months there were also a few sporadic strikes by coal miners. But it was in July 1989, when about 500,000 coal miners all over the USSR went on strike, that the strike became a pre-eminent weapon of economic protest. Thereafter, strikes became commonplace, expressing a wide range of grievances. In 1989, the economy as a whole lost 2.5 million workdays due to economic strikes alone.[8]

Coal miners were working in an industry that was surviving only because the state provided enormous subsidies, in 1988 equaling 5.4 billion rubles.[9] The main coal-mining areas were in the Donetsk Basin (Donbass) in eastern Ukraine, a major mining center since the nineteenth century, in the Pechora Basin of Western Siberia around Vorkuta and Norilsk, in the Kuznetsk Basin (Kuzbass) area, in the Kemerovo Oblast of the Western Siberian lowlands, and in central Kazakhstan, around the city of Karaganda. As long ago as 1979, the decision had been made to shift investments to the coal fields of Siberia and Kazakhstan and away from Ukraine. The increased investment in the high-productivity Kuznetsk coal fields was to be financed by reducing investment in the already low-productivity Donetsk region. The results were predictable. The Donetsk operations became more labor intensive; miners there were routinely working two Sundays a month just to keep output constant; the mines as well as workers' morale were in a state of disarray.[10]

There were also significant bread-and-butter problems affecting workers in Donetsk. The social sector in the Donbass suffered a great shortage of housing and other goods. From 1986 to 1988, 214 million rubles that had been allocated for public goods, including 35 million designated for housing, had not been spent. There was also an inadequate supply of food.[11] The issue of low wages was a high-priority one for miners. In many places, miners' wages had deteriorated relative to those of the rest of the labor force. For instance, the average monthly salary of miners in the Donetsk region city of Makeevka in 1988 was 240 rubles, which was only slightly higher than the average USSR wage.[12] Moreover, the deputy chairman of the Soviet coal miners' union said that the miners were disturbed by the large incomes that were being earned by those who were self-employed or were operating under lease arrangements with their enterprises, or those who worked in a cooperative. All of these people were making much more money than the miners.[13] Worker irritation about wages extended to the structure of the pay system. Bonuses had come to be about half of a miner's income. As long as the monthly plan was fulfilled, there was a handsome bonus. But if the plan was not realized, a miner's earnings might fall by as much as half. This system led not only to great insecurity among the miners, but also to their capricious treatment of equipment and supplies in order to maximize their chances of fulfilling the plan to get their needed bonuses.[14]

Miners in Donetsk were further troubled by rumors that coal extraction there had become too expensive, and that less expensive coal would be imported into Ukraine from Russia and Kazakhstan, from the Kuznetsk Basin and Karaganda where costs were lower. In fact, the Ministry of the Coal Industry had divided up the mines in the region into four groups, on the basis of a variety of factors having to do with each mine's potential survivability under the new regime of economic accountability. Fear spread rapidly through the Donbass when a number of mines were closed in April. The workers felt betrayed by the central government deciding their fate without any consultation. Many believed they could make many of the doomed mines work if only they were given complete autonomy in running the operations.[15]

Unrest in the Kuznetsk Basin had been building over a number of years. In the previous seven years, 803,000 people—or the equivalent of the population of the area's two largest cities—had left the Kemerovo Oblast because of the chronic housing shortage, the critical levels of environmental pollution, and the high cost of living in Siberia.[16] Indeed, on March 9, Prime Minister Ryzhkov was in the Kemerovo Oblast in the heart of the Kuzbass to speak to residents about the housing problems, the shortages and poor selection of food, and the absence of consumer goods.[17] He was reminded by a local official that conditions were so disagreeable that in the previous 20 years, 360 villages in the Kuzbass had ceased to exist because of the mass outmigration.[18]

There had been warnings of the miners' unhappiness before

the July explosion. On March 2, workers in a large mine in Vorkuta, in the far northern Pechora Basin, struck over issues of pay and working conditions. After their complaints in early February to the mine's council of the labor collective had been turned down three weeks later, they finally walked out. The workers wanted a new system of remuneration and additional pay for working the night shift, more railway cars to haul coal, more stable prices for their coal, and a 40-percent cut in managerial personnel.[19] The strike lasted five days and ended when the authorities agreed to adjustments in the wage system.[20]

More strikes broke out elsewhere. By the end of March, there had been eleven strikes involving 609 participants. All were of short duration, some lasting no more than a few hours. The issues involved wage rates, production quotas, pay for forced layoffs, evening and night shifts, as well as the poor supplies.[21] In April, there was another coal miners' strike, this time a five-day sit-down strike by miners in Norilsk, also in the far north. The central issue was, once again, a demand for a pay increase. The government sent the minister of Ferrous Metallurgy and the chairman of the USSR State Committee for Labor and Social Problems to negotiate with the striking miners. At this point, the miners' tone was conciliatory. A leader of a drilling team said, "We appreciated that our problems cannot be solved by a strike. We could have put the whole combine in a difficult position by continuing it. The appeal by the leaders of the ministry and the Krasnoiarsk Krai to start work convinced us of the need to seek new ways of settling the conflict."[22] But the miners' conciliatory attitude went only so far. After apparently solving the wage dispute, the miners put forward another demand, an additional wage increase of 30 percent. More negotiation finally resolved the wage issue.[23]

At the end of June, striking Estonian miners in a production amalgamation demanded that one section of their mine be closed because the unevenness of supplies reduced their work time and therefore their earnings. They wanted guaranteed work and therefore guaranteed pay. The section was closed and the miners demands were met. After the issue was settled, both the mine management and the trade union said they had been fully aware of the miners' concerns but had not recognized "that the workers' patience was wearing thin."[24]

Several observations are in order about the strikes up to the end of June. First, the miners' protests to this point were isolated and did not create a chain reaction either within a region or among regions. Second, the authorities failed to recognize that a storm was brewing among the workers; they failed to see that the conciliatory attitude of April had evaporated by the summer. Third, in spite of the imperfect way in which democracy and glasnost were functioning, the strikes that had occurred thus far encouraged some workers to believe they could fight back without fear of retaliation. Further, the strikes reflected the conviction that things were not going to get better on their own.

The July 1989 Explosion

Miners in the Kuzbass, specifically in Mezhdurechensk, went on strike on July 10. At issue were the shortage of goods, the ambiguous state of production conditions, and the inadequate quantity and low quality of food in the miners' cafeteria. The workers demanded a twenty-four-hour-a-day cafeteria, not only during the week but also on weekends; a reduction in the amount of time before new work clothes were supplied; supplies of meat and sausage in the mines themselves; the provision of padded jackets for winter work; and 800 grams of soap a month and a towel, to be provided at the mine's expense.[25] The disappearance of soap from the lives of the miners was a symbolic last straw. As the head of the Kemerovo strike committee said, "Can you imagine what it's like for a miner without soap? How much worse can it get?"[26] Initial negotiations produced a compromise agreement whereby each of the city's mines would become a state enterprise and be economically independent. The strike committee proposed an end to the strike based on this agreement, but the rank-and-file workers added additional demands. On July 13, in an open letter to the Soviet government that was published in *Izvestiia*, the Mezhdurechensk miners asked for, among other things, the provision of food for the people of Siberia and the far east sufficient to meet basic health standards. A final package of forty-one demands reflected the workers' anger over a number of economic and social issues. These included stable wage rates, pension supplements, longer vacations, and a higher price for coal so the mines could achieve viable economic independence. The most urgent demand was for more food.[27]

The Mezhdurechensk strike spread rapidly through the Kuzbass. On July 16, 80,000 miners had stopped working; two days later, the number of striking Kuzbass miners had reached 150,000.[28] The chairman of the Kemerovo strike committee defined the issue for that city's miners: "[L]et me note that many of the miners' demands boil down to giving the mining collectives a real right to be masters of the enterprises' destiny, up to and including the conclusion of barter transactions for above-plan fuel and the use of foreign exchange for the social needs of the city and of the region."[29] In order to achieve economic viability, the Kuzbass miners needed—and demanded the right—to sell coal at market prices. The cost of production in the Kuzbass region was the lowest in the country, but the state-determined price at which they were required to sell their coal was so low that local mines were either losing money or making very little profit.[30]

A poll of 216 miners in the Donetsk region, which was taken after the strike, revealed that their uppermost concerns were economic. Shortages, particularly of soap, and the miners' conviction that they were underpaid were the primary issues, followed closely by longer vacations and higher pensions. These bread-and-butter issues led 300,000 miners to go on strike in the Donetsk region until July 25.[31]

While it is tempting to focus on the uniformity of coal miners' demands, in fact, the situation was complicated by agendas that differed from region to region, town to town, and even from mine to mine. In Makeevka, local issues led to an agreement there that

Table 5.1

Miners' Views on Causes of Strike

Suggested Causes of Strike	Percent
Shortage of basic supplies	86
Low wages	79
Little vacation time	62
Inadequate pensions	56
High prices of supplies, unsatisfactory housing conditions, and poor relations with administration	39–41
Poor working conditions	33
Lack of social justice	32
Poor medical services	25

Source: David Marples, "Why the Donbass Miners Went on Strike," *Report on the USSR* (September 8, 1989), 31.

set fixed wages for low-productivity activities and miners who operated pneumatic hammers.[32] In Yenakievo, also in the Donetsk region, workers demanded that party officials in the city stop receiving favored treatment in the form of access to specially prepared cuts of meat and special food stores.[33] The miners in Karaganda, in central Kazakhstan, wanted the Karaganda Coal Association abolished and its buildings to be turned into children's facilities. They also demanded that the building that housed the Coal Industry Ministry be turned into a scientific center.[34] These demands of the Karaganda miners reflected the strong anti-bureaucratic feelings that ran throughout the mining communities; and while there were many grievances that all the miners held in common, each strike had its distinctly local flavor. Thus, as the strikes expanded into other regions of the country, negotiations to end them became that much more complicated because local grievances had to be dealt with one city or one mine at a time.

On July 19, miners in Rostov-on-Don, in Vorkuta, and in the western Donbass all went out on strike.[35] In the meantime, strike negotiations had been going on in the Kuzbass. A Kuzbass settlement was finally arrived at on July 21, and it was supposed to apply to the entire coal industry. There were nine major points: (1) the coal mines and pits were to be given complete economic independence in accordance with the Law on the State Enterprise, a process that was to be completed by January 1, 1990; (2) as of August 1, 1989, enterprises would have the right to sell above plan output at free-market prices within the Soviet Union and abroad; (3) the USSR State Committee on Prices and the USSR Coal Ministry were to raise coal prices to levels that would better reflect costs of production; (4) as of August 1, 1989, coal industry enterprises would have the right to establish output norms and evaluation standards independently; (5) retroactively, as of July 1, 1989, those working the evening and night shifts would get an additional 20 and 40 percent premium, respectively, over their regular hourly wage; (6) coal miners would have Sundays as their regular day off; (7) miners were to be paid for the time spent traveling from the shaft to the workplace and back at their regular hourly wage rate; (8) enterprises were recommended to make a one-time payment to the families of deceased miners and to retirees who had worked many years at the same enterprise, as well as to give workers additional leaves, the amounts to be decided by each enterprise; (9) enterprises were recommended to give women with children under the age of three years the right to leaves.[36]

While not all the miners went back to work at the same time, the agreement effectively ended the strikes. Miners in the Kuzbass returned to their jobs on July 21, and all the miners in Karaganda were back at work on July 22.[37] But in the Donetsk, miners did not feel that all their demands had been met. In particular, they wanted the issue of pensions resolved.[38] They were not satisfied with the government's assurances that national pension reform was part of the legislative agenda of the Supreme Soviet. They wanted the issue settled locally. Thus, as of July 25, only about half of the Donbass miners were back at work, and it was not until July 27 that all were back on the job.[39] Likewise, the Vorkuta miners in the Pechora coal basin refused to accept the agreement worked out in the Kuzbass because it did not meet some of their specific concerns. Among their more than forty demands, they wanted housing that was appropriate to the harsh climate of the far north and control over one-fourth of the hard currency earned from the export of their coal.[40] The miners of Mezhdurechensk were particularly angry that of the 29 million rubles earned in the first half of the year, the area's five mines were left with control over only 2.2 million rubles.[41]

Aftermath of the 1989 Coal Miners' Strike

While everyone went back to work at the end of July, it was clear that the country was now a changed place. The coal miners had not only articulated a radical economic agenda, they had also stirred a boiling political pot. And there were many who understood that the country was not the same. The coal miners' rebellion was part of a larger underlying political process that was changing the country. It is no coincidence that at virtually the same time as the miners were on strike, the most reform-minded politicians in the country were independently organizing around their own political agendas. On July 29, following right on the heels of the miners' strike, the so-called Interregional Group of Deputies held its first meeting in Moscow. The group, which consciously defined itself as representing the "left-radical" point of view in the USSR, had a membership which included Gavriil Popov, the mayor of Moscow, and Boris Yeltsin, who less than three years later would become president of Russia.[42]

The strikes had been significant in many ways. For one, they changed the relationship between the government and the working class: for the first time in the Soviet period, the government had conceded a right to strike. The mounting number of strikes and the toll they took on the economy became the catalysts for legislation to legalize strikes. On October 9, 1989, the USSR Supreme Soviet passed unprecedented labor legislation in an effort to contain a phenomenon that now eluded its control.[43] The legislation spelled out in detail the stages through which workers had to go before they were allowed to strike.[44] The goal seemed to be to ensure that wildcat strikes, which might escalate into quite damaging situations, could not take place. Workers had to present their grievances to the management in writing, and if management was unable to remedy the grievances, workers then had to take their complaints to a higher body. If the demands were still not met, there were two layers of arbitration prescribed. All of this was supposed to take no longer than fifteen days. If no agreement could be reached, workers had the right to strike after giving management five days' advance notice.

The right to strike was not unconditional. The USSR Supreme Soviet or the Supreme Soviets of the republics could postpone or suspend a strike for as long as two months. There were also a number of restrictions on who could strike and when a strike could take place. Strikes were forbidden if there was a "threat to people's life and health." They were also prohibited in such areas as rail transport, defense plants and other organizations associated with national security, urban transport, and government administration. There were conflicting views on how much these restrictions might limit the actual number of workers eligible to strike and therefore how limiting the law was on workers' behavior. One view was that these limitations affected as many as 70 percent of the work force and another held that it would affect about 35 percent.[45]

The strikes had had a serious short-term economic impact. An official post-mortem reported that one million worker-days were lost during the July strikes and that total financial losses were more than 200 million rubles.[46] And nothing had really been solved. Tension remained high everywhere in the coal producing areas.

In the short run, at least, it was an impossible situation for everyone concerned. The miners could not possibly have got many of the things they wanted instantly, because the government did not have the resources, or perhaps even the will, to meet their demands; and the miners' patience with deprived living and working conditions was exhausted, or nearly so. With miners' dissatisfaction undiminished, the government was faced with a rebirth of the crisis.[47] The protests began anew, even before the ink had dried on the July agreement. Miners in the Donbass complained early in August about living conditions, especially housing.[48] On August 3, the very day that the Soviet government formally adopted Resolution 608, the program of measures to solve the problems in the coal regions, 17 coal-mining enterprises in the Kuzbass held a two-hour warning strike because of their belief that the USSR Council of Ministers had failed to satisfy a July 18 agreement to suspend the construction of a controversial hydrosystem project.[49] The miners in Vorkuta also went on a brief strike again. The issues were unchanged. The workers demanded not only higher pay but also more consumer goods, especially soap, and more economic independence.[50] After two days, the Vorkuta miners suspended their strike until January 1, 1990.[51] The Donetsk miners, concerned about the pension issue and vacations, threatened to strike if the government did not take action by October 1.[52] A month later, they held a two-hour warning strike over these two issues, after deciding not to strike again for three weeks.[53]

At the end of October, miners in Mezhdurechensk in the Kemerovo Oblast walked out because a number of points in the July protocol were not being fulfilled, including the transfer of the coal mines to an independent status.[54] They were joined by Vorkuta miners.[55] In these instances, as in other cases, there was a clear difference between the perception of the government, which believed that the promises of the July agreement were being carried out, and the perception of the miners, who charged that the pace of implementation was slow in some cases and nonexistent in others.[56]

No doubt chastened by the renewal of strikes in some of the coal areas, Minister Shchadov gave a ninety-minute speech in Donetsk on October 25 in an effort to make the government's case that it was acting in good faith to meet the terms of the July agreement and to assuage the miners' most negative feelings.[57] But sporadic strikes persisted throughout the remainder of 1989 as the government and the miners sparred with each other over what the government had and had not accomplished. And all the time, the economic conditions in the country kept deteriorating as coal production slowed down. When the strikes resumed in November, there was a shortfall of 574,000 tons of coal in Vorkuta alone for the first half of the month.[58]

In some instances, workers emerged with new economic demands. The Vorkuta miners issued an additional five demands in November, including that workers be allowed unconditionally to keep their extreme-northern-region wage supplement when they moved from one mine to another; that young miners who had lived five years or more in the north be paid the full regional wage supplement retroactive to the time they had started work; and that those who had lived in the north for fewer than five years be paid a supplement based on the number of years they had lived there. There were also political demands, one of which called for punishment of management officials who did not fulfill the terms of Resolution 608.[59]

The government acceded partially to the economic demands. As of January 1, 1990, miners in the Pechora Basin would receive eighteen months' service credit for each year worked. In addition, those who left their jobs to work in southern mines would be allowed to keep their northern-region premium, although the amount of the premium would decrease each year they were in a southern mine. They would maintain their service record and their northern-region premium wages if they returned to their original job inside a month. The demand for the regional premium benefit for young miners was rejected.[60] Although these concessions met the requirements of most miners in the area, one of the largest mines in the region, the *Vorgashorskaia* mine, remained on strike until December 2. The mine was finally granted complete economic independence and the right to contract directly with a west European firm.[61]

As the year drew to a close, the government made another mostly fruitless effort to convince the miners that the issues that had given rise to the July strikes were being dealt with in a timely manner. On November 18, a conference was held at the Kremlin, hosted by Prime Minister Ryzhkov and attended by representatives of virtually all the coal regions in the USSR. The conference's primary goal was to assess the degree to which

Resolution 608 was being fulfilled. But, because of the economic instability caused by the coal strikes, it was also clear that the government needed to mend as many fences as it could. It was reported at the conference that during the first ten months of the year, the shortfall in coal deliveries was 14 million tons, including 1.2 million tons meant for the population. To appeal to the miners, much was made of the government's effort to meet their need for housing. Housing construction for the Coal Ministry was to be about 2.6 million square meters in 1989, with a 15-percent increase over 1989 planned for 1990 and 4–4.5 million square meters planned for 1995. The government also addressed the miners' exasperation in coping with the strictures on economic accountability and self-financing without prices that reflected costs of production. The promise was that a new wholesale price list would be produced in *1991* (italics are mine). In the meantime, prices were raised 15 percent, and there were plans for further increases in some prices in 1990.[62]

As 1989 ended, the relationship between the government and the miners was now eminently clear. The miners had virtually no trust left in the government. In the main, the miners had acquired a sophisticated sense of their power, although some of their demands, such as asking the government to punish those who did not fulfill Resolution 608, had a sophomoric tinge. The miners learned that they were powerful, and the government knew it needed the miners. In July, the miners had started out trying to find ways to ensure that their standard of living would get no worse. As the year progressed, the cast of their demands became quasi-political if not outright political in intent. What the miners did in 1989, therefore, was to move the working class from dutiful supplicant to an independent power group.

Strikes in 1990

Strikes continued after their legalization and became even more important. There were so many successful strikes that even a brief warning strike or the threat of a strike was sufficient to move the leadership to respond. For example, when in 1990 health workers and teachers threatened to go on strike because their standard of living had plummeted, the raises that had been set for them for 1994 were promised to them for 1991.[63] Few in the country seemed untouched by the abiding spirit of the strike. Journalists in Vladimir, demanding higher wages, threatened a warning strike, then called it off the day before it was to start when the oblast executive committee found 150,000 rubles to meet their wage demands.[64] Murmansk sailors who worked on nuclear-powered vessels went on strike for one day and were then joined by the crews of icebreakers as well as other Murmansk shipworkers. Their grievance was that they were being paid much less than sailors working on foreign routes who also received part of their pay in hard currency. If the government did not meet their demand for a portion of their pay to be paid in hard currency, they were going to shut off the ships' reactors.[65]

The economic impact of the strikes was apparent early in the year. While in 1989, the loss of labor due to both work stoppages and ethnic conflicts amounted to 7.3 million worker-days, in January and February of 1990 alone, 9.1 million worker-days were lost. The work time lost in this two-month period contributed to a one-percent decline in Soviet GNP over the same period in 1989.[66] After the first seven months of the year, the costs to the country were estimated to be a billion rubles, about 80 percent of it due to the conflict in Azerbaidzhan between Azeris and Armenians over control of Nagorno-Karabakh.[67] On average, 65,000–75,000 workers were on strike every day during the first half of 1990.[68] At the end of August, former Prime Minister Ryzhkov said that some 1,700 enterprises were affected by strikes, with direct and indirect losses amounting to 3 billion rubles.[69]

As strikes became routine in 1990, there was a clear shift in their nature as well as in the government's approach to them. At first, the strikes were grounded strictly in economic issues. But when these issues were not fully addressed, or when the workers' standard of living deteriorated more rapidly than the government's limited effort to assist them, striking workers began to develop a political agenda to get rid of the government leaders who did not meet their economic demands. At the same time, the government became extremely reluctant to enforce the laws against spontaneous strikes. For example, railroad workers threatened a warning strike for mid-October 1990 and then a general strike to begin on October 25 if their demands were not met. The Minister of Railways, N. Konarev, obviously did not want the workers to strike. First, he told the workers that their strikes were against the law. Next, he appealed to their sense of patriotism and told them that the strike would hurt the economy. Finally, he said that he appreciated their grievances and that the government would try to meet their concerns.[70] The more that control over the economy began to slip from its grasp, the more susceptible the government became to workers' pressure.

While wage demands were always high on the workers' agenda, several other issues were of consequence to them. The transport workers in the city of Voronezh went on strike in October, demanding a lowering of the retirement age by five years to fifty-five for men and fifty for women, an increased housing allowance, and improvement in the food service at the terminals, as well as a 60-percent pay increase.[71]

The breakdown in central planning and the unemployment that it threatened also led workers to organize and either strike or threaten strikes. When twenty-seven enterprises in the RSFSR's light and textiles industries were on the verge of ceasing operations because their raw material supplies were about to dry up, workers in most of the enterprises formed strike and job-action committees in the fall. Their branch trade committee threatened to strike on December 15, 1990. They had three major demands: 1.5 billion hard-currency rubles to be spent on raw materials, higher wages, and the right to sell half their output at free-market prices.[72]

The threat of a strike in a crucial but collapsing industry put the state in a bind. On the one hand, meeting the workers' wage demands—which it ultimately did—meant more inflationary pressure for the economy. On the other hand, if it refused to meet the workers' demands, there was a good possibility that this branch of the economy—which was already not producing enough to put in the stores—would be in even worse shape giving the general population even more reason to be disgruntled with the leadership. In a meeting between I. Klochkov, chairman of the Federation of Independent Trade Unions of Russia (FNPR), and Iu. Skokov, deputy chairman of the RSFSR Council of Ministers, it was agreed that if the light and textile industries collapsed, the entire consumer market would be in trouble.[73] A negotiated settlement was much the preferred solution.

The textile workers' strike illustrated the new balance of relationships within the country as the political system loosened and the economic situation eroded. Workers saw themselves as victims of the collapsing economy, but they also recognized that they now held power over the authorities who had the responsibility to pull the economy away from the brink. The authorities had become vulnerable and needed the workers if they and the economy were to survive.

The textile workers' strike also exemplified the government's consistent unwillingness to test the law on strikes against the resolve of the workers when a strike was threatened. Bauxite miners in Severo-Uralsk threatened a strike, saying that they would not deliver ore after January 1, 1991. They demanded a raise in bauxite prices, an improvement in social conditions, and a rate of pay given on a par with the higher-paid bauxite miners in the northern regions. These demands and the threats which lay behind them brought USSR Metallurgy Minister E. Kolpakov and the Sverdlovsk Oblast Soviet chairman, E. Rossel, to Severo-Uralsk to resolve the workers' grievances.[74]

The Coal Miners in 1990

After the great push that the miners had made in 1989, both extracting a great deal from the government, at least on paper, and demonstrating their capacity to organize effectively, 1990 proved to be a year of transition. In part, this was because the miners were watching and waiting to see what the government was going to do. It is also true that the miners had expended a great deal of physical and psychic energy, and they were exhausted. As the months of the new year went by, it became increasingly clear to the miners precisely what the government was willing and able to do, and therefore where the line of discord was to be drawn. The miners' attitudes hardened during 1990, and as they did, the strikes and the rhetoric became unabashedly political. The failure of the government to solve the economic demands of the working class politicized the coal miners. If there had been any shred of hope or trust left at the close of 1989, it was absolutely dead by the end of 1990.

Workers from all the coal regions complained about the food shortages. One of the worker delegates from Siberia said that in his town there was nothing but horse meat available.[75] Miners also complained that after they returned to work and stepped up production, the coal simply piled up because railroad cars were unavailable to haul it away. As a result of their coal not getting to the buyers, there were insufficient funds for wages. The miners were further hamstrung because they had no choice but to sell the coal to state-designated buyers; since the economic independence granted to the mines really hinged on them operating within the confines of the Law on the State Enterprise, they were not permitted to make direct contacts and sell their coal on their own.[76] The temperature of the miners continued to rise. In May, the Karaganda miners held a forum to air their grievance that most of the measures in Resolution 608 were unfulfilled.[77] The chairman of the Donetsk Strike Committee summed up the feelings of the miners when he said that "the guarantees are no more than good intentions," and that the "government has cheated the miners again."[78]

There was a shift in the way the miners stated their agenda. In 1989, they had focused narrowly on their own economic and social needs. In 1990, the problem was specified first as concern over the viability of perestroika and then more stridently as a need to rid the country of its political leadership. The economic interests of the miners thus went through a metamorphosis, from the miners' own needs to the broader conclusion that politics and economics were intimately linked. As one of their leaders put it, "[W]e understood that none of our economic problems could be solved apart from political ones, and that the solutions to them were being impeded in all ways by the command-administrative system."[79]

The government was aware that it was slowly losing the fight to retain the trust and therefore the allegiance of the miners. Throughout most of the year, high-level officials met with the miners in a public-relations effort to persuade them that the government was making progress in meeting the terms of Resolution 608 and to diminish the most hostile feelings toward the government when it was unsuccessful in fulfilling those terms. Gorbachev himself met with a small delegation of miners in early February to hear their grievances.[80] Early in March, a government commission toured the coal regions of Kazakhstan to monitor the implementation of the 1989 settlement.[81] Three months later, at the end of May, Minister Shchadov, Deputy Prime Minister Lev Riabev, and a number of miners met for a round-table discussion in Moscow.

It was a time of summing up, of examining what had been accomplished and what of Resolution 608 remained to be accomplished. On the plus side, bonuses for working the night shift had been doubled, compensation had been introduced for time spent going to and from the mines, the soap allowance had been doubled, and the issue of retirement benefits had been resolved. But a number of the promises had not been honored. In particular, the material-technical supply situation had little improved and miners continued to work in an environment that was often economically unstable and sometimes physically dangerous. It was agreed almost universally that food and medical supplies were extremely inadequate. The leave provision, which was supposed to provide fifty-seven days for those working in harmful conditions, was also unmet because the government had not yet introduced the appropriate legislation. Shchadov tried to assure the miners that the government's goal was to introduce extended leaves for miners on January 1, 1991.

The miners also regarded the new economic independence of the mines as a fiction. Nominally, one-third of all mines were placed on the same footing as other industrial enterprises, but the cost of production for most of the mines was higher than revenues from coal sales; the state's plan to increase coal prices by 60–70 percent in 1991 was regarded as inadequate for the mines' financial self-sufficiency. In fact, some wanted coal prices raised three to four times their current level, an increase which the government regarded as unwise because of the potential inflationary effects.

The government dealt with the financial problems of the mines by continuing to provide almost 8 billion rubles in subsidies. There were those who argued that the subsidies were a form of blackmail, keeping the miners beholden to and dependent on the government. If the state withdrew its subsidies most of the mines would choke to death on their losses.[82] Miners in Donetsk complained further that although they had been granted pay increases for working the night shift or in high-temperature conditions, the money for these raises was not coming out of any supplementary funds, which had been the promise of the government, but out of the income of the coal enterprise.[83] Meetings went on all year, but the longer that demands were unmet, the less fruitful were any government requests for patience and faith in perestroika.

It was in this context of cynicism that the miners held their first congress in June 1990 with an agenda that included the social situation of the miners, an assessment of the fulfillment of Resolution 608, and consideration of how the coal industry might be affected by a shift to the market economy.[84] In addition to rehearsing their unhappiness with the slow pace of Resolution 608's implementation, the miners voiced their fears about a future transition to the market, noting that the industry was being kept afloat only by huge subsidies and that many mines would have to close if those subsidies were withdrawn.[85] This was a complicated theme for the miners, because one of their most fervent demands was the right to sell their coal abroad at market prices so that they could earn the hard currency that would enable them to improve the quality of their lives. What the miners poorly understood was that independence not only implied the freedom of the market but its associated risks as well, which were currently diminished by state subsidies.

The concerns of the congress also revealed the degree to which so much of the movement had become politicized. One of the congress's actions was the decision to form a new independent trade union of miners, a goal that would not actually come to fruition until the fall.[86] The miners further distanced themselves from the past by passing a resolution which asserted that the Communist Party no longer ministered to their interests.[87] Miners had already entered the political arena and been elected as deputies to soviets, from local to republic levels.[88]

On March 1, Donetsk miners held a six-hour warning strike demanding the resignation of local party leaders and threatening a major strike if this demand was not met. Relatively few miners joined the mini-strike, however, out of apparent concern that a strike now could do further damage to the economy.[89] But in May, thousands of Donetsk miners did go on strike, albeit briefly, over the fear of chemical pollution in their mines. Earlier, fifty miners in nearby Gorlovka had been killed or injured in an explosion caused by the leakage of chlorobenzene into their mines.[90] On July 11 and 12, there were one-day "political strikes" all over the country, but it was clear from the rhetoric that the underlying issues were economic.

A poll of about 500 workers and other employees at five mines in Donetsk succinctly recorded the concerns of the miners.[91] The purpose of the survey was to determine how well the 1989 protocol was being implemented. As Table 5.2 shows, the failure of the government to provide economic freedom was first on the list of miners' complaints. The absence of wholesale price reform, which was necessary if economic independence was to succeed, and the desire for better housing followed.

When asked to assign blame for the "lack of fulfillment of

Table 5.2

**What in Your View is the Most Important Issue
of the Protocol?** (in Percent)

Full economic independence	23
Wholesale price reform	12
Improved housing conditions	12
Administrative staff reductions	10
Wage increases	8
Perfection of the pension system	7
Development of economic accountability	4
Public health improvements	4
Other (increased vacations, improvements in trade, better equipment, labor safety)	20

Source: Argumenty i fakty, no. 28 (July 1990), 6.

demands," 55 percent blamed "central organs," 14 percent, "local organs," 29 percent had no response, and the remaining 4 percent blamed either themselves or the trade unions. These feelings translated into a throw-out-the-villains sentiment after mid-1990. They also translated into a total lack of faith in the existing state trade union. When asked who could best protect their interests, 54 percent said an "independent organization," 32 percent said an "informal trade union," and only 6 percent named the existing trade union. As regarded the future use of strikes, 79 percent said they believed it was their right to strike and 74 percent thought that strikes would increase in scope.

As conditions continued to deteriorate into the autumn, the miners resorted more and more to barter, trapped as they were between state orders, which required 90 percent of their output, and the state supply system, which could not deliver the inputs they needed. Those who did provide inputs to the mines wanted side payments, such as consumer goods and equipment, which the miners did not have.[92] Indeed, the production levels in some mining areas were declining not only because of input shortages, but also because of the virtual absence of consumer goods. With no incentive, the miners refused to work a full complement of shifts, in some cases reducing the number of shifts to twelve or thirteen instead of the usual twenty-two. The incentive to work was further diminished in September by the cigarette and beer shortages.[93] Hopes that above-plan coal could be exported and exchanged for consumer goods were dashed in some places, such as Vorkuta, because the railroads did not provide rail cars to ship coal to port sidings.[94] And all the time what lurked in the back of the miners' minds was the unknown but greatly feared outcome of a free market which had not yet appeared. The 500-Day Plan, which had been unveiled in August, frightened the miners, not only because of the suggested speed of its implementation, but also because losses in the mines kept mounting and almost all of them could become candidates for closing in a free-market economy.[95] The rapid rise in prices in 1990, coupled with increased taxes on profits, also meant that coal-mine subsidies would have to increase, perhaps as high as 25 billion rubles in 1991. In the absence of subsidies—a threat posed by the 500-Day Plan's reform proposal—anywhere from 150,000–200,000 miners could lose their jobs.[96]

When the miners held their second All-Union Congress, Gorbachev admitted that the government had not done all it should have and asked for a patience that was no longer there. He said: "I have to admit frankly that not everything the government, the sector leadership, and the trade unions planned in order to improve the miners' living and working conditions is on target. A number of urgent, well-justified demands made by the previous congress have remained unfulfilled . . . fundamental changes can only be achieved by concerting our efforts—the government and the miners themselves. Dialogue and cooperation rather than confrontation are the key to success."[97] This was not a message with much appeal, and the congress, conceived in a spirit of antipathy to the government and the official trade union and their perceived ineptitude, ended on October 26 with the formation of an independent miners' union.[98]

The government recognized that the miners' fears and anger, expressed only in part by the creation of the new union, could translate into even more danger to the economy if another protracted strike took place. Minister Shchadov tried to provide some reassurance about the future, promising that, even in the face of the mines' mounting financial problems, there would be no layoffs, provided that subsidies—already doubled in 1990 from 8 billion rubles to 16 billion rubles a year—could be increased to 23 billion rubles.[99] It was only a piece of the message that the miners wanted to hear, and it did little to assuage their hostility.

Thus, 1990 ended with little actually accomplished. The mines did not have real economic independence; the miners' material situation—real income, food, housing, consumer goods, and medical care—was either no better or, as in most circumstances, worse; the supplies of raw materials continued to be maddeningly uncertain; and economic linkages had collapsed. Moreover, in trying to soothe the miners' anger, the government had taken a step away from the transition to the market. The miners had taken the government hostage, and the government believed that its ransom was a promise of full employment, if only the miners would side with the government's effort to extract subsidies from the budget. The government was trying to buy time. As it turned out, the full-employment trump card won few friends. It was a dismal year for the miners, and it would lead to another explosion in 1991.

The Strikes of 1991

In 1991, the strike became an even more favored weapon for workers in their effort to overcome the corrosive effects of inflation and goods shortages on their standard of living. Two polls early in the year of more than 2,000 people in 33 cities and 17 raions in 11 republics revealed how positively people viewed the use of strikes. People were asked how they would react if all strikes were temporarily banned. In January, 50 percent of the people polled said they would support a ban, while only 36 percent said they would be against one. But three months later, when the economic situation had further degenerated, only 38 percent said they would support a ban on strikes, while the same number were against a ban.[100] In Ukraine, the results of a poll taken early in 1991 indicated that more than 33 percent of the adult population would take part in a strike if the standard of living plunged significantly. Incredibly, more than half said they were ready for "mass resistance" if their social benefits were reduced.[101]

The increasingly favorable view of strikes correlated with the rapid decline in the economy and the simultaneous loss of faith in the government's ability to halt the slide. By 1991, a pattern had emerged: When prices rose sharply and steadily, workers demanded higher wages to compensate them for the deterioration in their real income; the government at first resisted, but in most cases conceded to workers' demands in order to ensure that critical sectors of the economy would not be crippled or come to a standstill. The position of the political leadership became more and more fragile as the number of people asking for its resignation grew. The leadership was in an untenable situation. In addition to whatever obligation they might have felt to honor principles of social justice, they were under great pressure not to allow the price of a piece of meat in a collective farm market to deplete a person's entire monthly income.

The strike was adopted as a weapon by the new independent trade unions. Thus, early in January 1991, the Federation of Independent Russian Trade Unions (FNPR) said that it would call for a general strike in the republic if the Russian parliament did not adopt laws guaranteeing workers protection against the consequences of the transition to the market, including legislation on income indexing and employment.[102] In late April, FNPR and the Democratic Russia Movement called for a republic-wide protest, to take the form in part, of strikes. The union's main demand remained the establishment of a system of social protection. But there were also demands for 24-day vacations, a 40-hour work week, and a rise of the minimum wage to 195 rubles.[103] In May, the FNPR supported the air-traffic controllers who threatened to strike over demands for a 300-percent wage increase, more vacation days, and a reduction in the retirement age to fifty.[104] (The government offered air-traffic controllers a 50-percent wage raise, and the controllers finally settled on a 60-percent increase.)[105] In the power struggle between the government and the workers, the latter seldom came away empty-handed. But their victories were largely hollow, because the workers were only one step behind the whole economy's careening slide to the bottom.

Inconsistent economic policies caught workers in a squeeze. Some prices rose, while others were not allowed to. Input prices increased for certain industries but output prices remained fixed, leading to large losses and jeopardizing jobs. And as we saw above, food prices kept climbing almost out of sight.

As the process of economic deterioration continued, the state's usual sources for providing workers with material support slowly disappeared. Workers depended on the state for a great many things, from subsidies for their enterprises to ensure their employment to vacation facilities and food and consumer goods sold exclusively through the enterprise. In the Perm Oblast, in the western foothills of the Urals, the metallurgical workers threatened a strike in February. In part, they were angry because they could not redeem their ration coupons for food. However, they remained somewhat tolerant of the shortages as long as they could get their main meals at their places of work. But when enterprises were unable to provide even this meal, workers openly threatened a strike, demanding the provision of food for the entire population of the oblast, the adoption of laws on indexation, and social protections.[106] In March, oil workers in Perm came into conflict with the oblast executive committee over many of the same issues, including the fact that workers' cafeterias were on the brink of closing and many of them were not serving the main entrees.[107] The same sense that entitlements were being violated led Leningrad sailors to plan a strike. The immediate cause was the five- to six-fold increase in the cost of lunches in their canteens as a result of the removal of the government lunch subsidy. The general director of the Merchant Marine Trade Association (*Torgmortrans*) had decided that until new wholesale prices for foods were set, lunches would be sold to the seamen at prices that reflected their actual cost; and the shipping line said that it did not have the money to subsidize the feeding of 40,000 people.[108]

No part of the economy remained untouched by strikes: workers for Latvian newspapers, Moscow magazines, the Moscow weather center, and the venerable Uralmash, the giant machine-building complex in Sverdlovsk, all went on strike over economic issues.[109] The health-care crisis even brought the city of Moscow's Medical Workers Trade Union to the brink of a strike. Scheduled for February 14, 1991, the strike was postponed for ten days only after the USSR Supreme Soviet allocated 9.8 million rubles to subsidize the purchase of pharmaceuticals, half of it to go toward imports. The issue of wages for doctors and other medical personnel was postponed. The fact that 65 percent of Moscow's medical personnel had said they would participate in a strike clearly got the attention of the government. The strike was even supported by the deputy minister of health, A. Moskvichev.[110]

As the number of strikes increased, the associated economic costs rose. From January through March 1991, strikes led to production shortfalls worth 218,422,000 rubles; in March alone, 1,169,000 worker-days were lost.[111] The government's patience with the strikes rapidly wore thin. In May, the Soviet parliament amended the 1989 law and imposed harsh penalties on those who either organized or participated in wildcat strikes. In addition to fines of up to 3,000 rubles, individuals could also lose their jobs. The law also gave the Soviet president the right to postpone a threatened strike and to suspend an ongoing one for two months. The same right was granted to the heads of the republic governments.[112] The Union government's effort to contain the strikes followed on the heels of legislation in Ukraine that banned strikes there altogether because they were seen to be leading to the republic's economic collapse. The worker's demands were to be discussed by a commission set up by the Ukrainian Supreme Soviet.[113] In a real sense, what the government had given in 1989 seemed to be taken back in 1991.

But there were no real teeth in the antistrike law; the momentum had already built up, and the confidence that workers had gained from their successful confrontations with the government was far stronger than the law. Indeed, in late March, when the metal smelters' union threatened a strike over wages and other earnings issues, the central government negotiated with the union to avert a walkout at the very same time it was preparing a law to prohibit such strikes. The settlement of the smelters' demands removed the restriction on wage increases during the year and allowed the smelting enterprises to charge market prices on 30 percent of their output.[114] The weakness of the government's resolve was demonstrated even more clearly in July when Leningrad dock workers canceled plans to strike after the government agreed to give them a 50-percent wage increase.[115] Although the threatened dock-worker strike would not have involved a large number of workers, its quick settlement must have made clear to every worker in the country that the government needed them much more than it needed to enforce hard-nosed antistrike legislation. Certainly, the dramatic June hunger strike by 90 copper miners near Cheliabinsk had gone against the new law. The miners stayed underground for a week until a people's deputy promised them that the Ministry of Metallurgy would not close their mine until the end of the year.[116]

The Miners in 1991

For the miners, 1991 started as unpromisingly as 1990 had ended. In the Kuzbass, a call for a political strike on January 18 over unresolved 1989 issues received very little support and did not take place.[117] When Donbass miners threatened to halt coal supplies, a strike was averted only when the Ukrainian government promised to raise coal prices immediately by 100–200 percent.[118] At the end of January, the Donetsk miners signed a protocol with the republic which not only formally raised prices, but also stipulated that subsidies for the year would amount to 12 billion rubles, somewhat below the minimum of 13.5 billion ruble figure that Ukrainian miners thought was necessary.[119] There was, however, no agreement on the miners' demand for a pay increase of 100–150 percent, and less than a week later, Donbass miners were out on strike.[120] There were differences between the demands of the Donbass miners, who emphasized economic issues, and those of the Kuzbass in Russia's Kemerovo Oblast, miners who called for the resignation of the central government and supported Boris Yeltsin.[121] In the Pechora Basin in the north, although there was no official declaration of a strike, work stopped in February because miners had not been paid since the previous December.[122]

Tensions in the coal-mining regions increased during the winter. There were warning strikes on March 1 in a number of areas, continuing in some places through March 3.[123] In Ukraine, the issue of the Donetsk miners' demand for a massive pay increase was still unresolved; in Kazakhstan, Karaganda miners were demanding an increase in pay equal to the Donetsk demand, compensation for price increases, and an improvement in the meat supply.[124] The strike in Karaganda, which lasted but two days, was called without any warning to local government authorities, contrary to the law—more evidence of how little respect the miners had for governmental authority.[125]

Most of the miners in the Pechora basin went back to work on March 4, suspending their strike until March 30. The miners there demanded direct talks on doubling their pay and increasing the retirement pensions of miners living in the most severe climates.[126] The miners in the Kuzbass weighed holding a one-day political strike on March 4, but this time their political demands, including the resignation of President Gorbachev and the rest of the central government, the depoliticization of the army, the KGB, and public education, were more explicitly tied to economic demands, which included a several-fold increase in pay and the adoption of a law on indexation, tying wage increases to inflation.[127] The central government adamantly opposed such a pay increase, in large part because it was estimated that it could cost as much as 15 billion rubles.[128] Likewise, Prime Minister Fokin of Ukraine refused to comply with the Donbass miners' pay demands, claiming that the more than fourfold increase in

Table 5.3

Monthly Rations, In Grams

	Kemerovo Citizens, Prisoners in the Correctional Labor Camps	
	with ration coupons	without ration coupons
Bread	Unlimited	19,500
Groats	900	3,600
Macaroni	300	600
Flour	700	300
Meat	600 grams of sausage	2,400
Vegetable oil	250	450
Sugar	1,000	600
Eggs	10 units	—
Butter	300	—
Fats	—	300
Fish	—	2,500
Potatoes	Unlimited	13,500
Vegetables	Unlimited	6,000

Source: Trud (March 30, 1991), 1.

coal prices now allowed underground miners to earn as much as 1,000 rubles a month, and that miners' salaries had gone up by 18 percent in 1990 even though coal production had fallen by 15 million tons. He furthermore refused to support an increase of subsidies above the 12-billion ruble level the industry had received in 1990.[129]

The miners' universal demand for massive wage increases was a consequence of the startling rise in prices, which had eroded their real income. Soviet miners used up about 4,200 calories a shift. In 1980 prices, a market basket of food to replenish those lost calories had cost 165 rubles a month. In 1991, that same market basket of food cost 350 rubles, or more than twice the 1980 cost, at a time when the average miner's salary was 334 rubles a month.[130] Miners felt further victimized by inadequate state food supplies. It was a bitter irony for miners, whose ration allowances entitled them to less food than prisoners were given. Table 5.3 shows the differences in the food allowances of Kemerovo miners and prisoners in the Correctional Labor Camps

(ITK). Almost without exception, the prisoners received higher food allocations from the state. Miners were further worried that the pay increases they had received earlier would be nullified by the price increases due in April. And they continued to feel that it was unjust for the new entrepreneurs and others to earn more money than they did; in their eyes, these were people "who contribute less but live no worse."[131]

While the pay issue was the main concern of the miners during this period, there were other problems that influenced their actions. In Kemerovo, the representative of one mine spoke of the absence of food and other consumer goods and the 5-percent sales tax as primary issues.[132] Miners in the Donbass wanted an increase in the number of underground jobs that would qualify for a more generous retirement pension.[133] And miners everywhere continued to demand that the promises made in the summer of 1989 be fulfilled.[134]

In March, with absolutely nothing being solved by way of resolving either the political or the economic demands of the workers, the strikes spread to other areas. On March 19, miners in the southern Urals went on strike. As well as a pay increase that would take account of the cost of living in the region, they demanded a repeal of the sales tax and Gorbachev's resignation.[135] The Donbass miners added a number of political demands to their previous economic ones, including the elimination of the Supreme Soviet, political and economic sovereignty for Ukraine, and the abolition of financial support for the central government.[136] Miners in Chervonograd, in the Lvov region, added the political demands of an end to the Soviet presidency, a dissolution of the Supreme Soviet and the Congress of People's Deputies, and Ukrainian sovereignty to its demands for high wage increases and piece-rate pay at state enterprises.[137]

Like two giants, the miners and the government collided. On March 21, the Soviet legislature asked the Ukrainian government to do what was necessary to stop the decline in coal production and asked the miners to drop their political demands.[138] In what can only be seen as part of a coordinated effort to send the miners a tough message, on the same day, as a result of a suit filed by mine administrators, the oblast court ruled that the strikes in the western Donbass were illegal.[139] Both these acts were surely prompted by the enormous economic losses suffered by the country. The direct losses from the coal strikes of 1989 and 1990 and the first quarter of 1991 amounted to about 2 billion rubles.[140] In March 1991 alone, coal production was down 3 million tons, and the state had lost 250 million rubles in profit since the strikes had begun anew.[141] It was no doubt this continued drain on the industry that led the USSR Supreme Soviet to intensify its antistrike efforts dramatically and swiftly. On March 26, it used the Law on Collective Labor Disputes as the basis for issuing a resolution to suspend the coal strikes for months. It was the first time that the government had actually used its muscle in an attempt to stop a strike. Although the resolution also had a somewhat conciliatory message—instructing the USSR Cabinet of Ministers and the Ukrainian republican government to work toward resolving the miners' economic and social demands—it made no reference to the political demands.[142] And as if to imply that the government was using the law only as a way of getting the miners' attention, both Prime Minister Pavlov and Chairman Leonid Kravchuk of the Ukrainian Supreme Soviet appealed to them to stop the strikes.[143]

A breakthrough of sorts came when the two sides scheduled talks for April 2 in Moscow. The government, however, said that it would not negotiate with groups that were still on strike.[144] This created an impasse: the miners remained firm in their determination to continue the strikes and received encouragement from Boris Yeltsin and from the bauxite miners of Sverdlovsk who went on a sympathy strike.[145]

One of the things that distinguished the strikes of 1991 from those of 1989 and 1990 was the degree to which the miners received visible support from others all over the country. That support came in the forms of contributions of various goods, particularly food—a generous offering considering the nationwide food shortage—and sympathy strikes. The Lithuanian Workers Union sent dozens of tons of food to striking miners and their families in the Donbass, Kuzbass, and Vorkuta regions.[146] Similarly, the People's Front of Latvia sent thirty tons of food and money donated from all over Latvia.[147] Muscovites donated food to coal miners in Siberia and Ukraine in spite of the well-known shortages that they themselves were experiencing at the time. Some people were even said to have donated their entire sugar and cigarette allowances to the miners.[148] In mid-March, the miners organized a solidarity fund, established by the Independent Trade Union of Mine Workers and the Interregional Strike Committee. The fund collected clothing, food, and money, the food going directly to the areas where the mines were located, and the money being deposited in a special independent trade union bank account.[149]

Throughout April, other workers went out on sympathy strikes. Workers in a cotton factory in Donetsk went on strike in mid-April in solidarity with the striking miners' political and economic demands.[150] A one-day solidarity strike took place in Vorkuta on April 18 by the workers in the mechanical works, the reinforced concrete works, and several consumer-goods enterprises.[151] The Moscow Trade Union Federation gave their enthusiastic support to the miners as well as sending 50,000 rubles to the families of striking miners.[152] The miners also received the backing of the leadership of the USSR Union of Cooperatives,[153] and a militant deputy minister of health in the RSFSR announced a hunger strike in solidarity with the miners.[154] Although there were those who were angry at the miners' apparent intransigence, by and large, the population supported them. The miners' resolute posture and the ubiquity of their support made it even more difficult for the government to bring them to their knees.

When the talks opened in Moscow, the miners arrived with nine demands: (1) a pay increase of 100–150 percent; (2) retirement after twenty-five years, with full benefits; (3) wage indexation; (4) an increase in family food allowances from 60 rubles a month to 120 rubles for those doing underground and dangerous work, and for all others a monthly subsidy of 70–120 rubles; (5) the availability of more nutritious food; (6) a decrease in workers' income taxes; (7) an increase in the housing stock; (8) improved technology in the mines; (9) the awarding of 10 percent of the production to the miners, to be disposed of as they chose.[155]

The final agreement represented a compromise. The government granted a total 100-percent wage increase over 1990 wages, to be paid in four increments of 25 percent each—for April–June 1991, for July–September 1991, for October–December 1991, and for January–March 1992.[156] As it turned out, the wage increase was partially tied to the level of the miners' production. In order for the last 25-percent wage increase to go into effect, coal extraction would have to increase from the 1990 level of 685 million tons to 712 million tons in 1991—no mean feat considering the production losses during the three months the miners had been on strike.[157] The agreement also allowed for monthly cost-of-living increases based on the nature of a worker's job, from 105 rubles for those doing underground work, down to 60 rubles for the least dangerous mining work. Other points of the agreement called for free vacation transportation for northern miners; miners employed in underground or other dangerous work to be able to retire after twenty-five years; the Ministry of Coal to be provided with more funds to build housing and recreational facilities; an allocation of 15 million rubles for wage increases and to offset taxes; and miners to be allowed to sell 5–7 percent of their production, depending on the kind of coal.[158]

As might have been expected, the response to the agreement was mixed. In many places, including Donetsk, Dnepropetrovsk, and Vorkuta, the miners were dissatisfied with it and refused to go back to work. Some of the displeasure was with the economic concessions and some was over the fact that the political demands had been ignored.[159] Miners in the regions where demands had been primarily economic in nature were more satisfied with the results of the negotiations than those in the regions where demands had been more political. Gorbachev himself met with miners from the Kuzbass and Vorkuta, the areas where political demands were strongest, in an effort to persuade them to go back to work.[160] But strikes continued in a number of places at varying levels of intensity.

The dissatisfaction with the negotiated economic package stemmed from several concerns. First, it was recognized by some that, given the large budgetary deficit and the inflation that already had the country in its grips, there was the potential for a hyperinflation that might eradicate the entire wage increase. Second, the terms under which foreign currency was controlled in the USSR greatly diminished any positive impact of the decision to allow the miners to sell up to 7 percent of the power-producing coal and up to 5 percent of the coking coal either at home or abroad at free-market prices. One estimate was that the miners could sell as much as 40 million tons of coal for about $2 billion; but the miners would be allowed to keep only a small portion of their hard-currency earnings because, by presidential decree, 40 percent of all hard-currency earnings had to go to service the nation's hard-currency debt, and, with another 54 percent going to the exporting enterprises, only 6 percent of their hard-currency earnings would be left in the hands of the miners.[161] Miners also felt they had not been sufficiently compensated for the fivefold increase in the cost of their "lunch bucket," the traditional foods that the miners take underground with them. The government's response, that the cost of the lunches was covered by the compensation clause of the agreement, did not satisfy many.[162]

The loss of faith in the central government's willingness and ability to satisfy their economic demands—much less their political demands—seemed complete. Like objects caught in a whirlpool, the miners and the government went around and around endlessly. On April 19, the coal miners in Ukraine agreed to end their strike after the government there acceded to their economic demands. The Ukrainian government had been persuaded, finally, to establish wage indexation, with a cap of 100–150 percent on the increases because of Ukraine's large budget deficit. The miners agreed to take their political demands to the central government.[163] At the Stakhanov mine, the largest in Ukraine, the average monthly wage of an underground worker had been

420 rubles before the strike began. On May 1, it rose to 570 rubles, a 30-percent increase, exclusive of compensation for price increases. At the beginning of 1992, the same wage was to increase to 1,600 rubles, a near quadrupling of an underground miner's pre-strike income.[164]

Despite its major economic concessions, the central government could not get the miners back to work. It was another nail in Gorbachev's coffin. Seven weeks after the coal strikes in Ukraine were over, the more militant miners of Vorkuta and the Kuzbass held out, and coal production in many mines in the Russian coal regions was at a standstill. In late April, the Kemerov regional soviet went so far as to say that it wanted to raise the pay of certain miners to an astounding 6,230 rubles a month, but the central government was utterly opposed and froze the wages fund of the Kemerov Oblast Soviet.[165] A new major issue was introduced on April 23 by the miners in Vorkuta, who demanded that the central government sign an agreement transferring authority over their mines to the RSFSR government.[166]

The impasse in Russia continued until Boris Yeltsin stepped in forcefully. He arrived in Novokuznetsk on April 29 to begin discussions with the miners about transferring jurisdiction of the coal mines in the Kuznetsk Basin from the central government to the republican government and on May Day, ironically enough, he signed an agreement effecting the transfer.[167] A day later, the central government announced it would ratify the agreement; the following day, it agreed to transfer the Vorkuta mines to the RSFSR as well.[168] The final agreement put all the Russian mines under the republic's political control.[169]

The strikes were over. It had cost the country dearly, financially and spiritually. It was one of Gorbachev's darkest hours; only the humiliation he suffered during the August coup attempt could match it in emotion and magnitude. But it was a great triumph for Yeltsin, surpassed only by his success in rallying the people against the leaders of the coup.

The issues did not disappear, of course, nor did the implications of the crippling strikes. By the end of July, in the

Kuzbass alone, output was down by 15.5 million tons compared with the first seven months of 1990, and 1.5 million worker-days had been lost through strikes. At the same time, miners' wages had gone up, overall, 68 percent, increasing the disparity between productivity and remuneration.[170] In July, the coal ministry and the miners' new union signed an agreement for 1991–92, which provided for a 100-percent increase in pay to the end of 1991 and increases of 100–180 percent starting on January 1, 1992. The agreement also specified differential compensation for certain workers involved in extraction, transportation, and processing and reduced the work week to thirty hours for everyone. Several social security guarantees were also included in the agreement, such as a lump sum payment of one year's earnings or a minimum of 10,000 rubles for the family of a miner who died on the job and guarantees of home fuel for miners' families.[171]

How can one summarize the tumultuous and historic events in the coal industry that marked the two years from mid-1989 to mid-1991? On the one hand, the strikes reflected the erosion of perestroika and Gorbachev's decline in power. But the strikes also contributed to that process. Indeed, Gorbachev's failures as both economic and political leader cannot be understood without assessing how his policies affected the miners and how their anger and rebellion affected the economic and political landscape. Their loss of faith was only the most visible measure of an entire nation's despair.

The 1991 Belorussian Strikes

In April 1991, following the nationwide rise in prices of consumer goods, the normally quiet and deeply loyal republic of Belorussia was the scene of mass protests by workers. In this case, what began as a protest against the price increases quickly turned into a call for radical political changes. The incidents in Belorussia are important to examine, if only because it seemed so unlikely that such massive action would occur there. That it did only served to dramatize how universal was the dissatisfaction with government policies to solve the economic crisis.

On March 28, the chairman of the Belorussian Council of Ministers, V.F. Kebich, made a televised address to prepare the population for the coming price increases, explaining that the reason for the new prices was in the higher wholesale prices of imported goods, which were outside of the republic's control.[172] He also told Belorussians that fault for the new prices lay at the doorstep of the central government and that the blame for the other problems of the economy were also located there. At the same time, he outlined a series of compensation measures that the republic government was taking to soften the blow of the price increases. These included raising the minimum wage and increasing food subsidies. But the people were not to be mollified. The depth of the population's anger was badly underestimated.

On April 3, the workers at the Kozlov electrical engineering works in Minsk went on a strike that quickly spread to workers in other enterprises in the city.[173] By the next day, there were 10,000 people filling the central square in Minsk to demand abolition of the 5-percent sales tax and a doubling or tripling of wages. In addition, they called for the resignation of all the top leaders in the central and republic governments.[174]

The Belorussian government was clearly jarred by the hostile response from the workers and, the very same day, began discussions with the trade unions on how to ease the impact of the price reform. While the most notable of workers' demands to be dealt with was that wages be raised to levels commensurate with the price increases, reducing the price of food in workers' and students' cafeterias and lowering the prices of children's articles were also discussed.[175] Kebich said that 65–70 percent of the republic's population would get full compensation for the price increases, but that it was not possible to assist the rest of the population because of the republic's large budgetary deficit—3.5 billion rubles out of a total budget of 16 billion rubles. On April 5, he said that the cost of children's goods would be cut in half and that these items would be sold only with ration coupons. The government also agreed to rescind the 5-percent sales tax on food, children's products, apartment rents, and public catering.[176] The central government's April 9 decree specifying the compensations for the price increases provided for the payment of 360 rubles a year to a family with children up to the age of six, up to 400 rubles for a family with children aged six to thirteen, and up to 460 rubles to a family with children between the ages of thirteen and eighteen.[177] But Belorussians saw these as meager palliatives. In their eyes, the economy had fallen to pieces and every family was devastated by the impact of the arbitrary 200–300 percent price increases; they had lost faith in their government. The agreement between the Belorussian government and the republican trade union council also provided for step-by-step increases in wages in industry, a package of concessions expected to add at least another 3.5 billion rubles to the Belorussian republic's budget deficit.[178] The government said that the compensation payments would cost an additional 14.6 billion rubles.[179] Nevertheless, the decision was made to double wages, starting with a 30-percent increase in April.[180]

The trade unions were only partly appeased, and it did not take long for them to expand their demands. On April 9, Vladimir Goncharik, head of the republic's trade unions said that the unions and the government should continue to discuss the issue of raising wages, that the economic independence of enterprises should be expanded, and that privatization should be accelerated.[181] The strikers also demanded that the 5-percent sales tax be repealed on all goods.[182] The strikes were suspended for ten days on April 11 while negotiations continued between strike committee representatives and the Belorussian Supreme Soviet.[183]

In the tense and polarized environment that engulfed Minsk, negotiations were bound to fail. On April 23, a demonstration involving a reported 20,000 people took place in the main Minsk square. It was announced that more than forty of the city's enterprises had stopped operating, either totally or partially. The strike committee chairman said that the strike could not go on indefinitely because "We are not going to destroy the well-being of the workers with our own hands."[184] This second wave of strikes lasted only from April 23 to 25, although there were those who believed that the workers should not ease their pressure on the government. When the strikes started up again on May 20 and 21, workers from only a few enterprises answered the call and the strikes were essentially over.[185]

What was the lesson of the Belorussian strikes? Primarily, the government seriously underestimated the anger of the workers. The price increases were like a match to the tinder of rage that had been building for a long time. Belorussia, like everywhere else, was left to its own inadequate devices when central planning broke down. Its economic growth had become dependent on metals imported from other republics and the export of its tractors, automobiles, motorcycles, and farm machinery. At the same time, it used energy—coal, oil, and gas—which it also had to import from other republics. Thus, when the individual republics began to go their own way, the Belorussian economy slowly ground to a halt and only by constant efforts at bartering for both final goods and raw material inputs did it survive.[186] Belorussia had become a beggar. The price increases were the last straw.

Belorussian workers felt betrayed by the central government. Only two weeks prior to the April 2 price increases, 83 percent of them had voted with Gorbachev on the referendum to maintain the Union. They had put their faith in the central government, and the central government then violated their trust. Belorussians had also been told that the pain of the price increases would be largely mitigated by compensations. As it turned out, there was very little recompense provided and the cost of even basic goods was going to eat up monthly income.[187]

The protests in Belorussia were a very powerful nail in perestroika's coffin, because even a previously quiescent and consistently loyal population had demonstrated that they were fed up. The population was unwilling to accept any changes that would leave them less well off, promises of a better future notwithstanding.

Conclusion

The Russian word for "strike," *zabastovka* is derived from *basta*, the Italian word for "enough." Soviet workers had indeed had enough. Enough of shortages, inflation, the threat of unemployment, and the sense that they had no control over their lives. Deprivations were no longer vitiated by full employment and stable prices, a loaf of bread and a bottle of vodka. And so they struck.

Notes

1. Moscow Television Service in Russian (July 24, 1989). From FBIS-SOV-89-140 (July 24, 1989), 39.

2. R. Livshitz and V. Nikitinsky, *An Outline of Soviet Labour Law* (Moscow: Progress, 1977), 196–197.

3. *Komsomol'skaia pravda* (June 2, 1989).

4. See, for example, Betsy Gidwitz, "Labor Unrest in the Soviet Union," *Problems of Communism* (November–December 1982), 32–35.

5. *Izvestiia* (January 15, 1991), 2.

6. See *Report on the USSR* (June 1, 1990), 32; (July 14, 1989), 30; and (August 25, 1989), 37.

7. Ibid. (May 26, 1989), 38. The government committed itself to improving the buses, providing land for housing, and providing breaks for the drivers during the day.

8. *Rossiiskaia gazeta* (March 7, 1991), 3. This figure does not include the massive number of work days lost because of interethnic conflicts. In the first half of 1989, there were 2 million man days lost because of strikes, but from July to November 1989, there were 5.5 million man days lost, suggesting about 5 million days lost because of ethnic conflicts. *Izvestiia* (December 14, 1989).

9. *Izvestiia* (July 28, 1989), 2.

10. David Marples, "Emergence of Coal-Mining Crisis in the Donetsk Basin: Planning and Investment Decisions," *Report on the USSR* (August 11, 1989), 10–12.

11. David Marples, "Why the Donbass Miners Went on Strike," *Report on the USSR* (September 8, 1989), 31.

12. *Trud* (July 21, 1989), 1.

13. Hamburg *Stern* (July 27, 1989), 116–117. From FBIS-SOV-89-144 (July 28, 1989), 59.

14. *Izvestiia* (July 27, 1989), 2.

15. *Pravda* (July 8, 1989), 2.

16. *Sotsialisticheskaia industriia* (March 28, 1989), 2.

17. Moscow Television Service in Russian (March 9, 1989). From FBIS-SOV-89-047 (March 13, 1989), 49.

18. Ibid. (March 10, 1989). From FBIS-SOV-89-047 (March 13, 1989), 50.

19. *Trud* (March 10, 1989), 2.

20. *Izvestiia* (March 10, 1989). From *Report on the USSR* (March 17, 1989), 35.

21. *Trud* (May 5, 1989), 2.

22. *Sovetskaia Rossiia* (April 9, 1989), 2.

23. *Trud* (April 25, 1989), 2.

24. Moscow TASS in English (June 30, 1989). From FBIS-SOV-89-126 (July 26, 1989), 81–82.

25. *Pravda* (July 13, 1989), 6.

26. *Sobesednik*, no. 31 (July 1989), 10. In *Current Digest of the Soviet Press* (*CDSP*) 41, no. 30, 5.

27. *Izvestiia* (July 14, 1989), 3.

28. *Pravda* (July 16, 1989), 6; *Sovetskaia Rossiia* (July 18, 1989).

29. *Pravda* (July 16, 1989), 6. From *CDSP* 41, no. 28, 4–5.

30. *Izvestiia* (July 17, 1989), 6.

31. Ibid. (July 21, 1989), 2 and Moscow TASS in English (July 25, 1989). From FBIS-SOV-89-142 (July 26, 1989), 66.

32. Moscow TASS in English (July 19, 1989). From FBIS-SOV-89-138 (July 20, 1989), 49.

33. Moscow Television Service in Russian (July 19, 1989). From FBIS-SOV-89-138 (July 20, 1989), 51.

34. Moscow Domestic Service in Russian (July 21, 1989). From FBIS-SOV-89-139 (July 21, 1989), 50.

35. *Izvestiia* (July 21, 1989), 3.

36. Ibid. (July 19, 1989), 6. The text of the agreement can be found in *Sovetskaia Rossiia* (July 22, 1989), 2. From FBIS-SOV-89-140 (July 24, 1989), 47–49.

37. Moscow Domestic Service in Russian (July 21, 1989). From FBIS-SOV-89-139 (July 21, 1989), 41; *Pravda* (July 23, 1989), 6.

38. Moscow Television Service in Russian (July 23, 1989). From FBIS-SOV-89-140 (July 24, 1989), 56.

39. *Pravda* (July 25, 1989), 1; Moscow Television Service in Russian (July 27, 1989). From FBIS-SOV-89-144 (July 28, 1989), 58.

40. Moscow Domestic Service in Russian (July 23, 1989). From FBIS-SOV-89-140 (July 24, 1989), 65.

41. *Komsomol'skaia pravda* (July 14, 1989), 1.

42. Moscow TASS in English (July 29, 1989). From FBIS-SOV-89-145 (July 31, 1989), 50.

43. In the ambiguous state of affairs at the end of the 1980s, it often became necessary for the government to confirm *de jure* what had already occurred *de facto*. The same thing occurred in the case of the cooperatives whose full legal status only authenticated what was already occurring in the country. See Anthony Jones and William Moskoff, *Ko-ops: The Rebirth of Entre-*

preneurship in the Soviet Union (Bloomington, IN: Indiana University Press, 1991).

44. *Pravda* (October 14, 1989), 1–2.

45. Cited in D. J. Peterson, "The Supreme Soviet Passes Strike Legislation," *Report on the USSR* (November 3, 1989), 12.

46. Moscow TASS in English (August 1, 1989). From *Report on the USSR* (August 11, 1989), 39; Moscow Television Service in Russian (September 30, 1989). From FBIS-SOV-89-189 (October 2, 1989), 48.

47. For example, as of the end of September, some 164 coal enterprises had become completely independent, higher coal prices were planned for the fourth quarter of the year, and 1.05 billion rubles were allocated to make supplementary payments to coal miners. See Moscow TASS in Russian (September 27, 1989). From FBIS-SOV-89-187 (September 28, 1989), 52. At least 75 percent of the newly independent mines were located in the Kuzbass. See Moscow Television Service in Russian (October 26, 1989). From FBIS-SOV-89-208 (October 30, 1989), 63.

48. *Report on the USSR* (August 11, 1989), 39.

49. Moscow TASS in Russian (August 3, 1989). From FBIS-SOV-89-149 (August 4, 1989), 73.

50. Paris AFP in English (August 5, 1989). From FBIS-SOV-89-150 (August 7, 1989), 69.

51. *Komsomol'skaia pravda* (July 14, 1989), 1.

52. Moscow Domestic Service in Russian (September 27, 1989). From FBIS-SOV-89-187 (September 28, 1989), 86. A pension law was on the agenda of the fall session of the USSR Supreme Soviet. The law envisaged the right of miners to retire after twenty-five years in the mines, regardless of age, and receive a pension equal to 70 percent of their average wage. See *Trud* (October 1, 1989), 1–2.

53. *Pravda* (October 24, 1989), 4.

54. Moscow TASS in Russian (October 23, 1989). From FBIS-SOV-89-204 (October 24, 1989), 72.

55. *Izvestiia* (October 23, 1989), 3.

56. See, for example, the statement by Coal Minister Mikhail Shchadov in *Trud* (October 1, 1989), 1–2.

57. *Izvestiia* (October 27, 1989), 2.

58. Moscow TASS in English (November 15, 1989). From FBIS-SOV-89-220 (November 16, 1989), 83.

59. *Sovetskaia Rossiia* (November 15, 1989), 2.

60. *Izvestiia* (November 28, 1989), 8.

61. *Komsomol'skaia pravda* (December 2, 1989), 1.

62. *Pravda* (November 19, 1989), 2.

63. *Report on the USSR* (July 27, 1990), 36.

64. *Sovetskaia Rossiia* (September 12, 1990), 2.

65. Moscow Domestic Service in Russian (September 6, 1990). From FBIS-SOV-90-180 (September 17, 1990), 98–99.

66. *Trud* (March 25, 1990).

67. *Rabochaia tribuna* (August 30, 1990), 1.

68. Ibid. (September 5, 1990), 2 and Moscow TASS in English (September 14, 1990). From FBIS-SOV-90-180, (September 17, 1990), 68–69.

69. *Sel'skaia zhizn'* (October 12, 1990), 2.

70. *Gudok* (October 7, 1990), 1.

71. *Pravda* (October 24, 1990), 2.

72. *Trud* (November 21, 1990), 1.

73. Ibid.

74. *Izvestiia* (December 21, 1990), 3.

75. *Trud* (February 8, 1990), 2. He also admitted without apology that when he was in Moscow he had bought sausage to take home.

76. *Rabochaia tribuna* (March 31, 1990), 2.

77. *Izvestiia* (May 24, 1990), 6.

78. *Literaturnaia gazeta*, no. 20 (May 16, 1990), 13.

79. *Rabochaia tribuna* (February 11, 1990), 1–2.

80. *Trud* (February 8, 1990), 2.

81. *Report on the USSR* (March 9, 1990), 37.

82. *Rabochaia tribuna* (June 1, 1990), 1–2.

83. *Literaturnaia gazeta*, no. 20 (May 16, 1990), 13.

84. *Izvestiia* (June 11, 1990), 2.

85. *Trud* (June 15, 1990), 1.

86. *Izvestiia* (June 15, 1990), 3.

87. *Report on the USSR* (June 22, 1990), 29.

88. *Izvestiia* (June 18, 1990), 2.

89. Moscow Domestic Service in Russian (March 1, 1990). From FBIS-SOV-90-042 (March 2, 1990). Moscow TASS in English (March 2, 1990). From FBIS-SOV-90-043 (March 5, 1990), 108; *Report on the USSR* (March 9, 1990), 37.

90. Moscow Television Service in Russian (May 10, 1990). From FBIS-SOV-90-092 (May 11, 1990), 97. *Report on the USSR* (May 25, 1990), 29. *Pravda* (May 16, 1990), 2. Moscow Domestic Service in Russian (July 21, 1990). From FBIS-SOV-90-141 (July 23, 1990), 84.

91. *Argumenty i fakty*, no. 28 (July 1990), 6.

92. *Pravda* (September 9, 1990), 2.

93. Moscow Domestic Service in Russian (September 10, 1990). From FBIS-SOV-90-176 (September 11, 1990), 48–49.

94. Moscow Television Service in Russian (September 21, 1990). From FBIS-SOV-90-186 (September 25, 1990), 77.

95. See, for example, *Komsomol'skaia pravda* (September 30, 1990), 2; and *Izvestiia* (October 8, 1990), 1. In fact, coal mines had made a profit in only 20 of the 72 years of the Soviet period. Moscow Television Service in Russian (October 8, 1990). From FBIS-SOV-90-196 (October 10, 1990), 81. Of course, the miners could not have known that radical economic reform would never take place while Gorbachev was in power; when the era of perestroika ended, neither the nation nor the miners were any closer to the market than they had been a year earlier.

96. *Rabochaia tribuna* (October 21, 1990), 1.

97. *Pravda* (October 23, 1990), 1. From FBIS-SOV-90-207 (October 25, 1990), 50.

98. An interview with A. Sergeev, deputy chairman of the Executive Bureau of the Independent Trade Union of Miners, describes the background for the creation of the organization and its goals. See *Trud* (January 4, 1991), 2.

99. *Moscow News*, no. 48 (1990), 10.

100. *Moskovskie novosti*, no. 18 (May 5, 1991), 5.

101. *Izvestiia* (March 22, 1991), 1.

102. Moscow TASS in English (January 3, 1991). From FBIS-SOV-91-003 (January 4, 1991), 44.

103. Moscow TASS in English (April 25, 1991). From FBIS-SOV-91-081 (April 26, 1991), 45–46.

104. Moscow Interfax in English (May 17, 1991). From FBIS-SOV-91-097 (May 20, 1991), 27.

105. Moscow Interfax in English (May 21, 1991). From FBIS-SOV-91-100 (May 23, 1991), 40.

106. *Trud* (February 5, 1991), 1.

107. *Sovetskaia Rossiia* (March 12, 1991), 2.

108. *Pravda* (March 2, 1991), 3.

109. Moscow TASS in English (January 3, 1991). From FBIS-SOV-91-003 (January 4, 1991), 32; Moscow Domestic Service in Russian (January 5, 1991). From FBIS-SOV-91-005 (January 8, 1991), 20–21; *Izvestiia* (January 18, 1991), 8; Paris AFP in English (March 27, 1991). From FBIS-SOV-91-060 (March 28, 1991), 57.

110. *Izvestiia* (February 3, 1991), 3.

111. Moscow TASS in English (May 8, 1991). From FBIS-SOV-91-091 (May 10, 1991), 26.

112. Moscow TASS in English (May 20, 1991). From FBIS-SOV-91-098 (May 21, 1991), 32–33.

113. *Krasnaia zvezda* (April 18, 1991), 3.

114. Moscow Radio World Service in English (May 31, 1991). From FBIS-SOV-91-106 (June 3, 1991), 42.

115. *Komsomol'skaia pravda* (July 6, 1991).

116. *Report on the USSR* (July 5, 1991), 31.

117. Moscow TASS in English (January 18, 1991). From FBIS-SOV-91-014 (January 22, 1991), 118.

118. Moscow Central Television in Russian (January 10, 1991). From FBIS-SOV-91-012 (January 17, 1991), 86.

119. Moscow Domestic Service in Russian (January 28, 1991). From FBIS-SOV-91-019 (January 29, 1991), 74.

120. Moscow TASS International Service in Russian (February 5, 1991). From FBIS-SOV-91-043 (March 5, 1991), 41.

121. Moscow Central Television in Russian (March 5, 1991). From FBIS-SOV-91-043 (March 5, 1991), 41.

122. Moscow Central Television in Russian (February 16, 1991). From FBIS-SOV-91-035 (February 21, 1991), 82.

123. Moscow Radio in Russian (March 3, 1991). From FBIS-SOV-91-042 (March 4, 1991), 56.

124. *Izvestiia* (March 1, 1991), 3.

125. Ibid. (March 9, 1991), 1. In fact, the local coal association sued the miners for 9 million rubles in damages and asked that the miners' strike be declared illegal.

126. Moscow TASS in English (March 4, 1991). From FBIS-SOV-91-043 (March 5, 1991), 40.

127. Moscow Central Television in Russian (March 4, 1991). From FBIS-SOV-91-043 (March 5, 1991), 39–40. *Pravda* (March 5, 1991), 2. There was no general strike, although miners in some pits held three-hour work stoppages on each shift. See Paris AFP (March 4, 1991). From FBIS-SOV-91-043 (March 5, 1991), 39.

128. See, for example, the interview with Prime Minister Pavlov on Moscow Central Television in Russian (March 5, 1991). From FBIS-SOV-91-044 (March 6, 1991), 32; and the interview with USSR deputy minister of the coal industry, Alexander Fisun in *Rabochaia tribuna* (March 5, 1991), 1. The cost of a 100–150 percent raise would have been 5 billion rubles in the RSFSR alone. See *Rabochaia tribuna* (March 7, 1991), 1.

129. Moscow TASS in English (February 27, 1991). From *Report on the USSR* (March 8, 1991), 31.

130. This pay excludes any premiums that a miner might earn working the night shift and supplements for travel time underground. *Izvestiia* (March 5, 1991), 2.

131. Moscow Central Television in Russian (March 14, 1991). From FBIS-SOV-91-051 (March 15, 1991), 24.

132. Moscow TASS in Russian (March 11, 1991). From FBIS-SOV-91-048 (March 12, 1991), 64.

133. Moscow Central Television (March 12, 1991). From FBIS-SOV-91-052, 37.

134. *Izvestiia* (March 12, 1991), 3.

135. Moscow TASS in English (March 19, 1991). From FBIS-SOV-91-053 (March 19, 1991), 42.

136. *Pravda* (March 15, 1991), 6.

137. Kiev International Service (March 21, 1991). From FBIS-SOV-91-056 (March 22, 1991), 48.

138. Moscow TASS in English (March 21, 1991). From FBIS-SOV-91-056 (March 22, 1991), 21.

139. Moscow Central Television in Russian (March 21, 1991). From FBIS-SOV-91-056 (March 22, 1991), 49.

140. *Rabochaia tribuna* (April 6, 1991), 1.

141. Moscow Central Television (March 24, 1991). From FBIS-SOV-91-057 (March 25, 1991), 43–44.

142. *Pravda* (March 27, 1991), 2.

143. Moscow TASS in Russian (March 26, 1991). From FBIS-SOV-91-059 (March 27, 1991), 17. *Report on the USSR* (April 5, 1991), 22.

144. Moscow All-Union Radio in Russian (March 28, 1991). From FBIS-SOV-91-060 (March 28, 1991), 29.

145. *Report on the USSR* (April 12, 1991), 26–27.

146. Moscow TASS in English (March 9, 1991). From FBIS-SOV-91-049 (March 13, 1991), 40.

147. Riga Domestic Service in Latvian (March 28, 1991). From FBIS-SOV-91-061 (March 29, 1991), 49.

148. *Chicago Tribune* (March 15, 1991), 10.

149. *Izvestiia* (April 11, 1991), 6.

150. Moscow TASS in English (April 18, 1991). From FBIS-SOV-91-075 (April 18, 1991), 19.

151. Moscow All-Union Radio in Russian (April 18, 1991). From FBIS-SOV-91-077 (April 22, 1991), 75.

152. Moscow TASS in English (April 9, 1991). From FBIS-SOV-91-069 (April 10, 1991), 55.

153. Moscow Radio in Russian (April 15, 1991). From FBIS-SOV-91-073 (April 16, 1991), 31.

154. *Rabochaia tribuna* (April 16, 1991), 1.

155. *Trud* (April 3, 1991), 1.

156. *Pravda* (April 5, 1991), 1.

157. *Izvestiia* (April 5, 1991), 2.

158. *Rabochaia tribuna* (April 5, 1991), 2.

159. Moscow All-Union Radio in Russian (April 5, 1991). From FBIS-SOV-91-067 (April 8, 1991), 46.

160. *Izvestiia* (April 6, 1991), 1.

161. *Komsomol'skaia pravda* (April 9, 1991), 1.

162. *Izvestiia* (April 5, 1991), 2.

163. Paris AFP in English (April 19, 1991). From FBIS-SOV-91-076 (April 19, 1991), 35.

164. Moscow Central Television in Russian (April 30, 1991). From FBIS-SOV-91-084 (May 1, 1991), 36.

165. *Trud* (April 24, 1991), 1.

166. *Report on the USSR* (May 3, 1991), 25. This was a subject that Boris Yeltsin, then chairman of the RSFSR Supreme Soviet, had informally broached on March 10 in a meeting with the Kuzbass strike committees. *Report on the USSR* (March 22, 1991), 29.

167. Moscow TASS in English (May 1, 1991). From FBIS-SOV-91-085 (May 2, 1991), 49.

168. Paris AFP (May 2, 1991). From FBIS-SOV-91-085 (May 2, 1991), 49. *Report on the USSR* (May 10, 1991), 25.

169. *Report on the USSR* (May 17, 1991), 37.

170. Moscow All-Union Radio in Russian (August 1, 1991). From FBIS-SOV-91-152 (August 7, 1991), 37.

171. *Trud* (July 12, 1991), 1.

172. *Sovetskaia Belorossiia* (March 30, 1991), 1.

173. *Izvestiia* (April 5, 1991), 2.

174. Moscow TASS in English (April 4, 1991). From FBIS-SOV-91-066 (April 5, 1991), 70.

175. Minsk Domestic Service in Belorussian (April 4, 1991). From FBIS-SOV-91-066 (April 5, 1991), 71.

176. Moscow Central Television Vostok Program (April 5, 1991). From FBIS-SOV-91-067 (April 8, 1991), 88.

177. *Komsomol'skaia pravda* (April 10, 1991), 2.

178. Moscow TASS in English (April 5, 1991). From FBIS-SOV-91-067 (April 8, 1991), 89.

179. *Komsomol'skaia pravda* (April 11, 1991), 2.

180. Moscow All-Union Radio First Program (April 11, 1991). From FBIS-SOV-91-071 (April 12, 1991), 66.

181. Moscow TASS International Service in Russian (April 9, 1991). From FBIS-SOV-91-070 (April 11, 1991), 46.

182. Moscow TASS in English (April 15, 1991). From FBIS-SOV-91-073 (April 16, 1991), 49.

183. Moscow TASS International Service in Russian (April 12, 1991). From FBIS-SOV-91-072 (April 15, 1991), 50.

184. Minsk Domestic Service in Belorussian (April 23, 1991). From FBIS-SOV-91-079 (April 24, 1991), 54.

185. Kathleen Mihalisko, "Workers and Soviet Power: Notes from Minsk," *Report on the USSR* (July 5, 1991), 16.

186. *Izvestiia* (April 15, 1991), 2.

187. Kathleen Mihalisko, "The Workers' Rebellion in Belorussia," *Report on the USSR* (April 26, 1991), 21.

Conclusion

We began this book with the statement that the Gorbachev years were remarkable. The story we have just told of perestroika's cataclysmic effect on the Soviet population confirms the extraordinary character of this period. The one indisputable fact is that the economy effectively collapsed, not in spite of Gorbachev and perestroika, but at least partially because of it. The disintegration of the economy and, ultimately, the death of the nation were so complete that one can only be led to certain conclusions.

First, central planning had effected a kind of potemkinization of the Soviet economy, a patina of discipline and order, whose removal, revealed the fatal flaws of the system—one might perhaps even say, its internal contradictions. One of the most powerful reasons for the downfall of the economy was the demise of the old system of rigid central planning without anything new to replace it. Central planning had diminished ambiguity; it had defined boundaries which had been sufficiently honored to allow the economy to struggle through, year after year. Perestroika, on the other hand, bred ambiguity. The resulting uncertainty was absolutely incompatible with existing structures, institutional arrangements, habits of mind, and accepted values. Thus, confusion reigned in the economy.

When combined with the explosive forces of nationalism, the administrative disarray created tensions that doomed the possibility of economic success. The conflagrations between the center and the republics and between republics and some of their cities led to self-destructive divisions. Indeed, at some point during 1990, it is arguable that there no longer was a Soviet economy. Central planning, as inefficient as it was, had bound fifteen republics together in a grudging but nevertheless plausible national economic system. Perestroika unintentionally contributed to the dissolution of this fundamental relationship and, with it, the pre-tense of coherence and cohesion in the economy.

Second, perestroika suffered from being a revolution from above. It did not spring spontaneously from a wellspring of grievances felt by the general population as a program to right the economy. Rather, it was an invention of Gorbachev and other intellectuals and reformers who supported his general vision. As were all its predecessors, it was a program without a popular mandate or a consensus. Consequently, perestroika was not only problematic in and of itself, it also had the resistance of the status quo. But paradoxically, at least in some of its dimensions perestroika invited action from below, as in the instances of the enterprise autonomy promised in 1988, the new freedom for individual entrepreneurs, and the lease-holding that was encouraged in agriculture; and certainly individual autonomy was fostered by the political reforms which allowed free elections. In promoting the democratic spirit and a climate of initiative, Gorbachev was also sowing the seeds of his own destruction. The workers who struck across the country after mid-1989 demonstrated that when their economic situation worsened, they had the will and the capacity to protest publicly and, in some instances, to bring the system to its knees. Their angry reaction showed that a diminished standard of living was no longer acceptable.

Third, Gorbachev did not recognize that while he was using his political skills to maneuver constantly to the center—trying to please the most radical reformers on his left and the threatened old guard on his right—the consequences of the tentative measures he enacted were destroying the population's standard of living. And while he hesitated every step of the way and tried to plant himself firmly in the middle, the population was becoming increasingly radicalized and hence was moving away from him and perestroika to the left. Even though Gorbachev had the enormous power of the presidency behind him, he failed to use it in ways that would inspire confidence. And in alienating the population, he lost both credibility and authority. His indecisiveness may even have led many to see him as vulnerable and weak. Hence the boldness of the workers in striking with such audacity.

Fourth, Gorbachev was meddling with the traditional system of rewards, and therefore his only legitimate hope for success was that there would be far more beneficiaries of his policies than losers—and that those who would become winners would become so quickly. But whatever Gorbachev did required modifications within the system, and that meant he would have to protect those who were hurt by the changes while simultaneously carrying out major reforms. These were not easily compatible actions. Gorbachev wanted economic reform, but he needed the loyalty of workers, factory managers, and members of the defense establishment. And so he became the ultimate compromiser. By electing always to seek the middle ground, Gorbachev chose the most dangerous position. He was flanked on both sides by constituencies who despised either what he did or the consequences of what he did. The fact is that he never pleased any of these groups.

It would be unfair to leave any assessment of perestroika on this sour note. Because it failed so miserably on so many bread-and-butter issues, Gorbachev's accomplishments in the economic arena receded into the background. They should not be overlooked, however. First of all, Gorbachev made it respectable for economists within the Soviet Union to speak the language of market economics and to espouse radical change. Anything even approaching such thoughts earlier had had to be cloaked in Aesopian language, often with a large dose of ritualistic obeisance to the works of Marx and Lenin. Second, Gorbachev began to tear down the economic bureaucracy, which had been the heart and soul of central planning. While it by no means disappeared, it was in partial retreat by the end of the perestroika era. There was a corollary shift, albeit incomplete, of decision-making power away from the bureaucracy and toward enterprise directors. The movement toward decentralized decision-making was reinforced by the promotion of legal private enterprise and, with it, the idea of private property, the absolute essence of a capitalist economy. Gorbachev also removed most of the barriers between the Soviet Union and the rest of the world, inviting foreigners to invest in the Soviet Union in joint ventures.[1]

Gorbachev must be accounted a modernizer, because he understood that his country's prospects in the world were exceedingly limited if it continued to travel the same path it had been on since 1928. But he had a foot planted in central planning and he never fully renounced his long-held beliefs. Gorbachev's failing was that perestroika was too firmly glued to the past.

Note

1. For a much fuller assessment of Gorbachev's performance as an economic reformer, see John Tedstrom, "Gorbachev the Economist," *Report on the USSR* (August 30, 1991), 11–12.

Bibliography

Aslund, Anders. 1991. *Meeting Report from a Lecture at the Kennan Institute for Advanced Studies* 8, no. 15.

Bush, Keith. 1992. "Commonwealth of Independent States: Foreign Indebtedness." *RFE/RL Research Report* (January 10), 20–22.

———. 1992. "The Disastrous Last Year of the USSR." *RFE/RL Research Report* (March 20), 39–41.

Central Intelligence Agency. 1991. *Handbook of Economic Statistics.* Washington, DC.

——— and Defense Intelligence Agency. 1990. "The Soviet Economy Stumbles Badly in 1989." Mimeo. Washington, DC (April 20).

———. 1990. *Soviet Labor Requirements for the Information Era.* DCI/ICI 5386–89.

Defense Intelligence Agency. 1987. "Gorbachev's Modernization Program: A Status Report." Mimeo. Washington, DC. (March 19, 1987).

Gidwitz, Betsy. 1982. "Labor Unrest in the Soviet Union." *Problems of Communism* (November–December), 32–35.

Granick, David. 1987. *Job Rights in the Soviet Union.* Cambridge, MA: Cambridge University Press.

Gregory, Paul and Stuart, Robert C. 1990. *Soviet Economic Structure and Performance*, 4th ed. New York: Harper & Collins.

International Monetary Fund et al. 1991. *The Economy of the USSR: Summary and Recommendations.* Washington, DC: World Bank.

Jones, Anthony and Moskoff, William. 1991. *Ko-ops: The Rebirth of Entrepreneurship in the Soviet Union.* Bloomington, IN: Indiana University Press.

JWF News. 1991 (April).

Koriagina, T. 1990. "Tenevaia ekonomika v SSSR." *Voprosy ekonomiki*, no. 3, 110–120.

Kozlov, Iu. 1990. "Tenevaia ekonomika i prestupnost'." *Voprosy ekonomiki*, no. 3, 120–127.

Livshitz, R. and Nikitinsky, V. 1977. *An Outline of Soviet Labour Law.* Moscow: Progress.

Marples, David. 1989. "Emergence of Coal Mining Crisis in the Donetsk Basin: Planning and Investment Decisions." *Report on the USSR* (August 11), 10–12.

————. 1989. "Why the Donbass Miners Went on Strike." *Report on the USSR* (September 8), 30–32.

Mihalisko, Kathleen. 1991. "Workers and Soviet Power: Notes from Minsk." *Report on the USSR* (July 5), 15–21.

————. 1991. "The Workers' Rebellion in Belorussia." *Report on the USSR* (April 26), 21–25.

Moskoff, William. 1990. *The Bread of Affliction: The Food Supply in the USSR During World War II*. New York: Cambridge University Press.

Narodnoe khoziaistvo SSSR v 1989. Moscow, 48.

Peterson, D.J. 1989. "The Supreme Soviet Passes Strike Legislation." *Report on the USSR* (November 3), 11–13.

Pizer, John S. and Baukol, Andrew P. 1991. "Recent GNP and Productivity Trends." *Soviet Economy* 7 (January–March) 46–82.

Samuelson, Paul A. and Nordhaus, William D. 1985. *Economics*, 12th ed. New York: McGraw-Hill.

Schwartz, Harry. 1954. *Russia's Soviet Economy*, 2nd ed. Englewood Cliffs, NJ: Prentice-Hall.

Teague, Elizabeth. 1989. "Gorbachev's First Four Years." *Report on the USSR* (March 3), 1–5.

————. 1990. "New Incentives Lure Townspeople into the Fields." *Report on the USSR* (October 19), 17–19.

————. 1991. "Tackling the Problem of Unemployment." *Report on the USSR* (November 8), 1–7.

Tedstrom, John. 1989. "The Soviet Economy: Planning for the 1990s." *Report on the USSR* (December 22), 1–7.

————. 1991. "Soviet Foreign Trade in 1990." *Report on the USSR* (April 12), 10–13.

Transition to a Market Economy. 1990. Joint Publications Research Service, JPRS-UEA-90-034 (September 28).

Treml, Vladimir G. 1990. "Study of Employee Theft of Materials from Places of Employment." *Berkeley-Duke Occasional Papers on the Second Economy in the USSR*, no. 20 (June).

Periodicals

Argumenty i fakty
The Chicago Tribune
Current Digest of the Soviet Press
Ekonomicheskaia gazeta
Ekonomicheskie nauki
Ekonomika i organizatsiia promyshlennogo proizvodstva
Ekonomika i zhizn'
Foreign Broadcast Information Service. *Daily Report–Soviet Union*

————. *JPRS [Joint Publications Research Report] Report–Soviet Union–Economic Affairs*
Glasnost'
Izvestiia
Komsomol'skaia pravda
Krasnaia zvezda
Literaturnaia gazeta
Moscow News
The New York Times
Ogonek
Planovoe khoziaistvo
Pravda
Pravitel'stvennyi vestnik
Rabochaia tribuna
Report on the USSR
Sel'skaia zhizn'
Sotsialisticheskaia industriia
Sovetskaia Rossiia
Trud
Vestnik statistiki
The Wall Street Journal

Index

Abalkin, Leonid, 94–95
Agricultural harvest
  problems in, 38–41
Anger of the population, 62–64
Anti-alcohol campaign, 11
  and budget deficit, 16
  role in inflation, 91
Anti-Russian sentiments, 142–45

Belorussia, 97
  strikes in 1991, 221–24
Bread shortage, 32–33
Brezhnev
  Food Program, 29
Budget deficit, 15
  as source of inflationary pressure, 16–17

Central Asia
  unemployment, 139–42
  tensions with other ethnic groups, 142–45
Charity, 118–19
Cigarette shortage, 61–62
Coal miners
  strikes of 1989
    implications of 1989 strike, 194–96, 197
    in Donetsk Basin, 187, 188, 191, 196
    in Kazakhstan, 192
    in Kuznetsk Basin, 188, 190–91, 192, 193
    miners' views of causes, 192
    number affected, 183
    in Pechora Basin, 189, 196
    1989 agreement with government, 193
  strikes of 1990, 201–8
    complaints about food shortages, 202
    desire for economic independence, 205
    deteriorating economic conditions, 206–7
    Donetsk, 205
    fear of transition to market, 204

Coal miners *(continued)*
    first miners congress held, 204
    new coal miners' union, 205
    shift toward political agenda, 202–3
  strikes of 1991
    coal miner and prisoner rations compared, 214–15
    economic implications, 220–21
    effect of inflation on coal miners' standard of living, 214–15
    effort by government to use anti-strike law, 216
    Kuznetsk
      demand for resignation of Gorbachev and rest of government, 213
      political strike, 212
    miner demands, 217–18
    Pechora Basin, 213
    spread of strikes in March, 215
    strike threat in Ukraine leads to large wage increase, 212–13
    support for coal miner strikes all over country, 216–17
    universal demand for wage increase, 214
    1991 agreement and mixed reaction to, 218–19
Consumer goods shortages, 15, 55–62
  aggravated by rising incomes, 55–56
  ban on exports to protect domestic supplies, 58–59
  cigarette shortage, 61–62
  consequence of decline in inputs, 59–60
  decline in 1989 output, 55
  hoarding, 56–59
  imports to compensate for, 60–61
  increasing gap between income and goods, 56

241

William Moskoff is the D.K. Pearsons Professor of Economics at Lake Forest College and the former editor of the journal *Comparative Economic Studies*. His books include *Ko-ops: The Rebirth of Entrepreneurship in the Soviet Union; The Bread of Affliction: The Food Supply of the Soviet Union During World War Two; Labor and Leisure in the Soviet Union*; and the edited volumes *Reorganization and Reform in the Soviet Economy; Perestroika and the Economy: New Thinking in Soviet Economics*; and *The Great Market Debate in Soviet Economics*.